THE NEW
DESIGN
SOURCE
BOOK

Paper clip, 1899, Johann Vaaler.

'*Design may be thought of as the well-doing
of what needs doing.*'

W.R. Lethaby (1857-1931)

THE NEW
DESIGN
SOURCE
BOOK

PENNY SPARKE • FELICE HODGES • EMMA DENT COAD •
ANNE STONE • HUGH ALDERSEY-WILLIAMS

KNICKERBOCKER
PRESS

A QUARTO BOOK

Copyright © 1986, 1992, 1997 Quarto Inc

This new edition first published in North America in 1997 by
Knickerbocker Press, 276 Fifth Avenue, Suite 206
New York, NY 10001

ISBN 1-57715-016-3

This book was designed and produced by
Quarto Publishing plc
The Old Brewery
6 Blundell Street
London N7 9BH

Editor Keith Parish
Design Liz Barnett, Karen Byrne,
Phillip Chidlow, Nigel Soper
Picture Researcher Diana Korchien

Art Editor Nick Clark
Senior Editor Jane Rollason
Art Director Alastair Campbell
Editorial Director Jim Miles

Typeset in Great Britain by Leaper and Gard Ltd, Bristol
and QV Typesetting Ltd, London
Manufactured in Hong Kong by Regent Publishing Services Ltd.
Printed in China By Leefung Asco Printers Ltd

THE AUTHORS

Penny Sparke was born in Middlesex. She took her first degree at Sussex University, followed by a PhD on 'British Design in the 1960s'. She lectured on Design History at Brighton Polytechnic for six years until 1981, when she moved to her current position in the department of cultural history at the Royal College of Art, London. Her published works include *An Introduction to Design and Culture* (Allen & Unwin), *Ettore Sottsass Jnr* (Design Council), *Consultant Design* (Pembridge Press) and *Furniture* (Bell & Hyman). She has contributed to a variety of design magazines, including *Blueprint, Design, Domus, Mobilia, Industrial Design* and *Metropolis,* and has broadcast on both radio and television on aspects of modern design.

Emma Dent Coad was born and educated in London. For five years she was involved in fashion design. She then joined the Society of Industrial Artists and Designers' magazine, *Designer,* where she worked as a journalist for six years. She is now a full-time freelance, working on design magazines in Britain and the United States, and she has broadcast on radio and television. A specialist in Spanish design she is the author of *Spanish Design and Architecture* and *Javier Mariscal: Designing the New Spain.*

Felice Hodges was born in America and has been a resident of Britain for many years. She studied Art History at Cornell University, New York, specializing in twentieth-century art. She then joined the editorial staff of *Antique Collector* magazine and was a regular contributor on a wide variety of subjects. Her publications include the *Phaidon Guide to Glass* (Peerage Books). She has lectured and broadcast extensively on various aspects of collecting. She is currently a freelance writer, specializing in design and antiques.

Hugh Aldersey-Williams is a design and technology writer. He is the European Editor of the American magazine *International Design,* and was author of *New American Design* and *World Design: Nationalism and Globalism in Design* (both Rizzoli).

Anne Stone was born and educated in London. She studied the history and theory of art at Sussex University, and then worked for a number of years in the antiques business. She was a regular contributor to *Antique Collector* for several years and her published works include *The Antique Collector's Handbook* (Ebury Press) and *Antique Furniture* (Orbis). She currently lectures on the decorative arts and her particular area of expertise is British furniture in the eighteenth and nineteenth centuries.

CONTENTS

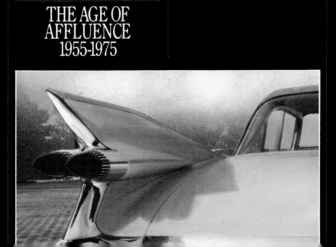

INTRODUCTION

s we move into the 1990s and look back at the decade that we have just left behind, it is clear that we cannot talk about an '80s Style'. Nor, indeed, does it seem likely that the last decade of the century will engender a consistent design movement, from an aesthetic point of view at least. Unlike their predecessors of half a century earlier, who were fired by the necessity to produce one style that would stand for the spirit of the age in which they lived, today's architects and designers immerse themselves in a number of stylistic options culled both from the past and from their contemporary context. The sense of optimism and the faith in new technology which inspired the style-makers of the early century to espouse a single aesthetic, based on the idea of machine production, no longer motivates designers in the much more ambiguous and ambivalent 1990s. Today's public needs objects which reflect its fragmentation, its pluralistic tastes and its new priorities. Style-makers are aware of this changing climate. Their responsibility, is to react to these varied and constantly shifting demands and to create artefacts that will satisfy them — an increasingly difficult task.

With this in mind, *Design Source Book* sets out to illustrate and explain the main styles of the last hundred years, presenting them both as a stimulus for today's designers, who are in constant search of renewed visual inspiration, and to show how designers have continually shifted their focus from the past to the present, to the future and back again to the past in search of styles to delight, shock and comfort the buying public. Whether they shared the high-minded idealism of the Arts and Crafts movement or participated in the commercial crassness of American streamlining, designers in this century have looked around them for visual sources and found them in such disparate areas as fine art, engineering and mass culture.

Design Source Book charts the succession of styles since 1850 — from the Arts and Crafts movement to Art Nouveau with its Celtic origins, to Functionalism with its commitment to the machine, to Art Deco and its neo-Egyptian imagery through to the influences of materials and technologies (both old and new) and to the proliferation of mass styles which have appeared in recent decades — presenting them all as evidence of the continued eclecticism in the mass environment and as possible sources to be reworked yet again. More than ever before history is now part of the present and as new styles lose their potency old ones are continually revived, albeit with ever new disguises.

Developments in mass communications and the increasingly dominating presence of the mass media within everyday life has meant that not only can more people now participate in the adventure of style consumption but those very styles become redundant more quickly through their mass availability. Always on the look out for 'something different', today's consumers seek change and variation in the goods with which they surround themselves and which determine the nature of their 'life-styles'. Inevitably this puts pressure on the designer to come up with the goods and to stand in front of society, showing the way forward. In their pursuit of prophecy, designers often invoke the help of the past.

Design Source Book sets out, therefore, to show where today's styles have come from. It quickly becomes apparent that our environment is a complex phenomenon whose emergence has been determined by a set of forces which are essentially economic, technological, ideological and cultural. The role of designers is to act as creative filters and to judge the appropriateness of one style over another. *Design Source Book* will, we hope, help them to do so with increasing confidence.

'Lorenzo and Isabella', oil on canvas, 1849, by Sir John Everett Millais (1826-96).

CHAPTER ONE

FITNESS FOR PURPOSE

THE ARTS & CRAFTS MOVEMENT 1850-1900

'The movement, passing under the name of "Arts and Crafts" ...may be defined ... to constitute a movement to bring all the activities of the human spirit under the influence of one idea, the idea that life is creation.'

T.J. COBDEN-SANDERSON, 1906

INTRODUCTION

The Arts and Crafts movement was initiated as an ideological reaction to the effects of nineteenth-century industrialization, which it believed had robbed the worker of the ability to take pride in his craft and brought about a degeneration in the design and quality of goods being produced. It consisted of a small number of loosely allied and influential individuals who, through the example of their personal and collective endeavours, realized broadly similar social aims and artistic aspirations. The movement, which began in Britain, dominated an important sector of artistic activity and socialist thought in the second half of the nineteenth century and heralded the start of a new appreciation of the decorative arts throughout Europe and America.

The elusive style produced by the movement was born out of an attitude to the craft process and the craftsman and represented a search for a means to embody the natural unity between form, function and decoration. A guiding principle was that an object should be fit for the purpose for which it was made. In the quest for a solution, a style emerged that drew its inspiration from many different sources, both artistic and intellectual, and ranged from the well-researched historicism of Gothic to the abstracted organic forms derived from a strong vernacular tradition.

Form and shape were often simple and made use of plain, linear or organic shapes. This derived in part from the massive forms of early Gothic architecture, exemplified in the work of William Burges, Richard Norman Shaw and some of the early work of Morris & Co, and in part from the simplicity of the vernacular — even rustic — tradition. This can be seen in both the simple, strong lines of furniture such as Morris's 'workaday' pieces and the austere, linear outlines of Gustav Stickley's furniture. In the purest form of the style, decoration was derived from construction so that, on furniture, pegs and dowels formed surface motifs and patterns, on metalwork hammer marks gave a softly dimpled texture to the surface, and in pottery brilliant colour was fused to the body in the firing process.

Natural plant, bird and animal forms were a powerful source of inspiration for many designers. William Morris, regarded as the movement's most outstanding master, used them almost exclusively in the essentially flat, two-dimensional, formalized patterns of his textile and wallpaper designs. The Rookwood Pottery of America, on the other hand, was noted for its much more naturalistic treatment of animals and plants. Following the example of John Ruskin and the Pre-Raphaelite Brotherhood, many of these plants and wild creatures were taken from nature rather than mythological or other fanciful sources and could be found among gardens and hedgerows.

Above: *Earthenware bread plate decorated in the majolica manner with the homily 'waste not want not'. Designed by Pugin and made by Minton c. 1850.*

Left: *Painted chest on stand by William Burges, 1875, showing the type of plain, simply constructed but luxuriously decorated domestic furniture favoured by many Arts and Crafts designers.*

Below: *The Drawing Room, Standen (1892-4). The house and several rooms were designed by Philip Webb, as well as many of the furnishings including the electric wall brackets here. The standard lamps are by Benson.*

Among the second generation of Arts and Crafts practitioners working in the 1880s and 1890s there was more abstraction, and a noticeable element of movement and dynamism crept into the work of designers such as Arthur Mackmurdo of the Century Guild, paving the way for Art Nouveau. Other designer-craftsmen were intrigued by more exotic or mythical creatures and drew on these sources of inspiration when decorating their work. Characteristic of this type of decoration is the work of the ceramist William de Morgan, the pottery designs of Walter Crane and the colourful enamelled metalware of the architect-designer Charles Ashbee.

Members of the movement came from all walks of life and included architects, artists, writers, thinkers, designers, craftsmen and — in the United States — even a soap salesman who sold his business interests to devote his life to the cause. They were united in their belief in the supremacy of the craftsman and his way of life, and in the value of hand-crafted objects over those made by machine. Some went so far as to denounce machinery but others saw it as a useful aid which, if used properly, could benefit society.

Those who identified with the aspirations of the movement formed themselves into small, clubby groups in which they could discuss their ideas and share their experiences. The inspiration for these groups were the medieval craft guilds that were a prominent section of society in the Middle Ages. Like them, they aimed to encourage high standards of design and craftsmanship and, further, to educate people into a greater awareness of all the visual arts, in particular the decorative and industrial arts. They felt that this awareness would improve and enhance the quality of life for all and that such artistic interaction would lend greater dignity to both creator and recipient. In this way the Arts and Crafts movement went far beyond being a stylistic development to embrace the idea of 'style as something organically connected with society, something which springs inevitably from a way of life'. The craftsman was seen to be an artist, while artistic activity itself was seen as ennobling and providing a positive force for good in society.

Top: *Stained glass window designed by E. Burne-Jones depicting the Annunciation, c. 1860, St Columba's Church, Topcliffe, Yorks.*

Above: *'The Golden Stairs', by E. Burne-Jones, 1876-80. 'Mood' painting such as this is more typical of the Aesthetic Movement.*

Above left: *Rookwood Pottery vase decorated with 'freesias' by Hattie E. Wilcox, c.1900-01.* Right: *'Cray' printed cotton designed by Morris, 1885.*

INSPIRATIONS

The great Gothic churches of England presented the mid-nineteenth century designer with a ubiquitous source of inspiration. Pure and harmonious in every detail, they were eloquent testament to the productive life of the medieval artisan fulfilled in working to a common purpose alongside others of different craft skills. Gothic structures soon adorned domestic interiors and furniture. But pointed arches, columns and quatrefoils looked fussily pedantic in the domestic context and relief came from the other main inspiration of medievalism — the humble peasant cottage, simply furnished employing local materials and no artifice to disguise constructional methods. The escapist mood left designers vulnerable to the everyday charms of nature, and meadow flora and timid country fauna are constantly evoked. Medievalism is the key, then. Literary, calligraphic, heraldic and other sources are pored over as well as architecure, and even the crafts revived are feudal — tapestry-weaving, stained glass, plasterwork and carpentry (as opposed to cabinet-making).

Take a pew
Wooden interior fittings of churches, such as this pew *right,* provided readily available examples to furniture craftsmen of 'honest' joinery techniques used in unveneered local timbers, with decorative effects confined to shaping and chamfering. Use of mortises, pegs and dowels drew attention to structural form.

Courtly splendour
William Burges who reconstructed Cardiff Castle and his client the Earl of Bute were bound by a delight in all things medieval. The scheme produced a Gothic and Islamic fantasy of heraldry, painted glass, mosaics, painted tiles, wood-carvings, fabrics and large-scale furniture. This is the golden stalactite ceiling of the Arab Room *above,* in the castle's Herbert Tower (1876). Its walls are lined with cedarwood and various marbles.

Dominant shapes
Above right and left: Quatrefoil and trefoil, pierced through woodwork, painted on or inlaid into surface or used as shapes in their own right, for example as door-hinge terminals. A more complicated version echoes the form of a flowerhead.
Stylized scrolling leaf patterns in formalized arrangements.
Gothic arches on architectural-style furniture, sometimes used as a series forming an arcade.
Fleur-de-lys motif, again cut out, applied or inlaid.
Continuous regularly curling pattern of flower stem with symmetrical arrangement of flowerheads, used as border pattern.

Country seats
Simple rustic shapes were taken up by the movement and produced without embellishment by designers such as Voysey, Morris, George Walton and, supremely, by Ernest Gimson, as in his plain rush-seated country chair, *above.* Settles and trestle tables were also favoured.

Beastly beauty
Animal life in William De Morgan's ceramics are treated with heraldic formality, so that both subject matter and manner reflect his interest in the medieval and mythical. A fiery arabesque licks around the fearsome outline of the dragon on this ruby lustre bowl, *above.*

Set patterns
Owen Jones' 'The Grammar of Ornament' (1856) stands as a monument to Victorian eclecticism. Decorated with colour lithographs of design patterns culled from the cultures of the world, it was an invaluable source for designers. The Persian border, *above left,* finds echoes in Arts and Crafts wallpapers, fabrics and plasterwork; border from an English medieval manuscript, *above centre;* detail of a 12th-century stained glass, *above right.*

abcdefg

ABCDEF

Sample of 'Old English', *top,* a typeface with Gothic points and obvious thick/thin strokes. The quill-pen style adorns pennants on William Morris crewel-work hangings. 'Golden Type', *middle,* an influential typeface derived from 15th-century Venetian specimens by Morris for his Kelmscott Press, 1890. Medieval illuminated initials, *bottom,* provided a model for formalized, flat, unshaded decorative designs.

THE THEORISTS

The concern felt about the low standards of design in all spheres of the decorative arts had been expressed throughout the first half of the nineteenth·century. It was neither new nor surprising therefore when, in the middle of the century, it reached a more critical and fervent pitch. As early as 1836 a Parliamentary Select Committee had been established to examine the problem. To compound the issue, there was real concern over the nation's moral state as, at the time, it was generally believed that a nation's moral and ethical condition was reflected in its art. If one was bad then so was the other.

Among the many voices raised was that of the architect Charles Cockerel, whose bluntly expressed belief that 'the attempt to supersede the work of the mind and the hand by mechanical process for the sake of economy, will always have the effect of degrading and ultimately ruining art' was shared by many. The decline in quality in the decorative arts was attributed to an excessive degree of industrialization, which demanded that quantity be pursued at the expense of quality.

The decline in manufacturing standards, it was thought, was compounded by a decline in design standards. This was held to be due to the lack not of talent but of educational and creative leisure facilities that would draw it out. Cockerel criticized the government for failing in this respect and cited Continental governments that had 'been always better and more systematically directed to arts and manufacturers' by establishing academies and academic positions that encouraged the necessary learning, 'thus diffusing taste through every class of society from the manufacturer to the purchaser.'

The Government did take notice, however, and out of this developed the beginnings of the modern art school system and of museums such as the Victoria and Albert Museum, London, which were intended to encourage and promote good design for the industrial arts. In the following year, 1837, a Government School of Design was established. The aim of the school was to train designers for working with industry but, by the middle of the century, it was clear that it had signally failed to achieve this. The writer and expert on ornament, Owen Jones, reiterated the problem in 1856 when he proposed that 'no improvement can take place in the Art of the present generation until all classes, Artists, Manufacturers, and the Public, are better educated in Art, and the existence of general principles is more fully recognized.'

It took the theories of the Arts and Crafts movement under the guidance of William Lethaby, who became principal of the Central School of Arts and Crafts, London, in 1896 and later of the Royal College of Art, to

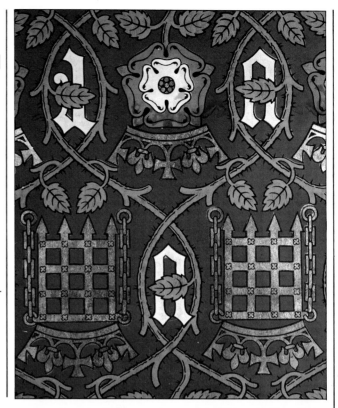

Right: Rose and portcullis wallpaper designed by A.W.N. Pugin. This pattern, which incorporates the initials V and R, was one of several variations designed for the Houses of Parliament. Historical emblems such as the Tudor red rose provided an appropriate vocabulary of motifs for Pugin. Other emblems included the white rose, the white stag and the fleur de lys.
Below: The gallery and stained glass lantern above the Chaucer Room in the 15th-century Octagon Tower at Cardiff Castle. It is part of an extensive scheme of interior reconstruction carried out by William Burges for the Earl of Bute from 1865.

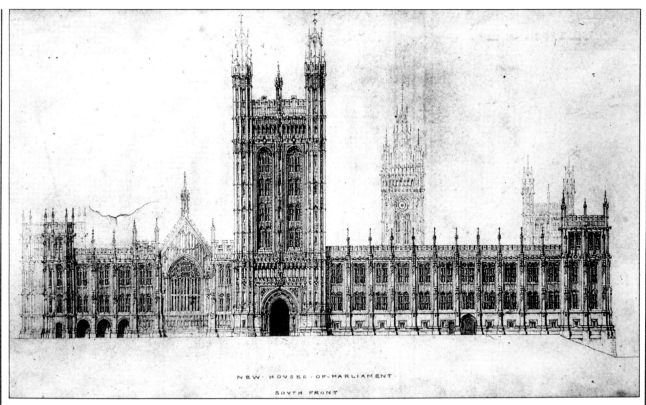

NEW·HOVSES·OF·PARLIAMENT·
SOVTH FRONT

Left: *Print of the South Front of the Houses of Parliament by Pugin, 1836. Pugin was a well-known scholar of medieval art and architecture and was often called upon for his knowledge. The façade of the new Houses of Parliament shows a classical building decorated with a wealth of Gothic detailing.*

Below: *Decorative detail from the interior of St Giles Church, Cheadle. This Roman Catholic church was designed by Pugin for Lord Shrewsbury, who was its generous benefactor. Pugin toured East Anglian churches for the purpose of studying medieval ecclesiastical architecture at about the time of this commission and may have used his researches for this project. His work was always thoroughly researched.*

equip designers for working with and for industry. Lethaby's example provided the impetus and inspiration for later generations to follow in the twentieth century, in both Britain and Europe.

The Gothic example

Among the first to raise their criticisms in England was Augustus W.N. Pugin (1812-52), while in France Eugène-Emmanuel Viollet-le-Duc (1814-79), put forward his design theories. Pugin linked the decline in aesthetic values to a decline in the nation's moral standing, and the belief that a 'nation's art was a symptom of its moral health' was widespread by the middle of the century. The answer lay through reforming society, and the model Pugin chose to follow was Gothic. But Gothic art and architecture were much more than just a style: for Pugin they were a symbol of a truly Christian society. It was only by returning to Gothic art and architecture that the ills and failures of the nineteenth century could be overturned. To this end he became a vigorous champion of the art of the Middle Ages. This was to have a long and continuing influence, first through John Ruskin and later through generations of architect-designers such as William Burges, Richard Norman Shaw, William Morris and, indirectly, the later followers of the Arts and Crafts movement.

The Gothic style provided Pugin with a vehicle through which he could channel his vision of reforming society. He illuminated his ideas through designs for artefacts and architecture that provided the inspiration and example for later Arts and Crafts practitioners. His best-known scheme was a design for the decoration of the new Houses of Parliament, rebuilt in 1835-7 to replace the original structure razed by fire the year before. Their Gothic style was identified as the national one. Because of its religious associations it was regarded as spiritually and morally uplifting, in strong contrast to the dark satanic mills of nineteenth-century industrialism.

Pugin published one of his most influential books, *Contrasts; or a Parallel between the Noble Edifices of the Fourteenth and Fifteenth Centuries and Similar Buildings of the Present Day*, when he was only 24. In it he contrasted Gothic with other architectural styles and demonstrated his belief in the social structure of the Middle Ages which, because it was stable, honest and good, was therefore capable of producing good art and architecture.

In his eyes, only good Christian men could produce good buildings. This book and later publications such as *The True Principle of Christian or Pointed Architecture* (1841) nevertheless reveal Pugin's ideas on design to have been in advance of their time and they were not properly understood until later in the century, when Gothic Revival architects like Burges, Shaw and Morris took them up.

His most radical suggestions included 'the two great rules of design ... First that there should be no features about a building which are not necessary for convenience, construction or propriety; second that all ornament should consist of enrichment of the essential construction of the buildings.' Another idea put forward by

SPIRIT OF ARTS AND CRAFTS

Leaving aside William Morris' progressive ideas about a carpenter being as good a gentleman as a lawyer, the movement he initiated was essentially revivalist. This is evident both in its aesthetic, with constant allusions to medievalism, and in its intense pride in execution and production by traditional methods. You may observe the rediscovery of ancient techniques and be struck by unusual blendings, but don't look for new techniques or new materials. Practitioners delighted in working with natural materials unmodified by industry. The art that conceals art is not at work here, even when the commission came from the wealthy patron on whom the movement ironically came to rely.

1900 Watercolour rendering of a design for a cottage interior by M.H. Baillie Scott, *above*. It keeps faith with the movement's interest in ruralism and simple furnishings, with a plain sideboard on the left and settles for fireside sitting and for dining. Colour is provided by fabrics and a painted frieze with bold floral patterns.

1877 The 'Artichoke' design of this wallhanging, by William Morris, *above*, embroidered in crewel wools on linen, is typical of his formal, repetitive patterns, clearly outlined and in a strong but sombre palette reminiscent of Flemish tapestries.

1907 The Greene brothers were among several American designer-craftsmen who subscribed to Arts and Crafts ideals. This walnut armchair, *right*, with straps and pegs in ebony, was part of the Greene & Greene scheme for the Blacker House.

1895 Ceramic tiles by William de Morgan, painted in 'Persian colours', *above*. De Morgan began working for Morris & Co as a designer of stained glass and tiles in the early 1860s but soon set up his own kiln to produce the wares himself. As well as using this sparkling Islamic-inspired palette he developed his own lustre-glaze technique and there are splendid bowls and vases by De Morgan on which a rich ruby lustre is set off by ochre and other pigments.

1865 The Gothic influence on this jewellery casket, *left*, is obvious in its architectural proportions, which even mimic a tiled 'roof'. Gothic devices are picked out in walnut inlays and gilding and the brass handles and strap hinges are typical of Arts and Crafts cabinet furniture. These details, together with the painted panels, depicting angels representing Day and Night, are in the style of J.P. Seddon.

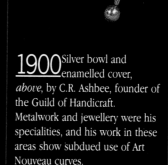

1895 Medieval knights, minstrels and swains, *below*, enjoy a somnolent idyll on this 'Sleeping Beauty' wallpaper design by Walter Crane, who made his name early in his career as an illustrator of children's books.

1900 Silver bowl and enamelled cover, *above*, by C.R. Ashbee, founder of the Guild of Handicraft. Metalwork and jewellery were his specialities, and his work in these areas show subdued use of Art Nouveau curves.

1891 Oak armchair by W.R. Lethaby, *below*, dating from the time of his association with Ernest Gimson. Displaying through-mortises on the arms and dovetailing on the front stiles, it makes no secret of its construction.

1903 Silver cup and cover, *left*, designed by C.R. Ashbee and bearing the hallmark of the Guild of Handicraft for 1902 and 1903, when the guild moved from London's East End to Chipping Camden, Gloucester. Apart from the silver pins through the base, decoration consists of a charming free-playing motif of flowers and leaves, pierced and chased.

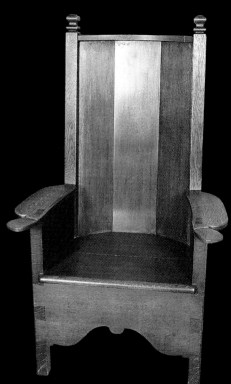

Pugin but not fully understood until later was that, where possible, local materials and methods of working them should be used, thus anticipating the emphasis put on traditional and vernacular arts and crafts by later adherents of the movement.

The Great Exhibition

In 1851 Pugin was involved in his last and most influential project—to design and arrange the Medieval Court for the Great Exhibition of 1851. His magnificently caparisoned stand was one of the chief attractions of the fair which, over the brief five and half months of its opening, attracted to London more than six million visitors from home and abroad. Tragically the stresses of working under so many pressures unhinged Pugin's mind and he was consigned within the year to a mental asylum.

The Great Exhibition, housed in its stupendous iron and glass structure nicknamed the Crystal Palace, proved something of a catalyst for design direction in the later nineteenth century. It did not so much capture the spirit of the styles to come as focus on the problems that had been rumbling in the background for almost half a century. Henry Cole, who, with the Prince Consort, was one of the prime movers behind the exhibition, believed strongly in the need to encourage and promote better design standards for manufactured goods, a task that the design schools were failing to do. Like a number of painters, sculptors and architects of the day concerned with improving industrial design, he submitted some of his own designs to the exhibition, working under the pseudonym Felix Summerly Art Manufacture.

Exhibiting manufacturers anxious to meet the high artistic aspirations of the exhibition's promoters went out of their way to commission designs suitable for 'art manufacture' from people like Cole who worked outside the pool of professional trade designers that they normally employed. Among the architects, artists and sculptors who contributed were Pugin, Alfred Stevens and Owen Jones.

Jones was an architect but was far more successful as a commentator on design and styles. Unlike Pugin, his antiquarian expertise was not confined to a specific aesthetic. He was interested in all styles. His best-known book, *The Grammar of Ornament* (1856), became a bible of ornamental styles covering every corner of the globe. It was superbly illustrated with coloured lithographs of every conceivable ornamental design and motif. It also contained some of Jones' 'propositions' on design largely derived from Pugin, a few of which were echoed in the Arts and Crafts movement. 'As architecture,' he wrote, 'so all works of the Decorative Arts should possess fitness, proportion, harmony, the result of which is repose.' He also put forward the idea, which again echoed Pugin and was later reiterated by Morris and others in the Arts and Crafts movement, that 'construction should be decorated. Decoration should never be purposely constructed'.

William Morris, social reformer

The designer, writer, poet and socialist William Morris (1834-96) was one of the most influential figures in the late nineteenth century. His ideas affected thought across a much wider spectrum than just art and design, encompassing politics, religion and aesthetics within a highly personal form of social idealism.

Morris was born into a generation deeply attracted to the mysticism, romance and magic of a medieval vision of art and life epitomized by glorious vistas of Gothic architecture. Much of his boyhood reinforced this vision. From an early age he was interested in churches and other old buildings and spent his holidays visiting them and taking brass rubbings. His interest in ancient buildings re-emerged when he founded the Society for the Protection of Ancient Buildings (called Anti-Scrape by his friends) in 1877. He also founded the Kelmscott Press which published books modelled in the style of medieval manuscripts.

University life at Oxford and the friends he made there, including Edward Burne-Jones (1833-98) and Dante Gabriel Rossetti (1828-82), were a continuing and powerful source of influence on the young Morris. Although his interest in medieval art and architecture never wavered, he abandoned an earlier idea of entering the church. After changing his mind several times he decided to become a pattern designer. His outstanding ability and great versatility in this field enabled him to apply his skills to a wide range of products, including wallpapers, textiles, book illustrations and printing.

An inheritance of £900 a year from his father in 1859 gave him the freedom to marry Jane Burden, whom he had met while working with Rossetti on a scheme for decorating the Oxford Union Debating Hall. Philip Webb (1831-1915), whom Morris had met while working briefly in the office of the architect George Street, designed a house for the couple at Upton, Bexleyheath, in Kent. The building and furnishing of the Red House, as it was called, encapsulated the spirit of co-operative artistic endeavour that was to become a precept of the Arts and Crafts movement. Webb's building was unusual, too, in that it broke with the more traditional country-house type then popular both in its modest size and use of vernacular and Gothic detailing. It seemed to re-unite nineteenth-century architecture with 'the common tradition of honest building'.

The Red House, which according to Burne-Jones was the 'beautifullest house in the world', brought together a number of people, each with specialist skills, in a loose association, the chief aim of which was to design and make all those things necessary to decorate, furnish and equip a home. The objects made for Morris' home embodied the ideas not only of Pugin and Ruskin — in their revealed construction and truth to nature and materials, for example — but of Morris and the Arts and Crafts movement. 'Have nothing in your houses,' Morris said, 'that you do not know to be useful or believe to be beautiful.' Their aim was to produce artistically designed, individually handcrafted wares, carried out in

a spirit of co-operation, joy and hard work. For Morris art was the 'expression of man's delight in his labour, a joy to the maker and the user'.

Morris' idea of designing and making articles, rather than being satisfied with the shop-bought wares of an unknown manufacturer, was not unusual, however. Many architects and designers, such as Pugin, Burges and Shaw, had done it, either for themselves or for special commissions. Indeed, Morris himself had done it for rooms he rented at Red Lion Square, London, the year before his marriage, and some of these items — mainly large pieces of furniture — formed the nucleus of furnishings for the Red House. They were cottagey and traditional in appearance, often drawing on vernacular or country forms such as the settle, a form much used by Arts and Crafts furniture designers.

Materials were taken from local sources. Colour was introduced through embroidery or painted designs, and ceramics were made from indigenous clays rather than refined porcelain bodies. Metalware objects were made of humbler materials such as pewter and brass and reflected Morris' affinity with the ordinary man.

Far left and left: *The Red House, Bexleyheath, designed by Philip Webb and built for William and Jane Morris, 1859-60. The Gothic revival appearance of the house echoed features already familiar in Butterfield's 'vicarage tradition' but the exposed brickwork and severe outline of the front anticipated 20th-century functionalism. The Gothic revival theme was carried inside, with arched doors and Gothic details applied to the stairwell. Furnishings were mostly designed by Morris, Webb and Burne-Jones. Their use of highly coloured textiles, ceramics, metalwares and painted furniture enriches the white walls, bare floorboards and exposed beams.*

Below: *Steel scissors made by G. Wilkinson and exhibited at the Great Exhibition. Elaborately engraved with the arms of Cavendish, they were held to have 'the charm of novelty'.*

Above: *The Medieval Court of the 1851 Great Exhibition, London, designed and supervised by Pugin, showed 'a style of decoration now almost totally neglected except in Roman Catholic churches...On his entrance the visitor was struck with the awe which is so often felt in a sanctuary.' It is depicted in a lithograph executed by Joseph Nash (1803-78) and printed by Dickinson Brothers.*

Left: *Lithographic print showing Beefeater guards awaiting the arrival of Queen Victoria by the Coalbrookdale Gates. Beyond, the magnificent Crystal Fountain by F. & C. Osler appropriately plays at the centrepoint of the whole exhibition.*

Right: *The exhibition was designed to show the 'Works of Industry of all Nations' and natural products such as furs were exhibited alongside engineering products like this large Ross telescope.*

Left: *Carved bloodstone vase with silver-gilt and enamel decoration, depicting Perseus and Andromeda. Made by Louis-Constant Sévin for Henry Thomas Hope and shown at the 1855 Paris Exhibition, it typifies the over-elaborate concoctions that the Arts and Crafts movement held in disdain.*

Bottom: *Mahogany armchair elaborately carved with national emblems and marquetry decoration, set with a painted porcelain panel of Prince Albert. Made by Henry Eyles of Bath and exhibited at the Great Exhibition.*

Below left: *Stained glass window depicting 'A Woman Playing a Harp' surrounded by flowers, 1872-4. Despite its small size this panel is typical of Morris' design style and shows the continued influence of the Pre-Raphaelite artists, some of whom were among his closest friends.*

MORRIS & CO

The success of the Red House project inspired Morris and some of his friends to form their own company, and the firm of Morris, Marshall, Faulkner & Co came into being in 1861. In its prospectus the firm described itself as being 'Fine Art Workmen in Painting, Carving, Furniture and the Metals'. Implicit in this was the idea that craft and the craftsman were of a standing equal to that of art and the artist and, to a degree, Morris was successful in raising the status of the artisan. 'Why in the name of patience should a carpenter be a worse gentleman than a lawyer?' he asked.

The firm's aim was to produce individually created, handcrafted artistic items that could be afforded by all. The group regarded themselves as a new breed of artist-designer who could turn their talents to designing all forms of domestic articles. Initially the firm operated from Red Lion Square and specialized in designing and making things in the neo-Gothic and medieval style, but later work shows little trace of its early Gothic influence and the firm developed a more organic, abstracted style.

Philip Webb, who joined the firm from the outset, was, after Morris, its most important and influential figure. He was responsible for designing much of the furniture, as well as some of the domestic items such as glass and metalwares.

The furniture made by Morris & Co fell into two categories: what Morris liked to call 'state furniture', which was grand and elaborate, and what he described as 'workaday furniture', which was 'simple to the last degree'. State furniture, which Morris admitted contributed to the 'swinish luxury of the rich', aimed to achieve a total richness of effect. It was for him the 'blossoms of the art of furniture' on which he spared no lack of elaborate carving, inlay or painting. These large, imposing pieces, which included bookcases, cabinets and sideboards, were simply constructed and tended to have large areas of flat panelling, which provided a magnificent alternative to canvas for the painters among the group to work on. Such co-operative endeavour met one of the high ideals of the movement, collective effort.

Most of these pieces were created in the early years of the firm's existence and were influenced by the solid, architectonic forms of early Gothic architecture so admired by Morris and Pugin before him. The painted ornament was carried out largely by members and friends of the Pre-Raphaelite Brotherhood, including Burne-Jones and Rossetti, both of whom worked for the company. Pictorial themes were taken from sources that re-awakened the medieval spirit and could be found easily enough in much of the popular fiction of the day, especially the novels of Sir Walter Scott and other romantic Gothic fiction. Chaucer was also resuscitated

William Morris (1834-96), socialist, poet, designer, typographer and master of several crafts, has inspired generations of artist-craftsmen up to the present day by his energetic and enthusiastic example. In spite of his mistrust of mechanization and his return to vernacular traditions and values, Morris' ideas on the nature and function of art and design in society affected thinking throughout Europe and America into the 20th century. Stylistically, much of his work was inspired by his love of medieval art and architecture, evidenced in this detail from 'The Orchard', a high-warp tapestry panel, c.1890, by Morris and J.H. Dearle. His pattern designs are imbued with a formal flat style which comes to life through his brilliant use of colour and the careful control of complex repeat patterns, as in this 'Blackthorn' wallpaper, designed in 1892. By contrast his admiration for the honest simplicity of vernacular, even rustic, furniture and decoration made his firm a world leader in the production of simply constructed pieces.

Below: *A satinwood and mahogany sideboard made by Morris & Co, c.1899. The light metal mounts which simulated 'old silver' were by W.A.S. Benson, who probably designed this piece. Benson, who became a director of the firm in 1896 after Morris' death, designed more commercial furniture and frequently used exotic timbers. He also designed for J.S. Henry, who specialized in making commercial furniture in the Art Nouveau style.*

Right: 'Saville' chair designed by George Washington Jack, c.1890, and upholstered in Morris' 'Honeycomb' fabric. Jack (1855-1932), an American, moved to London in 1875, becoming chief furniture designer for Morris & Co in 1890.

Below right and detail left: Embroidered crewel work wall hanging worked in wool on linen, c.1880, by Lady Margaret Bell and her daughters for the dining room of her home, Raunton Grange. The house was designed by Philip Webb and the frieze of embroidery that hung above the panelling, by Morris and Burne-Jones.

and the 'Prioress's Tale' was the subject chosen by Burne-Jones to decorate a wardrobe designed by Philip Webb and given to the Morrises as a wedding present in 1859.

Not all furniture made to the firm's designs was as elaborate as these large pieces. The firm, which became styled simply Morris & Co after 1875, also made much simpler pieces, many of them based on vernacular styles. These epitomized the rustic, country, traditional designs of Morris and this type of simple elegant furniture forms one of the links between Morris and the Arts and Crafts movement and the developments of the twentieth century. Characteristically the woods used were indigenous, such as oak or beech, and were often stained black or green in the traditional manner of much seventeenth- and eighteenth-century country furniture. Seats were caned or woven with rushes, tables were often simple trestle affairs and country pieces such as the settle were revived.

Among the firm's most successful products was the stained glass, with which Morris and his partners challenged the more conventional trade outlets. Using the 1862 International Exhibition to demonstrate its improved colour and the superiority of its designs, the firm posed a serious threat to the traditional stained-glass manufacturers. Many of the designs for commissions received later were for churches and other ecclesiastical buildings but a number of private commissions were made, including one for two rooms at St. James's Palace and another for the Green Dining Room at the new South Kensington Museum (now known as the Victoria and Albert Museum).

Morris' own involvement with designing and producing articles for the firm was chiefly concerned with pattern-making for fabrics, carpets and wallpapers. His interest in colours and the use of natural dyes, combined with his knowledge of printing, weaving and knotting, made him an acknowledged expert in all these fields. Although his skills were acquired almost by accident, since he was loath to ask of others what he could not do himself, these and other similar craft skills became almost a prerequisite for membership of the Arts and Crafts movement.

The firm expanded steadily throughout the 1860s and 1870s and acquired a showroom for exhibiting its products in Oxford Street in 1877. Expansion required the firm to make a number of moves over the years, including one to Merton Abbey in 1881. This was close to his friend and colleague William de Morgan, who was influenced by the ideas of the Arts and Crafts movement and whose own ceramic business contributed to the pottery production of Morris & Co. De Morgan (1839-1917) was respected for his finely crafted pottery, much of which was decorated with lustre colours, a technique he did much to revive. The motifs that he used came principally from flowers, plants and animals but he also deployed mythical and heraldic beasts in his designs as well as curious sailing ships that recalled the romance of the ancient Nordic sagas.

26

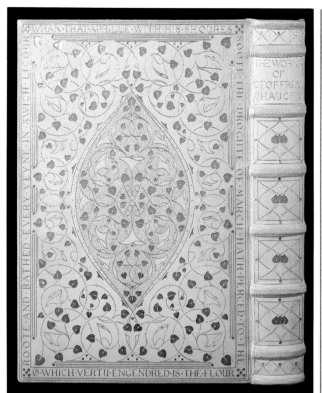

Left: 'The Works of Geoffrey Chaucer' bound by the Doves Bindery for the Kelmscott Press in 1896. Morris set up the Press in 1890 and it was his last interest over which he could exercise complete artistic control.

Below: Two panels showing figures based on Chaucer's 'Illustrious Women', designed by William Morris and embroidered by Jane Morris and her sister Elizabeth Burden.

THE CRAFT GUILDS

The Arts and Crafts movement came of age with the formation of the guilds and craft societies. The prototype for these was the Guild of St. George, inspired and established by the art critic and writer John Ruskin in 1872. He dreamed of reforming society by following the example of the medieval guild system, but he supplanted the spirituality of Puginesque Christianity with a temporal vision of the brotherhood of man. The idea of replacing industrialized Victorian society with one based on medieval guild masters and guildsmen was not well received and support for the project was so low that, in spite of Ruskin's contribution of £7,000 to launch it, the guild foundered.

Above: *Mahogany dining chair designed by A.H. Mackmurdo for the Century Guild, 1882-3 and made by Collinson & Lock, Fleet Street, London, who were 'manufacturers of artistic furniture'. This famous chairback design represented a new development within the Arts and Crafts movement and influenced many later designs and especially the development of Art Nouveau.*

Mackmurdo and the Century Guild

The Guild of St. George was nevertheless important as the inspiration and model for later, more successful societies. Among the first to follow its lead was the Century Guild in 1882. Like all the guilds, it was fired by Morris' enthusiasm for reviving hand craftsmanship and restoring the craftsman to his rightful place. In their first programme the members promised to 'render all branches of the arts the sphere no longer of the tradesman but of the artist'. Under the collective mantle of the guild its members agreed to make and promote their work as a democratic collective effort.

The impetus of the guild came from its two older,

Below: *Title page from A.H. Mackmurdo's book 'Wren's City Churches', published by G. Allen in 1883. The energetic design of the swirling, organic plant forms closely echoes that seen on his earlier chairback.*

more experienced members: the architect-designer Arthur Heygate Mackmurdo (1851-1942) and the illustrator-designer Selwyn Image (1849-1930). Mackmurdo was the dominant member of the group, designing many of the guild's products. (Because of the collective policy practised by the guild definite attributions are often difficult). Among those who joined it were Herbert Horne (1864-1916) — remembered particularly for his Blakeian *Angel with Trumpet* design — Kellock Brown, George Esling and Clement Heaton — all noted metalworkers (Heaton was also known for his fine enamelling) — and the sculptor Benjamin Creswick.

Like so many of his contemporaries who played a prominent role in the movement, Mackmurdo was an architect by training. His designs, executed either by the other members of the Century Guild or by firms sympathetic and acceptable to them, heralded the styles of the late nineteenth and early twentieth centuries, especially that known as Art Nouveau. Like Morris, whom he met in 1877, he taught himself the basics of many of the crafts for which he designed and could turn his hand to textiles, furniture, printing and book illustration. Some early designs for the guild included fabric patterns that demonstrate the sinuous line that characterizes his later work. Natural plant forms, especially abstracted flower-heads and limpid leaf motifs, flow across the surface in a firmly geometric and well-ordered repeat structure of a type much used by Morris. But the guild's work conveys a much stronger sense of movement and uses much sharper colours than anything Morris & Co produced.

Mackmurdo's title page for his book *Wren's City Churches*, published in 1883, was in advance of its time, anticipating not only Art Nouveau but also, in the strong lines of the woodcut, the technique if not the anguish of German Expressionism. The powerful undulating forms of flame-like flowers on waving stems flanked by etiolated peacocks set off the title, placed diagonally across the page. Although Mackmurdo is often regarded as the precursor of Art Nouveau, he rejected its extreme curvilinear style as 'a strange decorative disease' which was neither sympathetic with, nor representative of, his socialist ideas.

The Century Guild, lacking the formal legal structure of a company, such as Morris & Co had, was nevertheless successful in securing steady work and some important commissions. Projects such as the restoration of Pownall Hall, Cheshire, serve to illustrate a paradox of the movement that was never satisfactorily concluded. In spite of the professed aim of Morris and all who came after him to provide artistically designed goods affordable by all, the truth was that even if the ordinary man really desired such items it was doubtful that he would be able to afford them. Notwithstanding its anti-elitist stance, much of what was made and done in the name of social brotherhood and the Arts and Crafts movement was the 'work of a few for the few'.

In 1884 the Guild published the first issue of its magazine, *The Hobby Horse*. The joint editors of this issue were Mackmurdo and Horne, and Selwyn Image designed the front cover. It was hand-printed on good-quality paper and was intended to be published quarterly. Its next appearance, however, was not until 1886. Nevertheless, this first issue not only prompted Morris to comment that 'here was a new craft to conquer' but also it inspired a succession of 'art' magazines. The most prominent of them was *The Studio*, which had an extensive readership not only in Britain but also in Europe and America. It was through publications like this one, launched in 1893, that the teachings of the Arts and Crafts gospel spread.

From 1888 the Century Guild undertook no further commissions and virtually disbanded itself, freeing its members to concentrate on their own work. Despite its early closure after only six years it produced some of the most influential designs of the last two decades of the century, and it set an example in both its structure and aims for like-minded designer-craftsmen to follow.

Two of its members chose later to live abroad: Herbert Horne, who at 18 had been the youngest member to join, left for Florence in 1900, where he wrote a biography of Botticelli; and Clement Heaton, who had joined the Guild as a young man of 21, left England in the 1890s to work in his specialist fields of stained glass and enamelling. Heaton achieved recognition for his *cloisonné* work in Neuchâtel, later settling in America and, like other members who travelled abroad, helping to disseminate the precepts of the movement.

Right: *The Hall of Voysey's house 'The Orchard', Chorley Wood, 1900, for which he designed much of the interior fittings and furniture. While retaining much of the simplicity advocated by Arts and Crafts thinking, Voysey's use of light and space demonstrate an increasing affinity with the Modern Movement.*

Below right: *Oak sideboard by C.F.A. Voysey. It shows his characteristic designs for metal mounts, to which he paid special attention, and Mackmurdo's influence in his use of exaggerated verticals which are topped off with horizontal caps. The use of local or indigenous woods, left plain, echoes Charles Eastlake's instruction that timber 'be left free from stain or polish'.*

Below: *This house was part of a Garden Suburb development at Bedford Park, West London, laid out by Norman Shaw in 1876.*

The Art Workers' Guild

The Art Workers' Guild was formed in 1884 from a nucleus drawn from two separate groups. The smaller of them, the St George's Society, consisted of five young architects linked by common service in the offices of the architect-designer Richard Norman Shaw (1831-1912), who was himself a member of the Art Workers' Guild. William Lethaby (1857-1931) was the most interesting and influential figure in this group and the one who carried forward most resolutely and clearly into the twentieth century the ideas and aims of the movement through his links with art education. The Society joined a group called the Fifteen, founded four years earlier by the designer and writer Lewis F. Day (1845-1910) and the illustrator and designer Walter Crane (1845-1915). This august body also included such figures as Morris, Mackmurdo, Shaw, Edwin Lutyens, Charles Voysey and Charles Ashbee, all of whom, with the exception of Morris, were professional architects.

The aims of the Art Workers' Guild were and still are 'to advance education in all the visual arts and crafts, by means of lectures, meetings, demonstrations, discussions and other methods; and to foster and maintain high standards of design and craftsmanship ... in any way which may be beneficial to the community.' The members were concerned that the links between architects, artists and craftsmen were becoming estranged from industry, and they would meet in each others' houses to discuss this and related problems.

The emphasis of the guild has always been on personal contact between members and its size was restricted to an 'ideal number' that would 'allow every member to know every other member'. This clubby attitude was born of a need for frank and confidential exchanges of view rather than of any sense of elitism, although in practice that appears to be the case. The influence of the guild tended to be more subtle than that of any other. This was especially so as its members tended to work as individuals from their own offices, studios and workshops rather than within the collective framework, as Morris & Co or the Century Guild had done.

The strength of the Art Workers' Guild lay in the scope of its members, many of whom were not only skilled artists, designers, architects or craftsmen but were also participants in the great renaissance of art education, which is among the movement's finest legacies. Lecturers and principals of leading art schools figured prominently among the membership. Walter Crane held a number of influential positions in education, including the post of principal of the Royal College of Art in 1898.

Crane is probably best-known for his work as an illustrator of children's books and ranks alongside Kate Greenaway and Randolph Caldecott. But he was also an industrial designer of considerable repute, working in a number of fields including ceramics, textiles, wallpapers and carpet design. To a lesser extent, he designed stained glass and ornamental plasterwork for use in

buildings. His ceramic designs, which encompassed tiles, jugs, vases and dishes, included a range of decorative motifs varying from flowers and natural plant forms to medieval-styled knights and their ladies and a rich variety of fierce-looking mythical or heraldic beasts and birds. Many of these were executed in the strong rich colours associated with 'art' pottery and included the glowing ruby lustres popularized by William de Morgan.

A firm that specialized in the lustre colouring used in conjunction with Crane's designs was Pilkington's Tile and Pottery Co, but Crane also designed for Maw & Co, Wedgwood and Minton. His wallpaper designs were made up by Jeffrey & Co, who also did work for Morris & Co. Unlike those of Morris & Co, his designs were often full of rhythm and movement, showing a greater lyricism than those of Mackmurdo. They were widely popular and his work gained considerable acclaim on the Continent, as well as in Britain, where he is also held up as an influence on the Art Nouveau style.

Charles Voysey (1857-1941) trained as an architect in the office of John P. Seddon, a specialist in Gothic architecture. He had participated in some of the early neo-Gothic designed 'state' furniture made by Morris, Marshall, Faulkner & Co, including the 'Honeymoon' cabinet exhibited at the 1862 Exhibition. Like most of the second-generation members of the movement, Voysey retained little of the Gothic influence in his design work but adhered to many of the principles that the Gothic reformists had promulgated. In 1882 he set up his own architectural practice but at first concentrated on designing for textiles and wallpapers, which were made up by Jeffrey & Co. Many of these designs, again relying chiefly on bird and plant forms, demonstrate a sense of controlled movement within elegant abstraction.

Voysey's bold architectural style was particularly suited to furniture design. While some of his contemporaries embellished their work with painted panels, inset ceramic tiles, panels of embossed leather or metal

Top: *Wallpaper design by C.F.A. Voysey. A light palette gives his designs a flatter and more airy appearance than the fabric and wallpaper designs of William Morris.*
Above: *'Oswin' pattern designed by Voysey, c.1896.*

As well as being an architect of considerable success and influence, Charles Francis Annesley Voysey (1857-1941) was a noted designer of wallpaper, textiles, badges, bookplates, memorial tablets, furniture and metalwork. Like many of his contemporaries he was trained under the light of Gothic Revival principles of design and construction but stylistically his work owed much to vernacular art and architecture, and the brass teapot, of c.1896, *above*, has a simple charm in its decorative use of constructional details such as rivets. Throughout his life he remained sympathetic to the ideals of the Arts and Crafts Movement. His buildings were often characterized by a solidity of construction with strong spatial masses countered by interesting groups of horizontals and verticals, a device used to satisfying effect at The Hill, Northamptonshire, *bottom*. This economy of design extended to the other fields in which he worked and his bold simple forms heralded several design features of the twentieth century. Voysey designed this textile print, *below*, for Liberty & Co in c.1890.

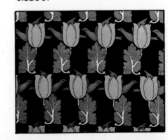

Left: *'Nympheas' printed cotton, designed by C.F.A. Voysey in the 1880s and made by Turnbull and Stockdale, showing a fluid pattern that anticipated Art Nouveau forms.*

and stained-glass windows, Voysey's pieces were austere and even hinted at the Japanese influence which was affecting the work of designers such as E.W. Godwin and Christopher Dresser, both of whom were closely associated with the Aesthetic Movement. He frequently worked in indigenous timbers and allowed the constructional form to provide the decoration in accordance with Arts and Crafts ideals. Like many of his contemporaries, such as Mackmurdo, Charles Rennie Mackintosh (1868-1928) — who in spite of being rejected by the movement forms a link between it and design developments of the twentieth century — and Charles Rohlfs (1853-1936) of America, Voysey exaggerated the vertical and horizontal planes and often allowed uprights on chairs and cabinets to extend beyond their normal limits, topping them off with a contrasting flat horizontal detail. Hinges were greatly elongated to form elegant strap plates reminiscent of the type used on medieval furniture. These he frequently decorated with motifs such as stylized flowerheads or hearts — which he also liked to use, usually cut out, as a decorative motif in chairbacks.

The Arts and Crafts Exhibition Society

Without the structure of a company like Morris & Co with its own showrooms, or the close working commitment of the Century Guild, some members of the Art Workers' Guild felt the lack of a forum for displaying and promoting their work. The prospect idea was mooted of holding a large exhibition, open to the public as well as to members. There was opposition to the idea — Morris himself was sceptical of the scheme's viability — so a splinter group was formed that favoured a programme of exhibitions to promote its work.

Under the initiative of one of its founding members, the architect-designer William Benson (1854-1924), the

Left: *Oak chair designed by C.F.A. Voysey, c.1906-09, showing his characteristically simple, linear style.*
Below: *Art pottery bottle vase designed by Christopher Dresser.*

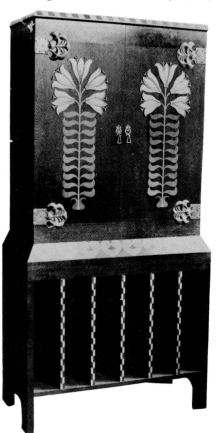

splinter group published its own circular *The Combined Arts*, through which members hoped to drum up support. The paper pointed out that 'Art Exhibitions have hitherto tended to foster the prevalent notion that the term "art" is limited to the more expensive kinds of portable picture painting, unmindful of the truth that the test of the condition of the arts in any age must be sought in the state of the crafts of design'. In November 1888 the new society, calling itself the Arts and Crafts Exhibition Society — after a phrase coined by another founder member, T. Cobden-Sanderson — held its first exhibition in the New Gallery, Regent Street.

Benson was a friend of William Morris and worked closely with his company. Under Morris' encouragement he specialized in metalworking and in 1880 opened his first workshop in Hammersmith, making a wide range of domestic metalwares, including dishes, kettles and stands, firescreens, coffee and tea pots, tureens and chafing dishes, as well as a wide range of light-fittings. These catered for the requirements of gas, oil and candle power but he also designed and made fittings for electrical appliances, then just coming into use. Features often included elongated stem motifs that anticipated the exaggerated whiplash forms of Art Nouveau. His metalwork was also incorporated into furniture designs, usually made in conjunction with well-known commercial manufacturers such as J.S. Henry & Co, although some were carried out by Morris & Co.

Left: *Music cabinet designed by M.H. Baillie Scott and made by the Guild of Handicraft, 1898.*
Below: *Green glass decanter decorated with intricately wound silver mounts, 1901. The sinuous organic form of the mounts is typical of Ashbee's work, most of which was executed by the Guild of Handicraft.*

Following Morris' death in 1896 Benson joined the latter firm and became a director.

Benson was among the small minority of early Arts and Crafts practitioners who were not anti-pathetic to mechanization, which he employed extensively in his own workshop. Nor was he as intolerant of commercial and trade links as some of his contemporaries, including Morris. In both attitudes he anticipated the stance of twentieth-century designers who stressed the need to work with industry rather than against it.

Ashbee and the Guild of Handicraft

Charles Robert Ashbee (1863-1942), an ardent admirer and disciple of William Morris, was a fine and innovative designer whose work, along with contemporaries such as the Scottish architect-designers C.R. Mackintosh and Mackay Hugh Baillie Scott (1865-1945), attracted considerable attention both at home and abroad. In 1888 the young Ashbee, already a member of the Art Workers' Guild, founded the Guild of Handicrafts out of a nucleus drawn from his School of Handicrafts, established the previous year.

In accordance with Ruskin's and Morris' ideas this society was modelled along the lines of a medieval guild. Within its safe and comfortable structure Ashbee envisaged a group of happy craftsmen producing honestly handcrafted objects that would be a source of pleasure both to themselves and the community at large. The majority of his colleagues were drawn from

Above: Oak gate-leg table by Sydney Barnsley, exhibited at the Arts and Crafts Exhibition in 1896. Barnsley and his partner Ernest Gimson carried the simple vernacular traditions of Arts and Crafts design into the 20th century. Below: Embossed and chased silver bowl designed by C.R. Ashbee and made by the Guild of Handicraft, 1893. The heart motif and the loose sinuous design of the legs echo Art Nouveau.

the impoverished environs of London's East End and their first homes were in Whitechapel. At the turn of the century, however, when the back-to-the-land movement was at its height, Ashbee decided to move his happy band of urban East Enders to Chipping Camden, Gloucestershire. The move took place in the spring of 1902 and guild members, numbering about 150, produced some of their finest work in this rustic setting.

Ashbee himself provided most of the designs. He specialized in metalwork and jewellery and much of his work is marked with his initials, C.R.A. Like many of his generation within the movement his work bore little of the historicism that characterized its early years. Instead, he strove for a sense of organic unity and an abstraction of pure form that quickly developed into a style.

Jewellery, metalwork and furniture formed the mainstay of the guild's work. Rather than being refined and polished in their final stages, the objects would show evidence of the methods and processes involved in their crafting. Thus metalwares were often left with soft mottled hammer-marks. In accordance with the ideas of making handcrafted wares that were affordable to most, jewellery and most of the silverware was decorated with less expensive semi-precious stones or with brilliant flashes of coloured enamels.

Among the guild's most famous projects was the production in 1897 of some of the furniture, metalwork and light-fittings for the Grand Duke of Hesse. This was carried out in collaboration with Baillie Scott, who had overall control of the project. The austere geometric furniture forms recalled Morris' 'state' furniture, being richly decorated with panels of flat, stylized plant and flower forms. These were achieved either through the use of coloured inlays or through the use of sumptuous materials such as embossed leather.

Despite Ashbee's initial mistrust of commercialism, which for him meant the unregulated use of machinery to maximize profit margins at the expense of humanity, he came to realize the usefulness of mechanization provided it was carefully controlled. Like many of his contemporaries he forsook the notion of rising above any contact with the trade and recognized the paradox that the Arts and Crafts style, if not its ideals, was disseminated more effectively through commercial retail outlets such as Liberty's in London and Tiffany's in New York than through any alternative outlets that the movement could have set up. To this extent the role of shops like Liberty & Co is ambivalent. On the one hand they encouraged designs from leading designers, including some major figures within the movement such as Crane and Voysey, thus resolving the movement ideal of uniting art and industry; on the other hand they saw it no part of their business to pass on the socialist spirit of the movement. It was nevertheless through these channels that the elusive and often idiosyncratic styles were catapulted to international popularity, and from this diversity sprang not only the 'decadent luxuriousness' of Art Nouveau but also many of the more advanced developments of the twentieth century.

BEYOND BRITAIN

Left: *Front cover of 'The Craftsman' magazine, published by the Stickley brothers from 1901 to 1916. The designs and furniture from their craftsman workshop were discussed and illustrated in the* journal, *which did much to promote the Arts and Crafts movement in America.*
Above: *A Craftsman living room illustrated in the magazine,* left, *which stressed simple homely domesticity.*
Below: *Art pottery pieces made by the Rookwood Pottery, Cincinnati, late 19th century. The prunus blossom bowl exhibits the Japanese influence for which the founder Mrs Nichols was noted.*

Although Morris and his successors had a considerable impact in both Europe and America, the Arts and Crafts movement was essentially a British phenomenon. In the United States the influence was at first strongest in the great cultural centres of Boston and New York, but it spread to the industrial heartland of Chicago and across the prairies of the Mid-West to the sunny open spaces of the Californian coastline.

As in Britain, where numerous local arts and crafts societies had sprung up throughout the country, similar groups emerged in America. These included the American Art Workers' Guild (established 1885), the Arts and Crafts Societies of Boston (1885), Chicago (1897) and Minneapolis and the Industrial Art League. Many of them embraced the high ideals of the movement but they were never realized as fully as they were in Britain. There were attempts to emulate Ashbee's great rural experiment in enterprises such as the Rose Valley Association of Philadelphia, which supported itself by selling its own handcrafted pottery and furniture. Like the Chipping Camden group, the Rose Valley Association eventually succumbed to bankruptcy and was forced to disband.

Right: *Elaborately decorated stove which shows the popular taste for derivative period styles often amassed on a single object, roundly condemned by Arts and Crafts enthusiasts as commercial rubbish.*
Left: *Mahogany cabinet decorated with embossed and gilt leather panels designed by Edward Godwin and James McNeill Whistler. Both were influenced by Japanese art.*

Stylistically much that was produced followed design principles established by Morris and others. Furniture designer-craftsmen such as Gustav Stickley (1857-1942) brought Morris' craft ethic to their own brand of traditional simple, plain — even austere — workaday products. Both he and the Arts and Crafts patron Elbert Hubbard (1856-1915) had craft workshops in New York State: Stickley in Syracuse and Hubbard with his community of Roycrofters in East Aurora near Buffalo. Hubbard, formerly a successful soap salesman, was neither craftsman nor designer but he established and helped finance the Roycroft artistic community until his death in the *Lusitania* disaster in 1915.

Stickley was less successful and the company that he formed in 1901 to make furniture went into liquidation in 1914, two years before he closed down his influential publication, *The Craftsman*. The 'massive simplicity' and severely linear forms of his furniture, reminiscent of 'Shaker' furniture, anticipated the spare rectilinearity of one of the twentieth century's greatest architect-designers, Frank Lloyd Wright. Although Lloyd Wright's enthusiasm for machinery ('My God is machinery,' he said) puts him squarely outside the Arts and Crafts movement, he owed a debt to many of the design concepts put forward by it.

In Europe the work of many Arts and Crafts practitioners was familiar through publications such as *The Studio* magazine and the annually produced *Studio Year Book*. Exhibitions of arts and crafts were also widespread. The styles of the British artist-craftsmen were readily absorbed by Continental designers, but they were developed into the excesses of Art Nouveau.

This failure to appreciate the basic tenets of the Arts and Craft movement led to a cultural dead-end and it was left to the radical thinkers of the Modern Movement to search for functionalism and significant form.

AFTERMATH

Commercial concerns in Britain at the turn of the century were capable of mass-producing the handcrafted country look widely associated with the movement, but there were nevertheless those who continued to produce beautifully designed, well-made and handcrafted useful articles in the traditional way. Best known of these twentieth-century craftsmen were Sydney Barnsley (1865-1926) and Ernest Gimson (1864-1919), who maintained the tradition of making 'wonderful furniture of a commonplace kind', although their patrons were of a rich élite capable of affording their wares rather than commonplace people. They also expressed their traditional values by seeking out the 'simple life' of the country craftsman first advocated by Ashbee.

On a practical industrial level the main thrust of the Arts and Crafts movement was formally re-organized in 1915 into the Design and Industries Association. This was established once again to promote co-operation between the public, designers and workmen, and under its aegis fine craftsmanship returned to established commercial firms. In this the DIA was strongly supported by firms such as Heals, under the direction of Sir Ambrose Heal, a member of the Art Workers' Guild who did much to influence design direction in Britain in the twentieth century. The ideals and ambitions of the Arts and Crafts movement were never fully realized but have been of immense influence on design in the twentieth century.

Above: *Traditional armchair with rush seat designed by Gordon Russell.*
Right: *Small cabinet with geometric marquetry decoration in ebony, holly and walnut with silver mounts, designed by Ernest Gimson and exhibited at Debenham and Freebody in 1907. It was reviewed in the 'Builder', which called it a 'model of careful execution...depending on the accurate cutting and fitting of innumerable small pieces.'*
Far right: *Oak bracket clock. The tall uprights, heart motif and use of an oak echo Mackmurdo's extended verticals and preference for local materials.*
Below right: *Pair of chairs and mahogany and ebony display cabinet by Greene & Greene, Pasadena c.1910. Their furniture is distinguished by the decorative use of pegheads and oriental motifs.*

Above: *Cup and cover by Harold Stabler. As well as being a silversmith and enamellist, he was a noted potter and in 1915 a founder member of the Design and Industries Association, an organization whose aims were not so different from those dreamt of by Henry Cole and Prince Albert at the Great Exhibition.*
Left: *'Aragon' wallpaper design by Alan Vigers, 1901. This exhibits the same meandering repeat pattern that Morris often used, but with greater subtlety.*
Right: *Sweet chestnut tallboy designed by Ambrose Heal.*

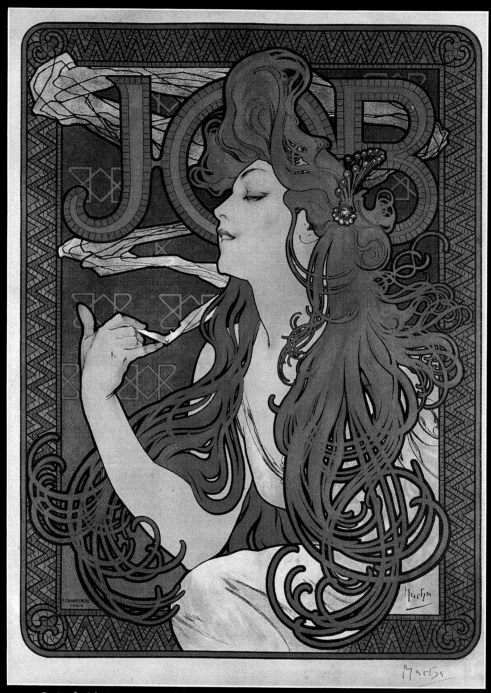

Design for Job cigarette papers, lithograph printed on silk, 1896, by Alphonse Mucha (1860-1939).

CHAPTER TWO

THE LANGUID LINE

ART NOUVEAU
1890-1905

'We stand at the threshold of an altogether new art, an art with forms which mean or represent nothing, recall nothing, yet which can stimulate our souls as deeply as the tones of music have been able to do.'

AUGUST ENDELL, c.1900

INTRODUCTION

The Art Nouveau movement swept through Europe and America in the 1890s, attaining its greatest popularity by 1900, the year of the Paris Exposition Universelle. Although the style was interpreted variously from country to country and made its appearance at different times, its widespread appeal lay in the expression of the shared aims of its advocates in pursuing an alternative art and decoration. It was a spirited and self-conscious period that looked forward to the new century but also drew upon the old one.

Like the English Arts and Crafts movement before it, Art Nouveau emerged as a co-ordinating force. It aimed to restore an equilibrium in the arts and crafts and it channelled its efforts particularly in the direction of the latter by producing luxury and utilitarian wares of artistic design and creating new architectural and interior schemes. Such 'progressive' concepts had been expounded earlier by John Ruskin and William Morris, but for the Art Nouveau designer the determining force was found almost exclusively in the treatment of surface decoration. The rich linear vocabulary of the style, with its multiplicity of floral and abstract ornaments and vigorous curves, was applied to a remarkable range of forms — from the novel cutlery designs of Henry van de Velde, to the organically inspired ironwork of Hector Guimard's Paris Metro stations. Art Nouveau permeated the city environment and spanned national boundaries to become the most assertive form of artistic expression of its time.

The sources of Art Nouveau were diverse. Although the movement sought to create new artistic forms and in so doing reject the retrospective inspirations of past generations, it embraced a number of traditional 'period' tastes. This eclecticism encompassed foreign and exotic arts and also incorporated contemporary trends. Such a rich and often incongruous mixture of designs and approaches appeared with varying intensity and sometimes in arbitrary combinations throughout the works of Art Nouveau's chief exponents.

The merging of contemporary attitudes

The Arts and Crafts movement contributed greatly to the Art Nouveau concept of a unity and harmony across the various fine arts and crafts media and to the formulation of new aesthetic values. The simple functionalism of the Arts and Crafts style was adapted by several Art Nouveau craftsmen — witness Charles Rennie Mackintosh's sparsely adorned Glasgow-style chairs and tables and the rustic designs of the Belgian Gustave Serrurier-Bovy.

In contrast the English 'Decadent' movement, inspired by the esoteric values and satirical wit of Oscar Wilde, influenced a number of Art Nouveau illustrators such as Aubrey Beardsley and Jan Toorop of Holland.

Symbolism was another literary and artistic trend of the late nineteenth century and it gave rise to a peculiarly mysterious and evocative Art Nouveau strain, as seen in the paintings of Fernand Khnopff in Belgium and Gustav Klimt in Austria. In addition, Symbolist traits were assimilated into the applied arts — for example, some of the glass wares created by Emile Gallé in France. These *études*, as he called them, were frequently highlighted by lines of poetry added to the textured surfaces for greater impact. The symbolism of line itself, in various rhythmic patterns, became a dynamic force for the Art Nouveau designer in conveying vitality and emotion. As early as 1889 Walter Crane instructed his colleagues to 'lean upon the staff of line — line determinative, line emphatic, line delicate, line expressive, line controlling and uniting'. In all its aspects,

Above: 'The Kiss', a colour woodcut by the German graphic artist and designer Peter Behrens, 1898. The rhythmic swirls of hair dominate the composition and create a two-dimensional, purely decorative framework for the profiles. Such pervasive linear ornamentation was a hallmark of 'Jugendstil' design, conveyed here in a typically abstract manner.

from the attenuated configurations of the Glasgow school, to the whiplash curves of Henry van de Velde and *Jugendstil*, linearity remained the essence of Art Nouveau composition.

Many new and 'modern' concepts were embraced by the Art Nouveau designer in his search for alternative decorative forms and structures. Unlike his Arts and Crafts counterpart, however, who stressed the importance of hand-craftsmanship and the use of simple and traditional materials, he appreciated the benefits of mass-production and other technological advancements. In architecture, for example, glass and metal were imaginatively combined and were preferred to stone and wood. Iron, in particular, was used with flair and featured prominently on numerous buildings and decorative furnishings of the period.

Historical attitudes

The revivalist trends that had characterized the nineteenth century continued to influence Art Nouveau artists and craftsmen, despite the fact that the movement declared itself as the 'new art'. In France rococo elements figured heavily in the Nancy School designs of Emile Gallé and Louis Majorelle, the elegantly fluid lines and naturalistic details of which recalled the florid tastes of the eighteenth century. In England and Scotland Art Nouveau decoration delved further into the past for inspiration, to the *entrelac* motifs and intricately coiled patterns of Celtic art. Such complex ornamentation appeared most strikingly in the works of the Glasgow School and in the 'Cymric' range of metalwares produced by the London store Liberty and Co.

Gothic and Renaissance characteristics were incorporated into Art Nouveau architecture — for example, in the symmetrical building façades of the Belgian Paul Hankar and in the arched tracery designs of his colleague Victor Horta.

The influence of exotic art forms

The painter Gustav Klimt included a number of exotic elements in his works. His use of glittering gold *tesserae* for murals imitated the richness of Byzantine mosaic compositions, and his choice of symbolic motifs such as birds, stylized 'eyes' and bold swirls alluded to the calligraphic styles of ancient Egypt. In America, Tiffany's 'Favrile' range of luxury glass objects was highlighted by iridescent surfaces, in imitation of weathered Roman wares.

As well as having an interest in ancient forms, Art Nouveau designers looked to the Far East for inspiration, and especially to the art of Japan. The two-dimensional, richly patterned surfaces of Japanese woodblock prints had an enormous impact on Art Nouveau artists, who exploited these compositional aspects effectively to emphasize the bold colour contrasts and flat linear rhythms characteristic of the style. These striking qualities occur in the graphics of Alphonse Mucha, Peter Behrens, Pierre Bonnard, Aubrey Beardsley and numerous others.

Nature and women

Art Nouveau is frequently referred to as a 'feminine art', an opinion fostered largely by its adherence to a specific thematic content composed of languid female figures and an assortment of plants and flowers. Such motifs were employed internationally across the broad spectrum of artistic media and were subject to many interpretations. For the Nancy School, a highly naturalistic approach was cultivated in the treatment of exotic plant forms, as poignantly conveyed by the delicate surfaces of Gallé's furniture. In Glasgow, stylized roses became a hallmark of Scottish Art Nouveau, and elongated figures of women appeared commonly in the graphic designs of the Macdonald sisters and Herbert McNair. In Germany, *Jugendstil* plant forms were often abstracted into sweeping linear rhythms, sometimes imbued with symbolism — as in the metalwork designs of Hector Guimard and Henry van de Velde.

Alphonse Mucha portrayed a range of sensual women in his posters and decorative panels, posed seductively in sumptuous floral landscapes. Gustav Klimt favoured female figures for his exotic murals, as did his Austrian contemporary Egon Schiele, whose nude portraits conveyed a stark eroticism.

The rich and composite nature of Art Nouveau contributed to its immense appeal, and its varied stylistic aspects converged to create a unique art which was distinctive and immediately recognizable. The free-flowing linear formats of Art Nouveau captured the uninhibited spirit of its *fin-de-siècle* advocates and heralded the arrival of the new century at the Exposition Universelle of 1900. The following sections trace the evolution of the style from country to country.

Above: *Art Nouveau bedroom suite by the French firm La Maison Mercier Frères, c.1902.* Below: *Art Nouveau chair by the French designer Eugène Gaillard, c.1900. The dynamic, fluid lines penetrate both the construction and design of the chair, as demonstrated by the elegant curved supports of the back.*

INSPIRATIONS

The arts and artefacts of Japan were a crucial inspiration for Art Nouveau. The hedonists of the Aesthetic Movement, worshipping art as a cult, fell eagerly upon Japanese woodcuts, with their simple palette and asymmetrical outlines, the minimalist grid patterns of room partitions, the refined detail of craftwork and elegant accessories such as fans and kimonos. The style took the Arts and Crafts 'unity across disciplines' precept to fulfilment. Open-air earnestness had no part in it, however, for it flourished in the hot-house atmosphere that fostered Symbolism, a contemporary art movement that hinted at Freudian obsessions through vivid, sensuous images. In the 'new art' the organic curves of nature and erotic female forms were invoked to avoid back-reference to classical proportion or platonic grace. Roses, sunflowers, lilies and peacocks carried inconographic weight, while calligraphic motifs from Celtic and Arabian patterns suited the allusive, mystical purpose. In the hot-house it was the exotic creatures — dragonflies, scarab beetles, locusts, lizards — that survived best.

Feather cluster
The Aesthetic Movement of Oscar Wilde and Aubrey Beardsley found apt hedonist symbols in the peacock, *inset right*. Liberty & Co, who marketed this peacock feather print, *right,* were virtually the only firm to champion the style in England.

Ivy league
Representation of nature was the root and branch of Art Nouveau. Ivy tendrils, *above,* and other whiplash floral and herbal forms recur throughout this curvaceous style, both in literal and abstracted representation.

Winged muse
As a complement to plant life, Art Nouveau wares often featured exotic and even sinister insect life, such as the scarab beetle. The bees on this silver cloak clasp, c.1900, by Child & Child, *left,* are outlined in Celtic-inspired curves.

Common motifs
Calligraphically drawn whiplash tendrils terminating in abstracted flowerheads that suggested heart, rosebud and egg forms, *above.*

Japanese imprint
The refined woodcut prints of artists such as Hiroshige, *left*, had a profound effect on artists such as Beardsley, Whistler and the Impressionists, many of whom designed posters in the Art Nouveau idiom. The grid structures of Japanese interiors are echoed in this sideboard, *below*, by Charles Rennie Mackintosh.

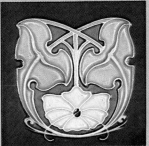

Celtic coils
Celtic stone cross illustrated in Owen Jones' 'The Grammar of Ornament', *above left*. The intertwined ribbon patterns of Celtic manuscripts, stone carving and metalwork, often terminating as fantastic beasts and birds, were a direct inspiration, witness this Minton tile, *above*. The intricate Arabian pattern, *far left*, provided another source, while the simple outlines of ancient Greek decoration, *left*, provided lessons in clarity.

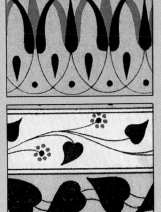

William Morris' second typeface, 'Troy' (1892), *top*, was based on fifteenth-century German founts. 'Boutique' (1900) and 'Auriol' (1901), *middle*, both capture the spontaneity of the Japanese brushstroke and the hand-daubed lettering of much Art Nouveau poster artwork. Though more formal, 'Herold' (1901), *above*, maintains the asymmetry, and rounded serifs far removed from classical chiselling give it soft curves.

ABCDEFG

ABCDEFGHIJKLMN

ABCDEFGHIJKL

ABCDEFGHIJK

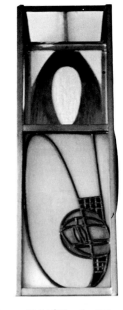

SCOTLAND

The most significant British contribution to the international Art Nouveau style was the work of the 'Glasgow Four' — Charles Rennie Mackintosh (1868-1928), Herbert McNair (1870-1945) and their wives Margaret Macdonald (1865-1933) and Frances Macdonald (1874-1921). This small group not only encapsulated Arts and Crafts and, later, Art Nouveau visions of a unity in the fine and applied arts, but also evolved new and highly original concepts in form and decoration. Through their paintings and graphic works, architecture, interior schemes, furniture, glass and metalwares they created a personalized and uniquely Scottish interpretation of Art Nouveau during the 1890s and early 1900s. This co-operative effort influenced many designers abroad — particularly the Secessionists in Vienna, with whom they were invited to exhibit in 1900.

The decorative hallmarks of the Glasgow style permeated the whole of their artistic expression, and certain stylistic elements and key motifs echo each other and recur with marked regularity. Surface ornamentation was confined mainly to austere linear patterns — especially slightly curving vertical lines that terminated frequently in egg shapes — and to grids and stylized roses. Colour schemes were subdued and virtually limited to pastel shades of pale olive, mauve, ivory-white, grey and silver. Elongated figures of women in contemplative poses also featured prominently in their designs, in keeping with the reflective mood of their interiors and furnishings. Although the decoration was defined in terms of set linear boundaries, the visual effect was not always simple — indeed, many surface patterns were complex and abstract, interspersed with symbolic forms which, like much of Art Nouveau, referred to the natural world. The interplay of long, bending verticals — like plant stalks — with egg and 'cell' motifs, stylized leaves and rosebuds imparts to each work a feeling of continual growth and vitality.

The linear style created by the Glasgow group was both innovative and insular, and appeared to incorporate little of the florid and dynamic decoration of Art Nouveau designers abroad. Their *oeuvre* was bound to many of the guiding principles of the English Arts and Crafts and Art Nouveau movements, and to the striving of both to create a new artistic harmony. The interiors designed by Mackintosh perhaps best serve to highlight this aim. His unification of architectural elements, furnishings and decoration produced a highly aesthetic setting, yet one that was adapted for everyday living. For example, his interior plan for the hall of Hill House, Helensburgh (1902-3) has the simple cube patterns of the furniture echoed in the same motifs on the carpet. The notion is extended to the rectilinear door and window frames, ceiling beams, wall panels and geo-

Above: *Light fitting by C.R. Mackintosh for Hill House, featuring rose motif, c.1902-3.*
Left: *High-backed chair by C.R. Mackintosh, c.1902.*

Above: *Painted cabinet by C.R. Mackintosh for Hill House, c.1902.*
Below: *Drawing of Hill House exterior, designed by C.R.*

Mackintosh, 1902-3.
Above: *Entrance hall of Hill House, 1902-3. Simple grid patterns dominate the interior.*
Below right: *Cover page for*

'Deutsche Kunst und Dekoration' by Margaret Macdonald Mackintosh, 1902. Tapering verticals enclose egg shapes, roses and a peacock.

metric light-fittings. The colour scheme is restrained and light; the whole effect is one of spaciousness and simplicity. It was a style that bore little resemblance to the dark and cluttered Victorian rooms of a few decades earlier. In its graceful restraint it drew upon a multitude of sources: the two-dimensional geometric patterns of Japanese woodcut design, the flat and twisted surface ornaments of Celtic art, and the plainer contours of Arts and Crafts construction.

Mackintosh was the most important and prolific member of the Glasgow Four. More versatile than his colleagues, he directed his talents beyond architecture, in which he trained, to painting, graphic design, interior furnishings and handicrafts. The Macdonald sisters and McNair also worked in a variety of media, including illustrations for books and magazines, decorative murals, furniture, glass and wrought-iron pieces. The group exhibited in London in 1890 with exponents of the Arts and Crafts movement, and subsequently abroad: in Liège in 1895, a year later in Paris, in 1900 in Lyons and Vienna, followed by Turin in 1902. The impact of these exhibitions was felt most strongly on the Continent and in Scotland, where their productions were received with much critical acclaim (in England the Arts and Crafts style appeared to remain the focus for artistic endeavours).

SPIRIT OF ART NOUVEAU

Inspired by the organic forms of plant-life, Art Nouveau evokes a distant, dreamy world from which strident urban preoccupations have been banished. The fluid whiplash line dominates both the form of things, from buildings and furniture to ceramics, glass and jewellery, and their surface decoration. Colours are subdued and subtly contrasted and interwoven, and there is a quest for shimmering light-effects, achieved with exotic materials such as mother-of-pearl, translucent horn and ivory and, notably, through experiments with iridescent glass. In the work of some practitioners, however, severe rectilinear grid patterns, derived from Japanese interiors, keep the burgeoning curves in check.

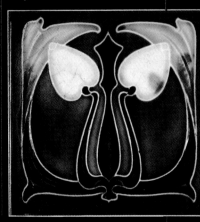

1895 Art Nouveau doorway in Paris, *left*, in which curling whiplash tendrils and the curvaceous human forms (of either sex) belie the essential rigidity of the wood and stone from which they are worked. The organic theme is sustained in the foliate swags of the surmounting iron balcony railings.

1900 Minton tile, *below*, decorated with a stylized floral motif, the flower-heads reduced to heart shapes.

1906 Official invitation to the launch of Cunard's 'Lusitania' at Clydebank, Scotland, *above*, featuring strangely retrospective sea vistas. It is clearly a product of its time in the calligraphic type and curving graphic panels.

1905 Parisian bedroom, *right*, designed by Hector Guimard, who believed in designing a complete scheme down to such details as fireplace and light-fittings. The bed and cabinets are elegantly carved in steamed pearwood.

1900 René Lalique's graphic invention and technical versatility are both evident in this exotic creation, a diamond and tourmaline pendant brooch, *above*, with *pique-à-jour* enamel.

1897 Side table in dark-stained pine, *below*, by C.R. Mackintosh, with Art Nouveau embellishments in wrought iron. The carpet is made to a Mackintosh grid design.

1905 American experiments in stained-glass techniques, inspired by the British Arts and Crafts interest in medieval glass, produced colourful results, especially in the work of L.C. Tiffany, where floral patterns meander across 'Wisteria' and 'Dragonfly' leaded glass lampshades and panes like this Tiffany Studio 'Trumpet Vine' window, *above*.

1895 'Whiplash' pendant, *right*, by the Manxman Archibald Knox, who was an expert in Celtic ornament and played an important role in developing the ranges of Cymric silverware and Tudric pewter.

1900 Gilt bronze lamp, *far right*, portraying the American dancer Loïe Fuller, who performed at the Folies Bergère, Paris, in the 1890s.

From the latter half of the 1890s Mackintosh was commissioned to create a series of decorative room designs for Miss Cranston's Tea Rooms (including the Buchanan Street Tea Room, 1896-7, in association with George Walton; the Argyle Street Tea Room, 1897, also with Walton; the Ingram Street Tea Room, 1901; and the Willow Tea Room, 1903-4) and buildings such as the Glasgow School of Art (1897-9, completed in 1907-9), Windy Hall, Kilmacholm (1899-1901) and Hill House, Helensburgh (1902-3). The interiors for the tearooms were designed in the characteristic Glasgow style, with delicate colour tones on the walls and painted furniture, interspersed throughout with linear patterns. The double doors created for the Willow Tea Room perhaps best capture the inventiveness and spirit of the Glasgow Art Nouveau style: a framework of slightly undulating verticals is accented by lively grid patterns, oval shapes and abstracted roses in silver, grey, white, mauve and green. The effect is striking. Similarly, the austere façade of the Glasgow School of Art is relieved by decorative iron railings and window frames that reflect the light, calligraphic approach.

Mackintosh's furniture demonstrated the same preoccupation with the interplay of lines, whereby shapes are made to conform to an overall geometric strategy. A large number of chairs, tables and cabinets were painted white and adorned sparingly to emphasize their bold rectilinear structure. Chairs frequently displayed unusually elongated backs, and long tapering arms and legs, either pierced with grid and other linear patterns or adorned with stencilled motifs. A small, white-painted two-tier table made by Mackintosh (in the Glasgow University Collection) also conveys this novel approach. The top is a simple circle and the second tier a square, the two levels being joined by tapering vertical lines, echoed below by long planks of shaped wood. The whole is free of surface ornamentation.

The Macdonald sisters' *oeuvre* was more limited, confined mainly to paintings, graphics and metalwares. They worked individually and sometimes in collaboration with each other and Mackintosh. The menu created for Miss Cranston's Tea Rooms (1901), for example, represents the joint efforts of Mackintosh and his wife Margaret, its stark black-and-white ornamentation and geometric contrasts epitomizing the Glasgow style. Many of their pictures depicted female figures, such as Frances Macdonald's *The Prince and the Sleeping Princess* (1895) in which the central figure of the princess is seen in quiet repose, surrounded by a network of swirling lines and flowers. The influence of the Pre-Raphaelites is especially evident in this work. The white metal plaques created by the Macdonald sisters for *The Iliad* (1899) further emphasize the figural content of their work and, as was often the case, elements of mysticism and a fairy-tale eeriness characterize the composition.

Herbert McNair's book illustrations also reflect the predominance of the female form. For example, in the drawing of the dustjacket for *His Book* (1896) a series of kneeling females are placed in Gothic-style niches,

Above: *Preliminary design for the mural decoration of Miss Cranston's Buchanan Street Tea Rooms by C.R. Mackintosh, 1897. The female figures are enclosed within 'entrelac' linear frameworks of verticals, coils and tangled foliage of elongated plant stalks supporting irises and roses. The delicate palette and use of elegant female forms create a subdued effect, in keeping with Scottish Art Nouveau.*
Right: *Detail of the interior of the Willow Tea Room, 1904, by C.R. Mackintosh. Undulating vertical outlines and oval abstract shapes in the mirrors are contained within the severe, white-painted grid of the wall panels.*

enclosed by their swirling locks of hair and by statuesque flowers on long stalks.

For brief periods during the late 1890s and early 1900s independent artists also worked closely with the Glasgow Four. Among them were the English artist Jessie King, whose book illustrations achieved considerable success, and Talwin Morris, who created interior furnishings (although in a style more akin to Arts and Crafts traditions).

By the end of the first decade of the twentieth century the innovative designs of the Glasgow School had waned considerably, largely as a result of their loss of artistic direction, and they eventually dispersed. Their unique style, however, contributed greatly to the development of Art Nouveau in Austria, and particularly to the geometric formats expounded by Josef Hoffmann and the Wiener Werkstätte. It is ironic that closer to home − in England − the influence of the Glasgow School was negligible, owing to the continued adherence to Arts and Crafts ideologies.

Above: *White-painted table by C.R. Mackintosh, 1902. Simple geometric shapes are offset by tapering vertical lines.*

Charles Rennie Mackintosh (1868-1928) was an innovative architect, designer and watercolourist, and the leading exponent of Scottish Art Nouveau. He developed a restrained calligraphic approach for his interior designs and furnishings, and pursued simple geometric formats which heralded the Modernist approach. Mackintosh's white and pastel colour schemes anticipated the cool, sophisticated interiors of designers such as Eileen Gray and Syrie Maugham. His use of repetitive grid patterns, circles and tapering vertical lines influenced many of his contemporaries abroad, namely the Secessionists in Vienna. The drawing for a music room project, *below*, dates from 1901. Although of recent manufacture by the Italian firm Cassina, the stark black and white chair, *above*, is of pure Mackintosh inspiration.

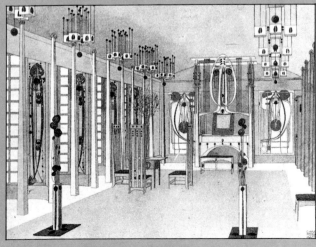

FRANCE

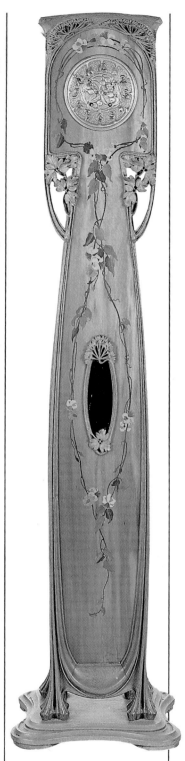

I n French architecture and the applied arts, Art Nouveau became the most important vehicle for artistic expression during the 1890s and early 1900s. The highly decorative nature of the style appealed immensely to French tastes and provided designers with a greater freedom to explore ornament, colour and form. As a result a wide and luxurious range of objects and buildings was created during this period, which highlighted not only the enthusiasm and inventiveness of individual artistic personalities, but also the movement's unique development in France.

The exponents of Art Nouveau worked in a variety of media. Numerous small and intimate *objets d'art* — glassware, jewellery and furniture — emphasized the overall fluidity and delicacy of form and decoration which characterized French *fin-de-siècle* design. In graphic work, particularly posters, the style was often interpreted more vigorously — for example, with the introduction of flat areas of bright colour and the use of bold expressive lines. The vivacity of these illustrations was also translated into an architectural vocabulary, as noted frequently on the ornamental façades of buildings and in details of ironwork fixtures and fittings. In all, the influence of Art Nouveau penetrated almost every form and surface. By virtue of its emphasis on decorative and aesthetic values, the style captured the imagination of France's finest artists, designers and craftsmen.

The development of Art Nouveau was focused on two distinct areas of the country. The first was in Nancy and revolved around the productions of Emile Gallé and his followers; and the second was in Paris, where numerous artists and designers banded together under the patronage of Samuel Bing, who both commissioned and exhibited their works at his celebrated gallery L'Art Nouveau (the name that later lent itself to the 'new art' movement). Within this geographical framework several distinctive personalities emerged for whom the style was a platform from which to diversify and expand their creative talents.

The Nancy School

The achievements of Emile Gallé (1846-1904) rank among the most outstanding in the realms of Art Nouveau furniture and glassmaking, and his scientific knowledge of botany and keen interest in the natural world are reflected throughout his output. Gallé's decorative content was confined mainly to exotic plant forms and insects, and these motifs featured prominently on his detailed marquetry designs for cabinets, tables, chairs and screens. The shapes and structures of many of these pieces demonstrate Gallé's adherence to traditional 'period' styles — for example, French eighteenth-century taste under the influence of rococo. But their curvilinear surface patterns of flowering plant

E mile Gallé (1846-1904), through his furniture and glass designs, created a visually striking and highly original Art Nouveau style inspired by nature. Novel glass techniques in surface texturing and colour enabled him to achieve a wide range of effects, from the subtlest relief-work to pieces of sculptural form. The supreme delicacy of his compositions was matched only by the virtuosity of his colouring, where overlying films of clear and muted shades appeared in breathtaking combinations, sometimes further offset by splashes of brilliant hues. Gallé's naturalistic approach extended also to his marquetry for furniture, and his influence on other Nancy School craftsmen — notably Majorelle and the Daum Brothers — was considerable.

Gallé's mastery of glass techniques is demonstrated by the plate, *above*, comprising a double overlay of glass which has been wheel-carved to varying depths to achieve exquisite detailing and a range of colour tones. Inspired frequently by Roman and ancient forms, Gallé also looked to the decorative styles of the Near and Far East, as seen on the vase *below* with its arabesques and niche motifs based on Islamic prototypes.

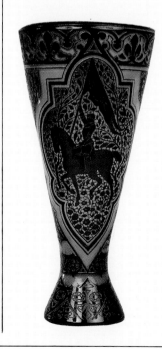

Above: Mahogany longcase clock by Louis Majorelle, inlaid with coloured woods and carved with naturalistic foliage, c.1900. The flowing contours and floral embellishments typify the Nancy style.

stalks and intertwining leaves create an effect that is both original and characteristically Art Nouveau.

In glassmaking Gallé explored a more adventurous range of decorative possibilities, inspired in part by the plasticity of the material, which lent itself admirably to the fluid, asymmetrical forms of Art Nouveau and permitted meticulous surface ornamentation in a wide spectrum of colours. A wide range of luxury wares was produced throughout the 1890s at Gallé's glassworks in Nancy, and during this mature period of his career some of the finest pieces were created. Many examples demonstrate Gallé's freer use of line and preference for rounded shapes, echoed in the undulating contours of superb relief decorations. Common motifs included large and naturalistic flowers, leaves, plant stems, butterflies and other winged insects, placed against matt or textured backgrounds of merging opalescent hues. His colour range at this time was limited to shades of mother-of-pearl, apple green, pink, violet, orange and burnt amber, and subtle tonal variations of these.

Gallé's successful productions inspired other glass manufacturers in Nancy to pursue similar decorative effects. Most notable among them was the factory of Daum Frères, under the artistic direction of the brothers Auguste (1853-1909), and Antonin (1864-1930). The relief surfaces of their glass wares hold an imaginative array of naturalistic motifs based on plants and insects. Vases were rendered frequently as slender, tapering forms in keeping with the elongated patterns of shooting stems and branches.

Louis Majorelle (1859-1926) was another important member of the Nancy School. In the 1890s he produced outstanding furniture and ironwork designs which, in their construction and ornamental detail, express a rhythmic fluidity. An interplay of rounded contours and swaying lines impart a sculptural quality to each work. Like Gallé, Majorelle's *oeuvre* incorporated exotic and traditional elements, including neo-rococo motifs, Japanese stylizations, and an overriding interest in organic forms. Other furniture and interior designers of the Nancy group included Emile André (1871-1933), Eugène Vallin (1856-1922) and Jacques Grüber (1870-1936), all of whom worked in the Art Nouveau idiom with an emphasis on curvilinear structures and naturalistic floral decorations.

Below: *Handle of flowing asymmetrical form in polished iron, a material much favoured by Art Nouveau craftsmen.*
Below left: *Glass lamp and vase by Emile Gallé, embellished with relief-carved decorations of fruit, leaves and flowers. Areas of high relief are polished to contrast with the matt-textured grounds.*
Below right: *'Etagère' of walnut and fruitwood by Emile Gallé, decorated with marquetry in various woods and with ormolu mounts.*

Developments in Paris

During the early 1890s, numerous exhibitions in Paris were devoted to both the fine and applied arts. These helped to foster not only a growing appreciation for fine craftsmanship but, more importantly, elevated its status to that of a valid means of artistic expression. Such endeavours to unify the arts and crafts culminated in the opening in 1895 of Samuel Bing's shop L'Art Nouveau, in which paintings, interior schemes and furnishings were featured side by side in appropriately 'modern' surroundings. Bing's inaugural exhibition was international in its scope and included, for example,

Right: Paris Metro station by Hector Guimard, of cast iron and glass, c.1900.
Below: 'France-Champagne' poster by Pierre Bonnard, 1891. Like Toulouse-Lautrec, Bonnard used emphatic lines and flat areas of colour for impact.

works by the Belgian Art Nouveau designer Henry van de Velde. But in the following years the gallery became an important meeting place for numerous French artists and craftsmen, among them Georges de Feure, Eugène Gaillard, Eugène Colonna, Auguste Delaherche and Charles Plumet. In their graphic designs, furniture, pottery, interior furnishings and accessories a sophisticated and elegant Art Nouveau style was cultivated. De Feure's posters reflect this elegance in their soft, pastel colours and subject matter consisting largely of female forms and stylized plant motifs. Gaillard's furniture is more abstract and dynamic in effect, and bears a striking likeness to the sculptural qualities of Majorelle's work — but even here, a softer, more refined and 'feminine' approach is conveyed.

In jewellery, the creations of René Lalique (1860-1945) exemplified the delicacy and luxuriousness of French Art Nouveau at its best. Like his contemporaries, Lalique employed a rich decorative vocabulary inspired largely by nature. Frequently, however, his plant and insect motifs were rendered into fanciful forms: an exotic bird is perched on top of a haircomb, as if emerging from it, while a lizard is transformed into the handle of a *lorgnette*. His choice of materials was equally imaginative and included, in various combinations, semi-precious stones, coloured golds, enamels, natural pearls of irregular shape and translucent horn.

In architectural design one of the most acclaimed exponents of Art Nouveau was Hector Guimard (1867-1942), perhaps best remembered for his superb cast ironwork for the Paris Metro stations, created in 1900. The entrances, banisters, signs, columns and electric lights reflect an overall harmony in their organically inspired forms and abstracted details. Similarly, Guimard's celebrated designs for the Castel Béranger building demonstrate this flamboyant approach in, for example, the asymmetrical ironwork of the main entrance — a gateway accentuated by a mass of flowing, dynamic lines expressive of both Art Nouveau and his own personal vision. Like Gallé, Guimard's *oeuvre* was eclectic. He drew freely upon a multitude of stylistic elements inspired by Gothic and rococo tastes and the art of Japan.

In the sphere of graphic works, brief mention must also be made of some of the artists who encapsulated on paper the spirit of Art Nouveau. Henri de Toulouse-Lautrec (1864-1901) created a series of spectacular posters in the 1890s, using an Art Nouveau calligraphy and format composed of silhouetted shapes, forceful lines and flat areas of solid colour. Eugène Grasset (1841-1917) and Georges Auriol made significant contributions to the development of book and poster designs, and the creation of a new decorative typography. The graphic works of Pierre Bonnard (1867-1947) were also closely connected to the Art Nouveau movement, as exemplified by the well-known poster *France-Champagne* (1891), with its bold stylized lettering and broad rhythmic lines.

The combined talents of France's finest Art Nouveau

Right: *Poster for the 'Salon des Cent', 1894, by Eugène Grasset. The flower and female are characteristically Art Nouveau, and the expansive calligraphy is also typical of the style.*
Below: *Dress design by Roger Broders, 1912, from 'Costumes Parisiens' — an elegant creation of Chinese inspiration, of silk and chinchilla.*

Far left: *Gilt-bronze bust by the French sculptor Bouval. The pose is contemplative and mysterious, an idealized female form accented by the familiar Art Nouveau motifs of blossoms, leaves and free-flowing locks of hair.*
Right: *A 'plique-à-jour' enamel and gold brooch by the French jeweller Gaston Laffitte, encrusted with diamonds, rubies and a natural pearl, c.1900.*

artists and designers were brought together at the Exposition Universelle held in Paris in 1900. Indeed, the progression of the style — from the earlier naturalistic forms of the Nancy School to the more abstract decorations of Paris — reached its climax at the turn of the century. During the course of the next few years, however, the movement was to lose its impetus, overrun by the new wave of 'Modernism' which advocated the use of simpler linear designs and unadorned surfaces.

BELGIUM

During the 1880s and 1890s Brussels was an important international centre for *avant-garde* painters and writers. This cultural and intellectual milieu stimulated the publication of numerous arts journals, such as the review *L'Art Moderne*, and the founding of societies such as the *Cercle des Vingt* (1884-93) and its subsequent re-grouping as the *Libre Esthétique* (1894-1914). These various artistic organizations shared a common goal in their search for novel ideas and alternative means of expression, free from the historic 'period' styles of the past. In this spirit of experimentation and desire for originality a new aesthetic was introduced in the fine arts and literature. A significant trend to emerge at this time was Symbolism which, as its name implies, sought to explore the ambiguities of dreams, symbols and emotions. On canvas, these elements were translated into frequently disturbing visual images. The painter Fernand Khnopff (1858-1921) exemplified this style in many of his portraits, which reflect a psychological intensity and an air of disquiet.

In architecture and the applied arts, the creation of new designs and structures came under the influence of Art Nouveau. Its emphasis on freer linear ornamentation was a vehicle for the anti-historical attitudes of its advocates, and the style was readily embraced by architects, interior designers and craftsmen.

In contrast to both the voluptuous naturalistic decoration of the Nancy School and the restrained linearism of the Glasgow group, the Art Nouveau movement in Belgium assumed a more abstract and energetic form. Here, the style was conveyed by the use of bold curvilinear patterns which, on occasion, were rendered so vigorously that they appeared to dissolve the structure of the objects themselves. These encircling and forceful lines allude frequently to the Art Nouveau concept of organic growth by means of their spiralling and outward movements. But, in general, there is little specific use of a naturalistic vocabulary of decorative motifs, and there are few recognizable forms. The unique aspects of Belgian Art Nouveau can be assessed through the diverse interpretations of its chief exponents.

Victor Horta (1861-1947) was the most acclaimed architect of the Art Nouveau style in Belgium. One of his important and early commissions was the design for the Hôtel Tassel in Brussels, built as a family house for a Professor Tassel in 1892-3. The exterior façade is comparatively modest, highlighted by curved bay windows and decorative wrought-iron *grilles*. The interior, in contrast, follows exuberant Art Nouveau design to the last detail of ornamentation. The entrance hall and staircase contain stained-glass windows and mosaic tiled floors accented by swirling, convoluted linear patterns — echoed by the twisting whiplash motifs of the ironwork balustrade, the columns and capitals, the crested

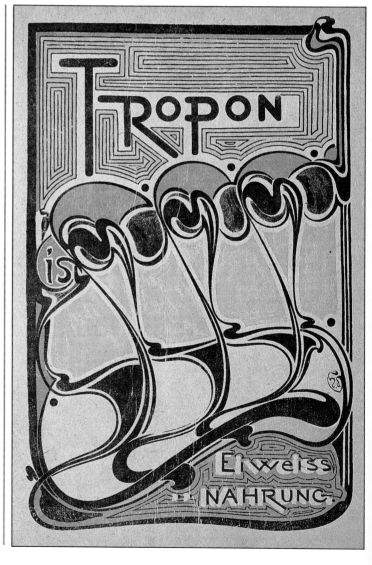

Above: *'Angels' Guard', a brightly coloured wool and silk embroidered appliqué designed by Henry van de Velde, and worked by the artist and his aunt. The tapestry was displayed at the Les XX exhibition in 1893, and recalls van de Velde's earlier career as a painter. In keeping with his curvilinear Art Nouveau style, the composition is reduced to abstracted, sweeping curves and parallel lines, worked in flat colours – charging the work with energy.*

Right: *'Tropon', the only poster executed by Henry van de Velde (an advertisement for a food product), 1899. The dynamic, repetitive curves dominate the composition, creating a fluidity and tension – qualities also found in van de Velde's Art Nouveau metalwork.*

Far right: *Detail of the wrought iron staircase by Victor Horta for the Hôtel Solvay, built for the millionaire Armand Solvay on the Avenue Louise, Brussels, 1895-1900. As well as being an architect Horta was a master of decorative ironwork, as illustrated here by the complex arrangement of elegantly twisting curves and swaying terminals.*

54

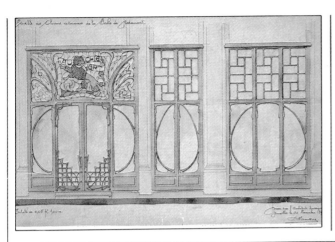

Left: *Architectural drawing of the glass porch for the Grand Hôtel, Brussels, by Paul Hankar, 1898. The glazing bars of the windows are Art Nouveau in inspiration, but the decorative friezes above incorporate foreign elements — note, for example, the Japanese fence pattern.*

Victor Horta (1861-1947) cultivated a highly decorative and refined version of Art Nouveau in the fields of architecture and interior design. The sheer exuberance of his style resulted in many important commissions for public and private buildings in Brussels. Like van de Velde, Horta pursued an abstract, curvilinear approach — infused with elegance and delicacy, and with frequent reference to the organic forms which recur throughout much of international Art Nouveau.

In his interior schemes, Horta combined glass and ironwork in novel ways, creating a cohesion of form and design from every vantage point. The wrought iron balustrades, *above,* found in many of his houses best capture his free-flowing style, with their intricately coiled patterns of curves and counter-curves. The ironwork

door handle *below,* for example, is a mass of undulating curves and web-like configurations, and shows the meticulous detailing for which Horta was renowned throughout Europe.

archways and the rounded contours of the staircase. The total effect is one of unity and harmony from all vantage points. The building was considered a landmark in Art Nouveau architectural design, not only as an early manifestation of the style but also as a complete synthesis of novel form and decoration.

Horta's next commission was another private house in Brussels, built for Armand Solvay in 1895-1900. Here, the facade itself becomes an undulating surface, featuring a central recess. The windows are outlined by gentle arabesques, and stylized ironwork *grilles*. Elements of the construction of the building are also permitted to become part of the overall decorative scheme — for example, the bolts and rivets of metal supports are prominently displayed. In Horta's Maison du Peuple (1896-9), built for the Socialist Workers' Union, an adventurous combination of 'modern' materials and designs was employed. The facade is almost entirely constructed of glass, and the long auditorium inside is augmented by a latticework of iron beams. Horta also turned his talents to furniture and textiles, and his dual role as an artist/craftsman embodied one of the fundamental principles of Art Nouveau, the unification of the arts and crafts.

Paul Hankar (1859-1901) was another specialist in Art Nouveau architecture and decorative furnishings in Brussels. Unlike Horta, who rejected historical influences, Hankar's *oeuvre* encompassed a wide cross-section of foreign elements, among them the art of Japan, and the English Arts and Crafts style. His house design for the painter Ciamberlani in the Rue de Facqz is neo-Renaissance in character with a symmetrical, ornamental facade and large circular windows. The house itself no longer exists. The Maison Niguet of 1899 (also later destroyed) is more typically Art Nouveau with its decorative iron-and-glass facade and exuberant linear style. In contrast, a small table designed in 1893 demonstrates Hankar's interest in Japanese construction. Here, the elongated legs and apron are accented by a series of delicate parallel lines in a fence-like pattern.

Henry van de Velde (1863-1957) was one of the foremost theorists and practitioners of the Art Nouveau style in Europe. Indeed, his versatility as painter, architect and craftsman was demonstrated throughout his *oeuvre*. He travelled extensively on the Continent, and in 1895-6 was commissioned by Samuel Bing to create four decorative interiors for the inaugural exhibition of the shop L'Art Nouveau in Paris. The fundamental principles by which he worked — to bring art and industry closer together for the benefit of all people (as expounded earlier in England by the social reformer William Morris) — were seen to guide and inspire him in all his creative pursuits. Van de Velde developed his own special form-language, which used abstract curvilinear shapes. In his tapestry *Angels' Guard* (1893) the bending road through the forest becomes a forceful central motif, echoed in the swaying, rhythmic lines of the trees and the flowing robes of the figures. Similarly,

Above: *Wrought-iron staircase by Victor Horta for the Hôtel Tassel, Brussels, 1893. Every element of the design exemplifies Horta's curvilinear approach—like parts of a fugue, the rhythmic arabesques respond and interact to create a harmonious whole.*

Above right: *Façade of the restaurant of the Grand Hôtel, Brussels, by Paul Hankar, 1896.*
Above far right: *Silver candlestick by Henry van de Velde, who designed outstanding utilitarian metalwares and jewellery in the Art Nouveau style.*

Far right: *House on the Avenue de Tervueren, Brussels, by Paul Hankar, 1898. Large circular windows were a feature of Hankar's 'oeuvre', inspired by Renaissance architecture. The spherical motifs recur on the ironwork 'grilles' and entrance gates.*

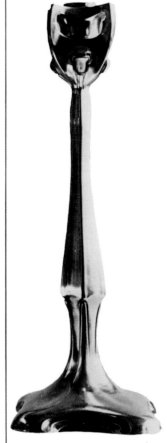

his 1897 design for a desk is composed of broad sweeps of curving contours that dominate every aspect of the construction. In his well-known poster *Tropon, l'Aliment le Plus Concentré* (1899) the successful combination of art and industrial design is evident. Here, the advertised product becomes a triumph of Art Nouveau calligraphy, composed of energetic whiplash curves and arabesques in brightly contrasting shades of orange, dark pink and brown.

In metalwares, van de Velde's exuberant style precisely suits the material, which he invariably rendered into fluid forms — like liquid silver. His famous six-branched candelabrum of 1900 (in the Musées Royaux d'Art et d'Histoire, Brussels) maintains a continuous momentum in the twirling strands of its base, which rise up to encircle each branch and nozzle, almost swallowing every structural element. Van de Velde's designs for cutlery, jewellery, inkstands, teapots, light fixtures and other utilitarian objects all convey the intense, rhythmic nature of his Art Nouveau style.

The furniture maker Gustave Serrurier-Bovy (1859-1910) was also associated with the Belgian Art Nouveau style. Many of his pieces of the late 1890s combine the influence of Japanese designs with the simpler constructions of the English Arts and Crafts movement.

Sketches in his design books for cabinets, tables, chairs, desks and fireplaces refer frequently to the structural use of repetitive arch patterns and sparse rectilinear decorations. These restrained effects were shortly to become the hallmarks of Modernist productions.

The metalwares and jewellery designs of Philippe Wolfers (1858-1929) bear a striking likeness to the fanciful Art Nouveau creations of René Lalique. In their choice of decoration and subject matter, both craftsmen relied on nature as the source of inspiration, employing a rich array of materials such as pearls, enamels, semi-precious stones, coloured metals and ivory. Wolfers also created small sculptural works of ivory and silver, in keeping with the exotic nature of his Art Nouveau style.

The success of the Art Nouveau movement in Belgium was reflected in the applied arts and throughout numerous architectural and interior schemes that transformed Brussels and other cities. Van de Velde's important contributions to the development of the style in the 1890s further ensured its widespread popularity in Europe. However, his departure from the country at the turn of the century preceded the decline of the movement, and by the early 1900s many of Belgium's Art Nouveau designers had died or abandoned the style in favour of simpler, more abstract formulae.

GERMANY

German Art Nouveau — or *Jugendstil* — developed later than its Continental counterparts and was not fully assimilated in the applied arts and architecture before the late 1890s. Until then many German designers were still committed to the revivalist trends of the second half of the nineteenth century and were firmly rooted in neo-baroque traditions and neo-rococo styles. However, as already witnessed in other countries, the desire to create new and unified arts and crafts became an overriding force by the 1890s, and for Germany the arrival of progressive Art Nouveau ideologies provided a fresh alternative to historicism.

From about 1895-8 a number of national events contributed to the rapid growth of *Jugendstil*. Several important arts journals were published, among them *Pan*, founded by the art critic Julius Meier-Grafe in Berlin in 1895, followed in 1896 by the weekly magazines *Die Jugend* (from which the term *Jugendstil* is derived) and *Simplicissimus*. These journals not only supported the new movement but provided artists with the opportunity to show their work to a receptive public. In the same year Henry van de Velde was invited to lecture in Germany, and in 1897 his celebrated interiors (designed originally for Bing's shop L'Art Nouveau in Paris) were shown at the Decorative Arts Exhibition in Dresden. These Art Nouveau settings exemplified in every detail an aesthetic and decorative coherence and, as the first of their kind to be shown in Germany, their impact was considerable.

Jugendstil evolved in two distinct phases. In its earlier manifestation, confined mainly to the years before 1900, the style bore a close resemblance to English Arts and Crafts decorations, with an emphasis on naturalistic and representational forms. This predominantly 'floral' art was interpreted most directly in graphics and the applied arts. Here, a peculiarly sentimental range of 'folk' themes and subjects was adhered to — flowers and budding plants appeared frequently in springtime landscapes, while swans and other birds, fish and animals alluded to an imaginary world of fairytale and fantasy. In contrast, *Jugendstil*'s later development favoured a more abstract and dynamic linear content, more in keeping with the 'Modernist' trends that swept through Europe in the early 1900s. This secondary phase was inspired largely by the ideologies of van de Velde, and his permanent residence in Germany after the turn of the century helped promote the non-representational aspects of the style. Although *Jugendstil* was a relatively short-lived phenomenon in Germany, the movement nevertheless assumed an intense and concentrated form.

Like many of his contemporaries, Otto Eckmann (1865-1902) turned away from painting and directed his talents to graphics and the applied arts. He made

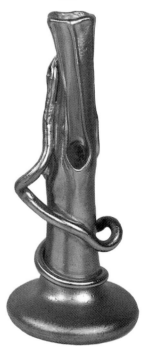

numerous illustrations for *Die Jugend* and *Pan* magazines in the florid manner of *Jugendstil*. Eckmann's unique calligraphic approach is best characterized by his treatment of contoured lines, which convey energy and tension in their sudden tapering and thickening. Such biting lines do not occur in the controlled Art Nouveau decorations of the Glasgow School, nor do they mimic the graceful curvilinear styles of the French. For subject matter Eckmann relied on plant and animal forms, as exemplified in his tapestry *'Five Swans'*

Top left: Cover of the Munich magazine 'Jugend', September 1896, from which the term 'Jugendstil' was derived. Bottom left: Silver centrepiece adorned with a band of peacock blue and green 'plique-à-jour' enamel and bold geometric friezes in relief, by Krall of Berlin, c.1900.

Left: *Iridescent glass vases attributed to the Austro-Bohemian firm Loetz, in imitation of Tiffany's 'Favrile' range, c.1900.*

Above: *Façade of the Atelier Elvira in Munich by August Endell, 1897-8 (destroyed). The central ornamental frieze possesses an almost surreal quality, and bears a striking resemblance to some of Gaudi's flamboyant architectural decorations in Spain. The pagoda-style door and windows, with their web-like glazing bars, recall Art Nouveau tastes.*

Right: *Hall staircase of the Atelier Elvira, with frenetic linear decorations in ironwork and plaster. The electric lights appear almost to quiver, emerging from a mass of frayed curls and jutting points.*

(1896-7). Here, the swans and bending stream are stylized and yet conceived literally — unlike the curving road in van de Velde's *Angels' Guard*, which is translated into an abstract force. Throughout his graphic work Eckmann explored a wide range of linear effects. In his binding for the book *Der Sänger* (1899) by A. Wildbrand waving lines of varying thickness radiate from a central point, like giant blossoms, and the same decorative technique is extended to the lettering of the title.

Hermann Obrist (1863-1927) employed a similar vocabulary of naturalistic motifs in his numerous designs for embroidery. His celebrated wall hanging of a cyclamen plant — entitled *Whiplash* by a contemporary critic — demonstrates Obrist's accurate observations of, and respect for, nature. From its convoluted roots to the delicate wisps of tapering stems the cyclamen appears charged with energy — a startling revelation of pulsating rhythm. This combination of naturalistic detail and abstracted form was indeed one of the most striking hallmarks of the international Art Nouveau style.

August Endell (1871-1925) displayed a more flamboyant approach in his decorative schemes. In his architectural design for the house Atelier Elvira in Munich (1897-8 — later destroyed by the Nazis as an example of 'degenerate art') the whiplash lines of *Jugendstil* had become increasingly abstract and fantastic. The entrance hall, for example, is highlighted throughout by a series of bizarre ironwork patterns, resembling plant roots and woody stalks. This complex imagery is extended further to the electric lights of the staircase, which radiate from the banister like shooting stars. The main entrance gate encapsulates these symbolic notions with its ornamentation of spiked shell motifs and wavering mass of linear configurations. Similarly, the unusual decorative frieze of the central façade is composed of distorted shapes and images. Here, there is no trace of the sentimental *Jugendstil* of Eckmann or of the forceful naturalism of Obrist but, rather, a Surreal quality is permitted to intrude into all elements of the design.

In the spirit of the English Arts and Crafts movement, numerous workshops devoted to the applied arts and to the design of utilitarian wares were established throughout Germany. One such co-operative was founded in Darmstadt, under the patronage of the Grand Duke Ernst Ludwig of Hesse, and attracted a number of architects and craftsmen such as Peter Behrens (1868-1940). Munich, however, remained in the forefront of artistic endeavours and many important *Jugendstil* designers continued to work here: Eckmann, Obrist and Endell were all based in the city, as well as Richard Riemerschmid (1868-1957), Bernhard Pankok (1872-1943) and Bruno Paul (1874-1968). In Berlin the movement focused on the activities of Henry van de Velde, whose influence extended beyond the abstract trends of late *Jugendstil* designs to merge finally with the Modernist tendencies of the early twentieth century.

AUSTRIA

Above: *Wooden plant stand by the Wiener Werkstätte, an unusual piece displaying the group's austere geometric style.*

Above: *Polished pewter lamp base by Joseph Maria Olbrich, c.1901.*
Left: *Two-armed candelabrum, again in pewter, by Albin Müller, c.1901.*

Art Nouveau in Austria assumed a quite different form from other Continental versions. It more closely resembled the sturdier Arts and Crafts productions of England and the austere linear approach of Glasgow. Its distinguishing features were to be found in the ornamentation of the surface itself which was often simplified to include only a few geometric shapes. Repeating patterns of small circles and squares featured prominently on two-dimensional planes and formed the basis of a rigid decorative repertoire that was observed throughout the fine and applied arts of the period.

The geometric aspects of the style were developed and adhered to by a small number of architects, artists and craftsmen working in Vienna. The group was known as the Vienna Secession and included, among others, the painter Gustav Klimt, and the architects and designers Otto Wagner, Josef Hoffmann, Joseph Olbrich and Koloman Moser. Their first joint exhibition was held in the city in 1897 and featured, in addition, the works of international artists such as Eugène Grasset, Fernand Khnopff, Auguste Rodin and Henry van de Velde. The Secessionists commissioned Olbrich to build a gallery for their annual exhibitions in 1898-9, and founded their own periodical entitled *Ver Sacrum*, which became an important creative outlet for their talents. The artistic output of the group was, indeed, considerable, and extended also to the designs of the Wiener Werkstätte — a decorative workshop founded by Hoffmann in 1903, inspired by the Arts and Crafts principles of England.

Otto Wagner (1841-1918) had established his successful career as an architect many years before the advent of Art Nouveau, and worked largely in the academic and revivalist traditions of the second half of the nineteenth century. During the late 1890s, however, his buildings demonstrated a brief flirtation with Art Nouveau ornamentation and a rejection of historical influences. These ideas were expounded in his popular book *Moderne Architektur*, written in 1895. In the structure and decorative façade of the Karlsplatz Stadtbahn station of about 1897 Wagner employed several Art Nouveau elements. Here, the curved metal outline of the main entrance and stencilled floral frieze bear a striking resemblance to the Metro stations created by Guimard a few years later in Paris. Similarly, the floral decorations on the façade of his *Majolikahaus* of 1898, in Vienna, with their richly coloured tiles, adhere to the naturalistic content of international Art Nouveau.

Wagner's students Joseph Maria Olbrich (1867-1908) and Joseph Hoffman (1870-1956) cultivated more rigorously new concepts in 'modern' architecture. Olbrich's innovative design for the Haus der Wiener Sezession captured the essential qualities of the Secessionist style by virtue of its geometrically inspired structure and sparse decoration. The exterior of the exhibition hall comprises a series of simple rectangular shapes surmounted by a massive dome. The arrangement is one of monumental order, interspersed with small, self-contained decorative friezes of foliage. The dome is

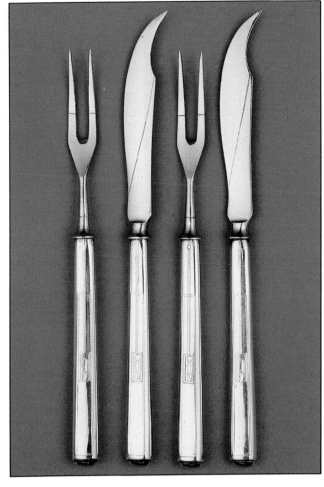

Left: *Wooden armchair by the Wiener Werkstätte. The interplay of geometric shapes – of intersecting parallel curves, verticals and circles – is free of all surface ornament. The effect is simple but striking.*

Above: *Nest of tables by the Wiener Werkstätte, displaying tall vertical legs and applied circular handles.*

Top right: *Parcel-gilt metal cheese service by Joseph Maria Olbrich, c.1900, adorned with incised abstract motifs on the handles. Numerous Art Nouveau craftsmen turned their attention to cutlery designs, creating decorative alternatives to the otherwise 'standard' forms. Here, functional elements assume ornamental qualities – note the swaying contours of the blades, and gleaming surfaces.*

textured in high relief with a carpet of leaves, framed by a bold cube pattern that occurs persistently throughout the Secessionist *oeuvre*. This important building, embodying the sentiments and aesthetic principles of its advocates, stood as a symbol of the new art.

Josef Hoffmann pursued these geometric formats in his graphic work, furniture, interior design, metalware and accessories. He was a frequent contributor to *Ver Sacrum*, for which he devised numerous vignettes in a stark linear style. Hoffmann developed an unusual decorative code that, like Mackintosh's Glasgow ornamentation, consisted of juxtaposed geometric shapes, straight lines and contrasting black and white tones. He favoured the use of squares and cubes, which occur with great regularity in his designs. In many of his interior schemes of the late 1890s, for example, cube patterns appear everywhere – on walls, partitions, windows, carpets and on furniture that is itself often rendered into simple block-like forms. Olbrich cultivated a similar range of geometric motifs in his graphic work and, as already hinted at by the dome of his Haus der Wiener Sezession, he favoured the use of bold circular patterns. Although these geometrically inspired compositions appear to contradict the asymmetrical, curvilinear mannerisms of European Art Nouveau, both trends were united in their rejection of historic 'period' styles and their striving for new modes of expression.

Sparse surface decoration was one of the dominant characteristics of Hoffmann's innovative designs, but for Gustav Klimt (1862-1918) geometric motifs were transformed into an exotic art of intense patterns and shimmering jewel-like colours. A critic later described him as 'an artist so typical of Art Nouveau that a more characteristic example of that international style could hardly be found. If Art Nouveau was an art of the surface … Klimt was its quintessence'.

Klimt executed numerous portraits of real and imaginary women in the early 1900s. Frequently, the figures are portrayed against flat, multi-coloured backgrounds of boldly patterned circles, squares, triangles and swirling lines. Indeed, this segmented ornamentation is often permitted to intrude on the subjects themselves — as in the large decorative frieze designed for Hoffmann's Palais Stoclet in Brussels, c.1905-8. In this work of mosaic and enamel an embracing couple emerge from a background of restless, irregularly coiled lines. Alternate decorative panels penetrate the surface of their costumes, composed of dotted circles and squares and swirling discs that appear in contrasting profusion. Klimt's use of glittering gold *tesserae* recalls the influence of Byzantine mosaic compositions, while motifs such as stylized swirls, eyes and birds placed in niches mimic the hieroglyphic tomb paintings of ancient Egypt.

These exotic forms occur throughout his paintings and murals of the period. In the picture entitled *The Kiss* of 1908 (in the Österreichisches Museum für Angewandte Kunst, Vienna) the richly patterned planes of the composition are imbued with symbolic content. The embracing couple kneel on a carpet of brightly coloured flowers, conveying an atmosphere of springtime and the renewal of life. The figures appear in a shimmering gold halo, accented by geometric motifs of rectangles and circles — an evocative sexual image symbolizing the birth and creation of mankind.

The sophistication and elegance of Klimt's compositions contrast with the stark graphic works of Koloman Moser (1868-1918), who preferred simpler linear formats, and monochromatic black-and-white contrast. Moser made numerous illustrations for *Ver Sacrum* and also executed a wide range of commercial designs for wallpapers, textiles, stamps, bank-notes, book covers and metalwares. In this last category he employed pure geometric shapes such as spheres, cubes and cylinders for the forms and structures of utilitarian objects. Often, these wares were stripped of all surface ornament, but in their highly polished exteriors and novel shapes an overall decorativeness was achieved. The functionalist approach of both Moser and Hoffmann was highlighted throughout their association with the Wiener Werkstätte, from 1903-15. The innovative works of this period embody a startling modernism that anticipated the Art Deco tastes of later decades.

Above: *Portrait of Adèle Bloch-Bauer by Gustav Klimt, 1907. Klimt executed numerous portraits of women, frequently placing his subjects against sumptuously decorated backgrounds embellished with gold and silver sequins — like glittering Byzantine mosaics.*
Left: *Mosaic panel of 'Minerva' by Leopold Forstner (1878-1936), founder of the Wiener Mosaik-Werkstätte. The subjects for his mosaics were derived frequently from mythological sources, displaying rich materials such as enamel, glass, precious metals and stones and mother-of-pearl.*
Right: *Silver-gilt and polished wood tea service by Josef Hoffmann, c.1905.*

Above: *Secessionist graphic work. The exotic subject and gold colouring typify the style.*
Right: *Poster for the Fourteenth Exhibition of the Vienna Secession, 1902, by Alfred Roller (1864-1935). The rich, segmented patterning dominates the whole surface.*
Left: *'Frommes Kalendar', designed by Koloman Moser. The flat areas of colour, bold rhythmic contours and two-dimensional aspects show the influence of Japanese woodcuts.*

63

OTHER PRACTITIONERS

There are other Art Nouveau designers who made significant contributions to the movement but do not fit into the main categories of this chapter. Other countries — the USA, Spain and Czechoslovakia for example — produced practitioners of international stature. Some of them are described here.

The luxurious productions of Louis Comfort Tiffany (1848-1933) achieved unrivalled success in the field of glass design, and his reputation as a master craftsman extended beyond his native America to Europe. Tiffany pieces were exhibited as early as 1895 at Bing's L'Art Nouveau shop in Paris, and later in the Exposition Universelle of 1900. Unlike Gallé, whose glass objects reflected a naturalistic content in their textured relief designs of flowers and insects, Tiffany pursued more abstract effects in the treatment of the decorative surface. In his celebrated 'Favrile' range of the late nineteenth and early twentieth centuries, hand-made vases and other luxury wares introduced new colour effects comprised largely of iridescent rainbow hues, in imitation of ancient weathered glass. Shimmering shades of blue, green, gold and pink were employed individually or in subtle combinations, sometimes highlighted by overlying patterns of stylized flowers, peacock feathers, and waving 'combed' threads of glass. The shapes of bowls and vases were rendered variously. A large number conformed to the flowing, elongated contours of

Art Nouveau, while others recalled the influence of ancient, oriental and later European prototypes.

Tiffany also created stained-glass windows, jewellery, and numerous lamps and light-fittings of glass and bronze. His lamp designs exemplified the sumptuous and flamboyant tastes of Art Nouveau with their intricate structures of elongated metal supports and delicate glass mosaics adorned with insects, spiders' webs and flowers. In their brilliant colours and subject matter, Tiffany's lamps resembled sparkling stained-glass windows.

The American graphic designer William Bradley (1868-1962) was invited, with Tiffany, to exhibit at the L'Art Nouveau salon in 1895. Many of his posters and book illustrations of the period were influenced by the graphic styles of his European contemporaries, among them Toulouse-Lautrec, Bonnard and Beardsley. In his design for the advertisement *Whiting's Ledger Papers* (c. 1900, in the Art Institute of Chicago) Bradley's attenuated linear style and use of bold tonal contrasts recalled the striking Art Nouveau designs of Beardsley. The repetitive vine pattern of the border, however, is more reminiscent of English Arts and Crafts design. Bradley devised numerous illustrations for book covers throughout the 1890s, notably for the *Chap-book* in 1893 and *The Inland Printer* in 1894.

Alphonse Mucha (1860-1939) contributed greatly to

Left: *Illustration for a bedroom interior designed by Will Bradley, from 'Documents d'Architecture Moderne', 1906. The solidly constructed furniture and decorations recall the English Arts and Crafts style, although the pastel colour scheme of olive, mauve and white is more indicative of Mackintosh.*

Bottom far left: *Three lamps of leaded glass and bronze by the Tiffany Studios, early 1900s. Spider webs, dragonflies and blossoms were favoured Art Nouveau motifs.*

Below left: *Cover of 'The Chap-book' for the Thanksgiving issue, 1894, by Will Bradley. Artists such as Beardsley, Toulouse-Lautrec and Beerbohm also illustrated for this journal. In 1904 Bradley wrote and designed 12 'American Chap-books'.*

Below: *Gold necklace decorated with translucent enamel and opals by L.C. Tiffany, c.1914.*

Louis Comfort Tiffany (1848-1933) was one of America's foremost designers of glass, metalware and jewellery in the Art Nouveau style. He started his career as a painter, but by the late 1870s an overriding interest in the decorative arts led him to the manufacture of stained glass windows and interior designs for public and private buildings. Tiffany pursued a wide range of Art Nouveau themes for his leaded glass panels, executed in jewel-like colours, and his immense success soon brought him important commissions from abroad. The French artists Bonnard, Vuillard and Toulouse-Lautrec created designs for Tiffany to execute in glass (exhibited at the Paris Salon in 1895) and Samuel Bing displayed his pieces at the grand opening of his *L'Art Nouveau* shop.

In the 1890s Tiffany experimented with glass-blowing and colour techniques, and produced shimmering iridescent surface effects for his 'art glass', an example of which is shown *above*. The luxury 'Favrile' range of hand-made wares was often highlighted by lustrous metallic sheens of gold, pink, peacock blue and emerald, in 'satin' finishes.

This silver berry spoon by Tiffany, c.1902, is typical of his sculptural style in this medium.

the widespread popularity of Art Nouveau through his graphic works and posters. This Czechoslovakian artist came to Paris in 1890 and thereafter received many lucrative commissions to design posters for Sarah Bernhardt and for theatrical productions. His first celebrated poster was for this actress's performance in *Gismonda* in 1894. This was followed by a variety of commercial designs that invariably depicted sensual women in floral landscapes. Like his colleagues in France, Mucha cultivated a luxurious Art Nouveau style comprising rich pastel shades and naturalistic ornaments. Frequently, these 'feminine' environments were infused with exotic elements, and alluded to a sophisticated world of *femmes fatales* and fairy-tale characters. In Mucha's composition *Woman with a Daisy* (c. 1897-8), for example, the figure assumes a mysterious pose,

Left: *'Temps du Jour' ('The Four Times of Day'), decorative panels mounted on a screen by Alphonse Mucha, 1899. Mucha's 'femmes fatales', posed luxuriously in the sumptuous floral landscapes of Art Nouveau, were popular throughout Europe.*
Right: *Mirrored 'coiffeuse' by Carlo Bugatti, c.1901. The waxed wood is inlaid with stylized flowers and star motifs. Its massive structure anticipates some of the exotic designs of the later Art Deco period.*
Right (middle): *Poster for Sarah Bernhardt's 'La Dame aux Camelias', 1896, by Alphonse Mucha.*
Far right: *Art Nouveau clasp by K.S. Bolin, Moscow, 1903, from a design by Paul Lienard.*
Below: *Banquette, c.1900, by the Italian Carlo Bugatti (1855-1940), whose flamboyant pieces reflect an immense individuality. The incised metal embellishments and geometric structure bear comparison to Secessionist designs.*

66

partially obscured by a jungle of tangled and intertwined flowers and stems. Each petal and leaf is clearly delineated and becomes part of an overall pattern that extends to the rich brocade of the woman's robe. This juxtaposition of flat areas of decoration reflected the influence of Japanese woodcuts, and was a technique employed effectively by Mucha and other illustrators of the period. Similarly, in his wallpaper design of red poppies, executed in 1902, the flowers and ruffled leaves are outlined individually in white, for greater emphasis and contrast. Every detail of the decoration is made apparent — as intricate as a mosaic composed of numerous parts. In Mucha's compositions entitled *Emerald* and *Amethyst,* from the series *Four Precious Stones,* 1900, the exotic female figures pose seductively among flowers, highlighted from behind by profusely patterned windows. Here, the complex surface ornamentation of interlinking circles and swirling discs recalls Byzantine mosaic work, and contributes greatly to the overall dramatic effect. These evocative Art Nouveau images of enchanting floral settings and sumptuous females captivated a wide audience and ensured Mucha's success as one of the best commercial artists of his time.

One of the most original and ostentatious exponents of the Art Nouveau style was the Spanish architect

Antoni Gaudi (1852-1926), whose breathtaking buildings and ironwork designs were executed in Barcelona in the late 19th and early 20th centuries. Gaudi's unique approach embraced a wide cross-section of exotic elements. His own extravagant tastes and heightened sense of drama were evident in most of his works, although his respect for traditional Spanish forms was never entirely abandoned. Indeed, the decorative features of Moorish architecture were frequently exploited and combined with the dynamic curvilinear mannerisms of Art Nouveau to create a tremendously diverse expression.

One of Gaudi's most important commissions was the Güell Palace in 1885-9, followed by Güell Park in 1900-14. In this building Gaudi retained a number of Moorish aspects, with forms such as the minaret and the relief-patterned walls of stylized scale motifs. The details of the ironwork embellishments, however, are pure Art Nouveau — and truly remarkable for their early manifestation of the style. The portals and wrought-iron gates, for example, comprise swirling, rhythmic lines and abstract configurations which bear a striking likeness to the energetic compositions of Endell for the Atelier Elvira in Munich and to Guimard's metalwork designs for the Castel Béranger in Paris. In a latter commission for the Casa Milá building of 1905-10, the façade is segmented by a series of undulating horizontal lines, creating an extraordinary rippling effect. This triumphant example of Art Nouveau architecture encapsulated the style not merely through its decorative details but by virtue of its entire structure, which was subjected to the ruthless rhythms of the design.

Below left: *Façade of the Colegio Teresiano, Barcelona, by Antoni Gaudi, an austere Gothic-inspired work of stone and brick, sparsely decorated with polychrome friezes and wall 'appliqués'. The pronounced arched windows form the basis of the design.*
Below: *Façade of the Casa Milá, Barcelona, by Antoni Gaudi, 1905-10. The concrete structure is rendered into sweeping curvilinear rhythms, its ironwork balconies in frenetic Art Nouveau configurations.*

Left: *A colourful ceramic-tiled iguana from Güell Park, Barcelona, by Antoni Gaudi, c.1900-14.*
Below: *View of the ceramic-tiled benches from Güell Park. A small fragment from the expansive tiled decorations, showing a 'fleur-de-lys' pattern, is also illustrated (bottom).*
Below left: *View of the Church of the Sagrada Familia, Barcelona, by Antoni Gaudi, c.1883-1926.*

Above (top): *Staircase and hall of the Güell Palace, Barcelona, by Antoni Gaudi, 1885-9. Note the profuse decorative ironwork on the balustrade, balconies and light fixtures.*

Above: *One of the bell towers from the Church of the Sagrada Familia, c.1924, by Antoni Gaudi, adorned with colourful ceramic fragments and applied geometric motifs.*

A decorative screen, c.1930, possibly by Sergei Petrovich Burylin (1876-1942).

CHAPTER · THREE
DESIGN FOR INDUSTRY

THE MACHINE AESTHETIC 1900-1930

'Thanks to the machine, to the identification of what is typical, to the process of selection, to the establishment of a standard, a new style will assert itself.'

LE CORBUSIER, 1924

INTRODUCTION

The first decades of this century were dominated by the attempts of many nations to inject art into industry. This was a double-headed policy aimed at both improving the quality of their manufactured goods and at making a bid for a position in the world marketplace. A number of European countries looked to the USA as that country's new production technologies and industrial organization were highly sophisticated and pointed the way for the rest of the world. Where 'taste' was concerned, however, the consensus was that Europe was still several decades ahead of the game.

A strong feeling, shared by designers, design critics and manufacturers alike, emerged at this time that the traditional concept of applying 'art' to the surfaces of manufactured goods had lost its relevance now that the machine, rather than the hand, dominated production processes. The logical alternative was, as many explained at the time, to evolve a simple, rational style which echoed the values and processes of machine production and thereby symbolized the new century in all its technological glory. The curves of Art Nouveau gradually faded in this period, therefore, giving way to a much simpler, more geometric 'machine aesthetic' and, where avant-garde architecture and the decorative arts were concerned, this became the dominant style of the first three decades of this century.

Below: *Johan Rohde's sterling silver jug of 1920 displays the same formal simplicity as many objects from this period.*

Above right: *An undecorated, geometrically shaped dressing table made of the new materials, chrome and glass, illustrated in Heal's catalogue of 1932.*
Right: *The dashboard of a 1908 Napier. The arrangement of the dials shown here is the result of functional necessity rather than 'design'. This kind of naïve* *'functionalism' was a great source of inspiration to the early Machine Aesthetes.*
Below: *Car bodies arriving at Ford's Highland Park plant in 1914. These black standardized components of Ford's 'Model T' were combined with the chassis on a moving belt system, the first in an automobile factory.*

Above left: *Marcel Breuer's cantilevered chairs, designed at the Bauhaus in 1928, were among the first examples of tubular steel furniture. Their austere, undecorated forms represented the search for modernity so central to the Bauhaus programme.*

Above right: *Le Corbusier's 'Pavillon de L'Esprit Nouveau' was exhibited at the Paris Exhibition of Decorative Arts in 1925. With its formal emphasis on simple geometry it was a striking contrast to the other more decorative contents of the show.*

Right: *Walter Gropius' Bauhaus building in Dessau, opened in the mid-20s, was a prime example of the new modern architectural style with its emphatic grid motif. The glass wall shown here let light into the studios behind it.*

INSPIRATIONS

Modernists were perhaps stimulated more than any other movement by contemporary painting. The Cubists Picasso, Braque and Juan Gris were seeking out the mystical essence of objects by breaking them down to their component geometric parts and juxtaposing images from several viewpoints on monochrome canvases. The result was an architecture of interlocking planes. Meanwhile in Italy the Futurists, attacking cultural apathy, extolled the excitement of speed, machinery and even war through an art that could be described as 'Cubism on the move'. The angular geometric motifs gave designers a dynamic iconography through which they could proselytize the cult of the machine, seen in Russia as an essential tool of a proletarian society. But the machine aesthetic was not entirely the child of artistic theory or propaganda needs. The impulse to reduce things to their essentials of standard parts to permit rapid serial production of consumer goods had long been appreciated in both the USA and western Europe. The new consumerism and developing business life brought an implicit aesthetic challenge: to create an uncluttered environment in keeping with modern living. The quest was for pure, rational form.

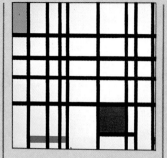

Primary reason
Gerrit Rietveld's experimental Red-Blue chair of 1917, *right,* is virtually a three-dimensional realization of the work of the Constructivist De Stijl artist Piet Mondrian, who spent a lifetime exploring horizontal/vertical relationships and colour juxtapositions within an asymmetrical grid, *above.*

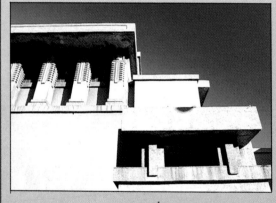

Graceful grid
The décor and furniture of a Japanese inn, *above right,* conform to a grid of horizontals and verticals. The architectural harmony of Japanese interiors was taken up by architect Frank Lloyd Wright. He devised an aesthetic specifically to suit machine products, with forms of simple, interchangeable geometric blocks. He applied it to furniture, interiors and architecture, as shown in this edifice, the Unity Temple at Oak Park, Chicago, 1906, *above.*

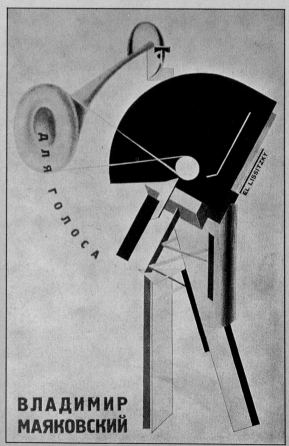

74

Н. Кочергин. Тифлис

 გაუმარჯოს კავკასიის
ხალხთა ძმობას!

Да здравствует братство
всех народов Кавказа!

N. Kotsherguin. Tiflis

Dominant shapes

The curving cylinder had been introduced by Thonet in the late 19th century in his bentwood furniture. A truer 'objective' aesthetic was arrived at in the designs for tubular steel furniture by Marcel Breuer and Mies van der Rohe, in which minimalist form followed function.

Circles and part-circles were prominent in Modernist design from cups to staircases.

The unembellished cube, rectangular block and grid formations reduced architecture to plain edifices of imposing height or low white expanses with horizontal ribbon windows.

The cone, an obvious Cubist elementary form, found its place in numerous everyday objects.

The cog and wheel were used as a graphic icon to suggest how the machine would transform society.

abcdefg

ABCDEFG

abcdefghij

**ABCDEFG
abcdefg**

Constructive ideas

The Russian art movements Suprematism and Constructivism owed much to the analytical cubism of works such as Picasso's 'Still Life with Chair Caning', 1912, *far left*. El Lissitzky, who designed the title page to 'For the Voice', *left*, with its characteristic dynamic diagonals, was greatly influenced by his Suprematist compatriot Malevich and passed on his ideas on abstract form, contributing with Mondrian to 'De Stijl' magazine and teaching graphic design at the Bauhaus.

Wheels of revolution

In 'The Red Worker', c.1920, a Russian poster by N. Kotscherguin, *above,* the inspiration is clearly political, the artist urging post-revolutionary society on towards functionalism and efficiency. The sun is drawn as a whirring cog.

Original design for 'Universal' typeface, *top,* by the Bauhaus typographer Herbert Bayer, 1925. It relies solely on geometry, rejecting symmetry, serifs, decorative ploys and even capital letters. 'Railway' type, *middle,* designed in 1918 for the London Underground by Edward Johnson – the first of the 20th-century sans serifs. 'Block', *above,* an influential design by H. Hoffman, 1908.

THE USA

The first signs of this new aesthetic had been visible as long ago as the early to mid-nineteenth century in the USA, where the rush to standardize production in order to meet the needs of the new mass market had been so accelerated that little thought had been given to the appearance of the products. A ready and willing market absorbed all the goods that America could produce and there was little need, at this stage, for a 'hard sell' or for highly elaborate products.

The American goods that were the products of the new industries displayed the machine aesthetic, albeit in a somewhat unsophisticated, unselfconscious way. The Colt revolver and the McCormick reaper, for instance, which were shown at the 1851 Great Exhibition in London, were both products whose forms openly demonstrated the standardization of their production and the interchangeability of their parts, as well as their utilitarian functions. In sharp contrast, however, the American 'applied arts' were as fancy as, or indeed fancier than, any of the garish British products on display at the Crystal Palace. A report on American manufacturing in this period was presented by a British commission, which remarked particularly on the specialized nature of American machine-tools compared with their British equivalents.

The period during which the new American machines displayed the simple aesthetic was short-lived but much discussed. In the 1850s, for instance, a sculptor called Horatio Greenough, an early proponent of 'Functionalist' theory, praised the work of American ship-builders and engineers and warned Americans against emulating the superficial 'stylish' excesses of European products. The brief 'proto-functionalist' phase of American design was, however, soon over and very quickly sewing machines and 'Hoovers' were all 'artistically' embellished with rococo or Art Nouveau surface details in imitation of the European decorative arts and in an attempt to satisfy what were considered to be 'women's tastes'. It was some time before the simple, undecorated, geometric forms of the machine aesthetic found their way back into machines. By the time that they did, they had already become a familiar style for architecture and the decorative arts.

The analogy of the machine and mass production

76

remained, however, a major influence on ideas about 'industrial style' and, by the time Henry Ford had manufactured his standardized black automobile on his moving assembly line, architecture had opted wholeheartedly for the 'machine aesthetic'.

Early Functionalist architecture

While Greenough was among the first of many writers to isolate the 'engineer's aesthetic' as a source of the new modern style in architecture and design, he had also anticipated the biological basis of Functionalist theory. This was picked up later by the Chicago architects Louis Sullivan (1856-1924) and Frank Lloyd Wright (1867-1959). In his book *Form and Function* Greenough compared a ship to an animal whose body is perfectly suited to the actions it performs and whose appearance is determined by the body's internal structure. A similar idea provided the basis of both Sullivan's and Wright's theories about 'Organic' architecture. They claimed, for instance, that the exterior form of a building is dictated completely by its internal components, which are in turn structurally determined. Just as a flower grows from the root upwards, so, they claimed, a building begins with a substructure and then acquires its outward appearance.

Sullivan's multi-storey Chicago buildings of the 1880s and 1890s — among them the Wainwright building and the Carson, Pirie and Scott store — were all, in essence, steel skeletons clothed in a concrete and glass shell. To this basic structural determinism was added, however, the functional disposition of the building: each floor, for instance, had a clearly defined purpose, the services all being housed near the top and the lower floors providing office space. This rational planning was reflected in the building's exterior form, and the rigorous grid format of these early skyscrapers was the first evidence of the emergence of a modern architectural style.

Wright's Prairie houses were as horizontal in emphasis as Sullivan's buildings were vertical. This younger architect defined Organic architecture as relating a building closely to the site on which it was built and to its own internal structure, which was in turn dictated by functional requirements. Wright stressed, for instance, the symbolic role of the fireplace as the central focus of the home and designed his houses to work out from that point. Wright, strongly influenced by the Japanese architecture and design that he had seen at the Columbian exhibition of 1893 in Chicago, adopted the Japanese grid as both a structural and a decorative motif in much of his work. Through his contact with Wright, Sullivan consolidated his own ideas about functional form and, in the first decade of the century, made his famous statement that 'Form ever follows Function. That is the law', thus anticipating much that was to come.

The undecorated, geometric aesthetic that accompanied so many of the new alliances between art and industry early in the century drew heavily on the architectural ideas developed in the USA at that time.

Above: *Louis Sullivan's Carson Pirie Scott store in Chicago, built at the turn of the century, was among the first steel-framed, curtain wall buildings to be erected in that city and quickly became an example of early Machine Age architecture. The entrance was, however, still Art Nouveau.*

SPIRIT OF THE MACHINE AESTHETIC

Designers of these early decades were caught up in the slipstream of their artist contemporaries. If Cubists could see everything in terms of spheres, cylinders and cones and present an object from several viewpoints at once, why should the designer remain distracted by irrelevant clutter? The age of the machine had arrived and whether the designer was a vessel for abstract theories, a fervent revolutionary or a communer with nature, there was a challenge to meet. The impact was twofold: it shows in the reduction of things to their basic components (in theory to facilitate mass production) and as a decorative inspiration, motifs standing as metaphors for the wheel, piston rod and other mechanical elements.

1937 Office designed by Frank Lloyd Wright, *above*, for the Edgar Kaufmann department store, Pittsburgh, and executed in cypress plywood. It shows his contrived respect for the grid format.

1930 Heavy-duty steel desk by Michel Dufet, *below*, takes the machine aesthetic to its ultimate form, anticipating 1980s 'ghetto chic'.

1905 Leaded glass 'Tree of Life' door panel designed by Frank Lloyd Wright for the Darwin D. Martin House, Buffalo, New York, manufactured by the Linden Glass Co, *below*.

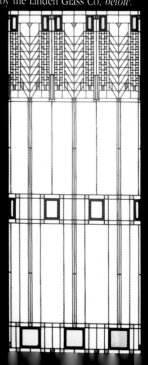

1931 Architecture reduced to its essentials of rectangles and cylinders in Le Corbusier's Villa Savoye, *top*. Broad internal spaces, *above right*, are all part of the quest for a state of platonic grandeur,

mathematical order'.

1911 Detail of the façade of the Fagus shoe-last factory at Afeld an der Leine, *above left*, a functionalist design by Walter Gropius in conjunction with Hannes Meyer.

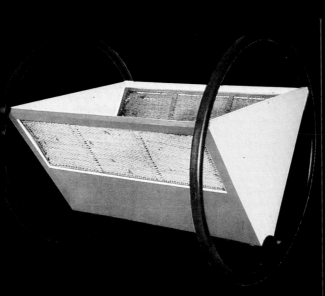

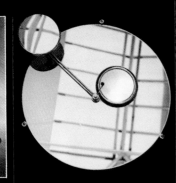

1922 Cradle for the modernist baby, *far left*, with rope-woven side panels and bentwood hoops, by Bauhaus student Peter Keler.

1926 Tubular steel and leather chair, *centre left*, by the Dutch Functionalist architect Mart Stam, one of the first designers to produce the cantilevered chair. It was manufactured by Thonet Bros, who also produced bentwood and cane furniture, *left*, to designs by Le Corbusier.

1923 Gestetner Ream Model duplicator, *left*, with mechanism left exposed.

1921 Cubist-inspired poster, *right*, by the American-born graphic designer Edward McKnight-Kauffer for London Transport.

1926 Sycamore chest by Eileen Gray, *below*, conceived with Functionalist simplicity but with a quirkiness in the angled steel handles and in the asymmetrical disposition of cupboards and drawers.

WINTER SALES are best reached by UNDERGROUND

1927 Eileen Gray delights in circular forms and motion in this classically minimalist 'Satellite' mirror, *above*.

1919 Glass beaker and saucer designed for Orrefors by Edward Hald, *above left*, the 'Girls Playing Ball' theme depicted with lyrically simple sweeping lines.

1915 Innovatory geometric forms and decoration in a porcelain teaset by Koloman Moser, *middle left*.

1930 Sterling silver cutlery set, *bottom left*, designed by Gundorph Albertus for Georg Jensen of Copenhagen – elegant functional forms with simple floral decoration.

GERMANY

The ideas of Sullivan and Wright were highly influential in the development of Functionalist architecture in Europe in the years after the First World War, but it was another aspect of the American achievement that shaped the German attitude towards 'art and industry' in the early years of the century.

While the Chicago architects were preoccupied with the idea of standardization as an abstract concept, the American automobile industry in Detroit and the furniture industry in Grand Rapids were actually using it as a major feature of mass-production proper. Henry Ford's ideas about the interchangeability of parts — which had their roots in Eli Whitney's production of firearms more than a century earlier — and the Grand Rapids approach towards the mass manufacture and standardization of unit furniture were transferred directly to Germany. It was these ideas that stimulated the emergence of a new furniture aesthetic in this period.

German furniture was manufactured in small workshops on craft principles but, within a few years, sawing and milling machines (among others) were introduced into furniture-making. In 1906 a number of the more progressive workshops joined together under the leadership of Karl Schmidt to form an organization called the German Werkstätten. This marked the beginning of Germany's attempt to extend craft into industrial design and to evolve a new, simple aesthetic for its products, by now made largely by machines from standardized components. The work of Richard Riemerschmid is the most significant in this context as it was he who exploited most fully the aesthetic potential of this new industrial approach in his highly innovative 'typenmöbel' (type-furniture). His standardized chairs, for instance, made of undecorated interchangeable wooden components, drew stylistically on vernacular chair-types and provided the first examples of cheap furniture aimed at a low-income market.

The Werkbund

The second major landmark in Germany's adoption of the machine and in her evolution of an appropriate design style for the new century was the formation, in 1907, of the German Werkbund, an organization set up as a pressure group to forge an alliance between art and industry. A major influence behind its formation was the publication in Germany in 1904-5 of a book entitled *The English House*. Written by a Prussian diplomat, Hermann Muthesius, it was a report of the time he had spent in England studying the architectural achievements of the Arts and Crafts Movement. Impressed by the way in which the British architects combined the simplicity of the vernacular tradition with modern services and rational planning, Muthesius saw in this example the way forward for a new twentieth-century design

aesthetic. In the book Muthesius emphasized the functional aspects of Arts and Crafts architecture, concentrating on such points as its practical planning and progressive and matter-of-fact use of services such as modern plumbing and electric lighting. He saw in these buildings the basis of a simple aesthetic which, inspired by the vernacular, was appropriate to the age of the machine.

Muthesius (1861-1928) was a founder-member of the Werkbund, along with Frederick Naumann and Theodor Fischer and a number of enthusiastic manufacturers. In the early years it set out to encourage manufacturers to use design and to educate both them and the general public in its general principles. From the beginning the Werkbund saw design as a fundamental element within the expansion of the German economy and the restoration of German culture and

worked to the brief of 'improving the design and quality of German goods' through lectures, exhibitions and other didactic means.

An early member of the Werkbund who has had a significant influence on modern industrial design in this century — not just in Germany but in the western world as a whole — was the graphic designer Peter Behrens (1868-1940). Behrens has often been called the first consultant industrial designer but his early work was as a promoter of the Art Nouveau style in posters and applied art objects. He was attached, in the early years of his career, to the artistic colony based in Darmstadt and adhered to that group's latter-day Arts and Crafts philosophy. When, however, he was approached by Emil Rathenau, the head of the AEG company (United Electric) to design a corporate scheme, the aesthetic he evolved for that project had a much more overtly 'industrial' feel to it.

Behrens' designs for AEG included a highly functional-looking building that owed its appearance more to the simple, utilitarian, anonymous style of engineers than the self-conscious aesthetic of contemporary architects; brochures; graphics (which were very simple and clearly laid out); undecorated steel cutlery, which was mass-produced for the firm's canteen; and a wide range of electrical products — kettles and fans among them.

With their overt mechanisms and 'unselfconscious' forms, unmodified by surface decoration, these wares had more in common with early American 'functional' goods than with Behrens' florid Art Nouveau designs of a few years earlier. This was the first time that a designer had made such a dramatic move from the applied arts to industrial design, changing his style from one that espoused decoration to one inspired by the machine and modern technology and therefore thought to be more appropriate to the industrial world.

The 1914 Werkbund exhibition

The gap between the individualism that had characterized late-nineteenth century ideas about decoration and the more 'objective' implications of the machine aesthetic reached a head in the debate between Henri van de Velde (1863-1957) and Hermann Muthesius on the occasion of the Werkbund exhibition in Cologne in 1914. While van de Velde held fast to his Art Nouveau-derived belief that the designer is essentially a fine artist who applies his skills to the objects of mechanized mass production, Muthesius was adamant that design for mass-production was not simply a question of 'applied art' but rather the result of a more rigorous understanding of the principles that govern that process.

In the Werkbund exhibition Walter Gropius and Adolf Meyer exhibited their model factory building with its exposed staircases shrouded in glass. Along with their factory designed for the Fagus shoe-last company a few years earlier, it was among the first European buildings to express itself exclusively through the aesthetic of new materials, steel and glass. Gropius (1883-1969) was soon to become, in fact, the major German spokesman on behalf of an architecture and design totally motivated by the machine. It was a few years later, at the Bauhaus in the 1920s, that he outlined his ideas more fully and became an important influence on the next generation of architects and designers.

Far left: *This advertising poster of 1914 for Kuno Bergman is a typical example of German graphic design from this period, combining, as it does, vestiges of Art Nouveau with a more geometric machine-inspired style.*
Below left: *Henri van de Velde's Werkbund theatre at the Werkbund's Cologne exhibition of 1914 showed, with its expressive forms, the last traces of 19th-century individualism.*

Below: *Peter Behrens' electric kettle for AEG designed in 1909.*
Below centre: *The AEG factory before Behrens' redesign.*
Bottom: *The AEG factory after Behrens' redesign of 1908 shows his commitment to the Machine Aesthetic.*

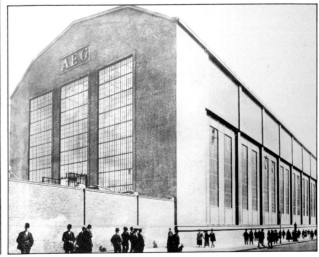

AUSTRIA

Among the numerous pavilions at the 1914 Werkbund exhibition was one designed by the leading Austrian architect-designer of the day, Josef Hoffmann (1870-1955). Austrian designers played an important role in the transition between Art Nouveau and the machine aesthetic as it was in that country that a number of men focused their attention on the thorny problem of what constitutes an appropriate architecture and design for the twentieth century.

In the late nineteenth century Vienna had been preparing itself for the move into the modern style. The Austrian Museum for Art and Industry had been founded in the 1870s and a major international exhibition had been held in the city in 1873. It was also in Vienna that the Secession artists and designers created their own sumptuous version of *Jugendstil*. Founded in 1897, the Secession group built its own building in the following year and set out to restore the so-called 'minor arts' to an equal footing alongside painting and sculpture. Their initial optimism had, however, faded a little by 1904, when there was a major disagreement among members about the role of 'design' in modern culture. A breakaway group, including the painter Gustav Klimt (1862-1918) and the designers Hoffmann and Joseph Olbrich (1867-1908) took upon itself the task of raising the standards of the decorative arts. In 1900 the magazine *Das Interieur* emerged as the mouthpiece for the group, showing Viennese architecture and applied arts to the rest of the world for the first time.

The Turin exhibition of 1902 — which featured a room setting designed by the Scottish architect, Charles Rennie Mackintosh (1868-1928), who was a major influence upon the Viennese group — was an important showplace for Austrian design and the rectilinear forms of its decorative objects rapidly became internationally familiar at this time. In the following year Hoffmann and Koloman Moser (1868-1916), with the help of funds provided by the Viennese banker, Fritz Waerndorfer, established the Wiener Werkstätte, which was set up on the model of C.R. Ashbee's Guild of Handicrafts and aimed to produce crafted objects in metal, leather, wood, ceramic and glass.

The Werkstätte's designs for small domestic objects were intended to act as a counter-blast to machine production but their innovative aesthetic emphasized, nonetheless, a simple geometry that had much in common with the abstract machine aesthetic, visible in products made in the US and in Germany. Unlike their American and German counterparts, however, they remained individualized exclusive objects, as a result never reaching the mass of the Austrian population.

The principle name associated with the Werkstätte is that of Josef Hoffmann, who produced some of that period's most stunning and timeless designs. The same

Above: Otto Wagner's Karlsplatz station for the Vienna Stadtbahn of 1898 Wagner's combination of Art Nouveau decoration and structural simplicity inspired the younger generation.

Josef Hoffmann (1870-1955), an Austrian architect whose work is currently being revived, studied under Otto Wagner and was a founder member, with Koloman Moser, of the Wiener Werkstätte in 1903. Much influenced by the architecture and designs of the Scotsman, C.R. Mackintosh, Hoffmann's work combined rich decoration with geometric simplicity and has often been described as rectilinear Art Nouveau. Some of his best-known designs include simple bentwood café chairs designed for the Thonet furniture company and his building in Brussels, the Palais Stoclet, *above*, of 1905-11, which combined simple geometry with sumptuous materials and decorative details, such as marble-veneered walls and mosaics by Gustav Klimt. Among his numerous smaller

objects were metal vases, trays and bowls which utilized his now famous grid motif and items like the little glass jar, *below,* of 1905. Like many of his Wiener Werkstätte colleagues, Hoffmann worked in a wide range of styles during his long career.

Below: *Secession building, Vienna, designed by Joseph Olbrich and built in 1897-8. It became a strong visual symbol for the new generation of Austrian architects.*
Left: *Detail of the Secession building.*

Above: *Textiles designed by a member of the Wiener Werkstätte, showing the way they turned geometric shapes into decorative motifs.*

Above right: *A metal inkwell designed by a Wiener Werkstätte member showing that group's debt to the organic motifs of Art Nouveau.*
Right: *A textile pattern designed by a member of the Werkstätte showing how proto Art Deco patterns characterized much of that group's work.*

geometric purism that was visible in German goods and the same interests in the abstract motifs in Japanese design that had inspired Wright a decade earlier characterized the whole spectrum of Hoffmann's work from architecture and furniture to small metal decorative objects that made repeated use of the grid motif and rectilinear shapes — trays, fruit-bowls, tea-pots, flower vases and cutlery among them.

In many ways the Viennese objects from this period occupied a middle ground between van de Velde's individualistic account of modern style and Muthesius' aggressively standardized approach. The Viennese designers combined both tendencies, and they gave this century a humanized modern style that kept a place for decoration.

The Viennese design movement was imported wholesale into the USA in the 1920s by Austrian emigrés such as Josef Urban and Wolfgang Hoffmann, Josef's son, and it quickly became an intrinsic component of the 'Moderne' style that dominated American interior design and decorative arts in the late twenties and early thirties.

Left: *The Paradiset Restaurant at the Stockholm Exhibition of 1930, designed by Gunnar Asplund. The strong machine style of the buildings at this exhibition owed much to German Functionalist architecture of the 1920s.*

SWEDEN

Austrian influence was also felt in Sweden in the early thirties as the Viennese architect Josef Frank made his home in that country in 1932. Once there he rejected his earlier preoccupation with architectural Functionalism, softening his approach to become a major protagonist of the 'Swedish Modern' style, which combined simple forms with light, usually naturalistic decoration and a respect for craft traditions.

In the first three decades of this century Sweden, like Austria and Germany, also developed a design philosophy based on craft principles. The new machine style was most appropriate for industrial products that had no craft traditions behind them. Where the older industries were concerned, however, the best work was, everywhere, by 1914, still being produced by craftsmen and, to a greater or lesser extent, reflected the fact in its chosen aesthetic.

The Scandinavian countries were craft-dominated but by the end of the nineteenth century they had absorbed some of the stylistic ideas that derived from the industrial sector and a light, democratic, modern Swedish style began to emerge as a result. At the Gustavsberg ceramics firm, for instance, the artist Gunnar Wennerberg was brought in to help the company evolve a modern style. He went directly to nature — to Swedish wild flowers in particular — for inspiration and created a series of light, fresh patterns that influenced much Swedish design in that period.

In 1915, however, a shift of emphasis occurred in Swedish decorative arts. The Swedish design body, the Svenska Sjlödforeningen, opened an employment agency for artists and craftsmen in an attempt to make contact with manufacturing industry. In fulfilling this role the organization was modelling itself on German Werkbund principles as it could see that Germany was making rapid headway in its sponsorship of the 'industrial arts' and winning a place on the world market. As a direct result of the new policy Wilhelm Kåge was introduced to the Gustavsberg works. Kåge (1889-1960) had worked as a poster artist in the Post-Impressionist style and saw his role at Gustavsberg as one of developing simple decorative motifs for cheap everyday ware. His 'worker's dining-set' of 1917, which bore a simple blue flower motif on a white background, was reminiscent of Swedish folk pottery.

It was the first sign of a direction in Swedish design, which found its full flowering in the democratic sentiment expressed by Gregor Paulsson in his book, written five years later, called *More Beautiful Everyday Things*.

The Swedes were searching for a design style that combined simplicity with humanism, beauty and democratic ideals, and Kåge dedicated the next twenty years to pursuing this end. Like him, the artists Edward Hald (1883-1981) and Simon Gate (1883-1945) were

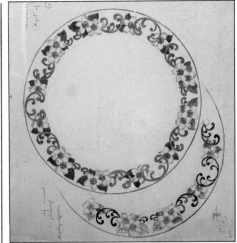

Left: *A soup tureen from Wilhelm Kåge's simple dinner service for working men designed for Gustavsberg in 1917. The decoration derives from traditional Swedish ceramics.*

Above left: *A floral design in gouache executed by Gunnar Wennerberg for Gustavsberg in 1905 as a ceramic border.*
Above right: *A neo-classical decorative detail from Simon Gate's glass bowl designed for Orrefors in 1921. The lightness*

and gracefulness of the engraved design typifies much Swedish glass of this period.
Below: *'Fireworks Bowl' designed by Edward Hald in 1921 for the Orrefors glass company.*

introduced to manufacturing companies by the Svenska Sjlödforeningen. In their case it was the Orrefors glass company that acted as patron for their forays into lyrical decoration on light simple glass forms. Like Kåge, they split their time between the design of elaborate one-off ceremonial pieces and simpler mass-produced ware aimed at a wider market.

Hald's most memorable pieces from the late twenties include his delightful 'Fireworks' vase with its image of a fireworks party etched onto the surface of its elegant form. Hald had worked with Matisse in Paris and had learnt from him the evocative nature of simple line drawing. Gate's contribution to Orrefors' production was both aesthetic and technical. He was responsible, for instance, for the development of the 'Graal' technique characterized by the bright colour it introduced into glass design. Mass-production was in these years still fairly restricted but Kåge, Hald and Gate succeeded nonetheless in establishing the groundwork for the democratic style which, by the end of the 1930s, was known internationally as 'Swedish Modern'.

The 1930 Stockholm Exhibition provided an important international showplace for Swedish design. From an architectural point of view it was dominated by Functionalism, but where the decorative arts were concerned a much more overtly humanistic aesthetic was in evidence. There was a significant gap in Swedish design between architecture, which looked to Germany and France for inspiration, and the manufacture of ceramics, glass and furniture, which looked to Swedish tradition. It was a schism that continued throughout the 1930s.

LONDON'S TRAMWAYS

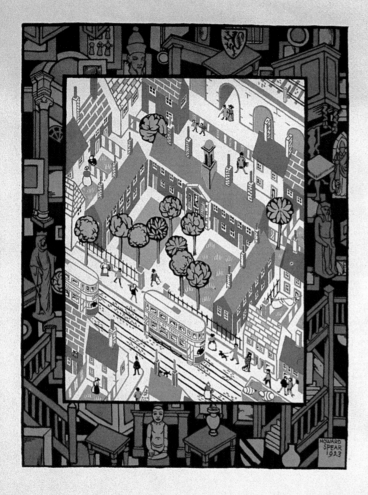

OLD FURNITURE AT THE GEFFRYE MUSEUM KINGSLAND RD. TRAM SERVICES 43, 45, 47, 49

DESIGNED AT THE L.C.C. CENTRAL SCHOOL OF ARTS AND CRAFTS

WATERLOW & SONS LIMITED, LONDON, DUNSTABLE & WATFORD

LONDON'S TRAMWAYS

THEATRE LAND LATE SERVICES BY TRAMWAY

DESIGNED AT THE L.C.C. CENTRAL SCHOOL OF ARTS AND CRAFTS

BRITAIN'S COAL
40 PER CENT
Raised from Collieries
served by
L·N·E·R

Far left: *A poster advertising London Transport's Tramway service in the 1920s. Headed by Frank Pick, London Transport commissioned many well-known artists and designers of the day to work on these progressive projects.*

Left: *A London Tramways poster for Theatreland showing how a dramatic image was combined in these designs with a simple, highly legible typeface.*

Below: *Although made in the late 19th-century, Christopher Dresser's simple spun brass chamber-sticks of 1883 looked ahead to the machine-inspired style of the early 20th-century.*

Left: *An LNER poster from the 1930s which combines an avant-garde image with a very clear message carefully laid out in a simple typeface.*

Below: *Christopher Dresser's silver teapot of 1881 anticipated the simple aesthetic that was pioneered by the British Arts and Crafts movement and admired greatly abroad.*

GREAT BRITAIN

Britain's most influential design activities in the period between 1900 and 1930 were the legacy of the Arts and Crafts movement, initiated a few decades earlier by William Morris and his followers. So entrenched had Morris' values become within British design thinking at the turn of the century that the transition from craft to industrial design that took place so smoothly in Germany was much delayed in Britain. A mistrust of Germanic rationalism and a decline in industrial expansion combined, in the period after 1900, to create a somewhat backward-looking approach to the decorative arts. Even Art Nouveau, that most international of styles, which exploited the aesthetic potential of new materials like wrought iron and glass, bypassed Britain almost completely and was described by Walter Crane, a leading member of the Arts and Crafts movement, as a 'strange decorative disease'.

It was, ironically, the Arts and Crafts architecture that had inspired Hermann Muthesius to visit Britain in the last century and report back on his findings which was now holding the country back. While in Germany a bridge was established between the 'functional' approach of the British architects and mass-production industry, for the country that originated Arts and Crafts the movement represented a cul-de-sac. When in 1915 the Design and Industries Association was formed in Britain as an equivalent of the German Werkbund it was peopled by many of the individuals who had earned their reputations in the previous century through their Arts and Crafts associations. C.R. Lethaby, for instance, was a founder-member of the DIA, as were Ambrose Heal, the retailer who had brought Arts and Crafts furniture to the metropolis and sold it to a 'discriminating' audience, and Gordon Russell, who was deeply steeped in Cotswold design ideals.

The DIA's slogan 'fitness for purpose' was based on ideas that Morris had outlined half a century earlier and most of the leading members remained in sympathy with that pioneer's design aesthetic. The result was that the association's influence was much less far-reaching than that of the Werkbund. While the latter body made enormous efforts to penetrate the 'new' industries and to translate craft ideals into the context of, say, the mass-production of electrical goods, DIA members restricted their reforming zeal to the products of the traditional industries. Thus while firms like Poole Pottery and, a little later, Harry Peach's Dryad furniture company were influenced by the association, moving, as a result, towards a simpler aesthetic for their products, there were no spin-offs in the new industrial sector.

Among the few innovative and influential designs to come out of the DIA circle was the work for the London Underground. Edward Johnston's simple sans-serif typeface was used for a corporate identity scheme which, through the twenties and thirties, changed the public face of the Tube network. The force behind this new programme was Frank Pick, the man in charge of London Transport's corporate style, who adopted a much more aggressive policy than most of his fellow countrymen towards the role of modern design within contemporary culture. His forward-thinking ideas had much in common with contemporary German thinking and he alone among DIA members had an influence on bringing Britain into line with progressive European ideas about design in the 1930s.

Apart from the work achieved by isolated individuals like Pick, British design in the twenties and thirties was characterized by the lingering influence of craftsmanship and, stylistically, by a series of revivals, from Georgian to Tudor. Where domestic style was concerned the Modern Movement touched only the intellectual middle-class sector of British society and never penetrated the mass of the British public. Britain remained, in fact, a follower rather than an innovator of style, right up until the 1960s.

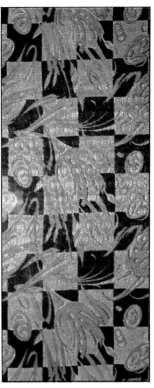

Above left: *An Arts and Crafts inspired chair designed by Gordon Russell in 1927.*
Above: *A Warner and Sons fabric from 1928.*
Left: *A British machine-style tea-set in silver from 1925.*
Below: *A Warner and Sons fabric from 1918.*

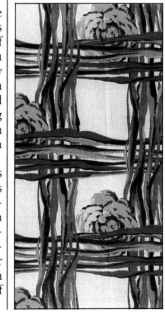

NETHERLANDS

By the First World War, ideas originated within avant-garde circles had come to completely dominate the applied arts and industrial design and the work in all these media that derived from the preoccupation with the machine became associated, collectively, with the concept of the 'Modern Movement'. It was under this umbrella that most of the important ideas about style were discussed in the years following the cessation of hostilities in 1917. The Netherlands had maintained a position of neutrality through the war and it was there that the Modern Movement first took on a special significance. Frank Lloyd Wright's ideas about functional architecture had been transported to Holland by the Dutch architect Hendrick P. Berlage and provided the foundation for the modern style that emerged in that country.

The Dutch Modern Movement was promulgated through a publication called *De Stijl*, which first appeared in 1917. Its name quickly became adopted as the general title for the movement in architecture, design and fine art which flourished in the Netherlands for the next decade or so. Alternatively dubbed 'Elementarism', this stressed the use of the minimal visual elements — horizontal and vertical lines (occasionally the odd diagonal crept in) — and basic colours. Together these constituted the essential vocabulary of the language through which the *De Stijl* artist set out to communicate 'universal truths'. There was a strong input of mystical thought, in particular theosophy, in *De Stijl*, which was manifested more overtly in the theoretical writings that accompanied the movement than in the works it produced. The movement engendered the production of a number of paintings, buildings and designs which have retained their purist appeal right up until the present day.

The painter most closely associated with *De Stijl* was Piet Mondrian (1872-1944), whose abstract compositions of those years achieved an unparalleled level of minimalism. They concentrated on the harmonious composition of line, mass and colour, thus exploiting the basic visual language that the architects, sculptors and designers were to extend into three dimensions.

The architect-designer who produced some of the most lasting *De Stijl* images was Gerrit Rietveld (1888-1964). Trained initially as a cabinetmaker, Rietveld translated Mondrian's 'Elementarist' principles into buildings and furniture designs, all of which emphasized the relationship between lines, mass and space expressed through minimal means. Structure also played an important role in the design of three-dimensional *De Stijl* objects. In his red-blue armchair of 1919, for instance, Rietveld concentrated on expressing the way in which the planes intersect each other in the construction of a sitting object. To make this visually

Above: *Gerrit Rietveld's 'Crate' furniture from the 1920s (reproduced here by the Italian company, Cassina). Rietveld was concerned with the spatial implications of the way planks of wood overlapped each other to create very simple furniture structures.*
Right: *Gerrit Rietveld's armchair of 1919 was made of stained panga panga wood with blue paint applied to the ends of each piece to emphasize the juxtaposition of planes.*

clear he exaggerated all the junction points by extending the elements a little further than necessary and by painting the planes at the end of them a contrasting colour. Rietveld's chair, often dismissed as supremely uncomfortable, functions in the end as a sculptural evocation of the abstract, essential qualities of a chair rather than as a sitting object *per se*.

By adopting the idea of construction determining external form as a primary metaphor in his designs, Rietveld was extending the theory of Functionalism into a poetic device and codifying the machine aesthetic into a visual language with its own intrinsic vocabulary. It was a language that was to dominate the style of much avant-garde architecture and design in the next few decades.

Right: *Jacket design in black and white by Vilmos Huszar for the first issue of 'De Stijl' magazine, launched in 1917.*

Below: *Rietveld's little side table for the Schroeder house was an Elementarist exercise. The circular base is red, and the square planes black and white with blue and yellow details.*

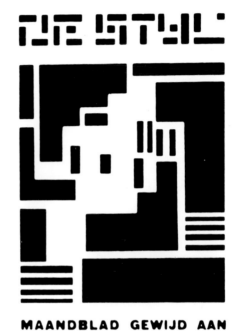

DE STIJL

MAANDBLAD GEWIJD AAN
DE MODERNE BEELDENDE
VAKKEN EN KULTUUR
RED. THEO VAN DOESBURG.

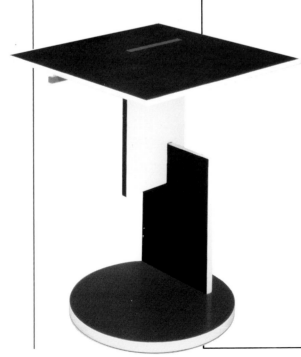

RUSSIA

РАБОТЫ СТЕПАНОВОЙ

РАБОТЫ РОДЧЕНКО

Прозкты спорт-одежды

Прозкты марки ДОБРОЛЕТА

Russian Constructivism emerged at the same time as Dutch *De Stijl* and developed a similar aesthetic, based once again upon the idea of the machine as a primary influence. Unlike the Dutch movement, however, the Russian design events after 1917 had their roots in the political changes that were taking place in that country. The post-revolutionary Russian artists and designers saw their task as one of building products for the new society in the same way as the engineer builds bridges and dams.

The idea of 'construction' was, therefore, funda-mental to the designs of men like Vladimir Tatlin (1885-1953), Alexander Rodchenko (1891-1956) and the Russian fashion and theatre designers of the day. They all worked for the new 'proletariat', creating an environment that was modern, efficient and functional. The abstract aesthetic that Russian painters like Kasimir Malevich had developed in pre-revolutionary Russia from European Cubist and Futurist experiments pro-vided the stylistic base for much of the new design. It was much more dynamic than its equivalent in Holland and, in Russia, the use of the diagonal was widespread.

Above: A spread from a Russian Constructivist book from just after the Revolution of 1917 entitled 'LEF' (left front of the arts). The left-hand page shows designs for sportswear by Stepanova and the right, logo designs by Rodchenko.

90

Malevich's 'Suprematist' style, characterized by its use of minimal colour — mostly black and white — and the use of abstract geometric motifs arranged dynamically on a monochrome background, appeared on the surfaces of ceramics and clothing, imbuing them with an optimistic, futuristic quality which suited the post-revolutionary fervour of the moment.

Although both Suprematism and Constructivism favoured the abstract, dynamic aesthetic and sought to translate the 'spirit' of the machine age into practical forms for everyday life, Malevich and Tatlin differed in their views about the role of the artist within modern society. For Malevich design was, in essence, an applied art inasmuch as his abstract motifs could be applied to the surfaces of any number of utility objects as well as providing the basis for an architectural style. Tatlin, however, saw design as being much more closely allied to engineering and, like the Americans before him, developed his new design aesthetic as an inevitable result of the application of the laws of construction, standardization and mass production.

For Tatlin the designer was not an artist but an anonymous 'worker' responsible for planning the new products for the new society. His designs included a worker's boiler-suit, a stove and a tower conceived as a major monument for the Revolution. Although never built, except in scaled-down versions, the tower was designed to include a radio station at its summit which would broadcast news of the Revolution.

Other Constructivist designers — Rodchenko, for example — worked on the designs of utilitarian constructions such as newspaper stands and cigarette kiosks which were the equivalents of Malevich's paintings. He was particularly influential in the area of graphic design and the new typographical style that emerged in Russia at this time and manifested the same compositional values as other Constructivist artefacts. Use of abstraction has, subsequently, been a major influence on progressive graphics internationally.

In the 1920s the Russian artists and designers continued to work in the service of the Revolution, helping to establish an art and design educational system which would, they hoped, provide the much-needed next generation of creative individuals. While in a country such as Holland, which had not experienced a social revolution, the ideas of the *De Stijl* group remained somewhat rarefied and dependent upon enlightened patronage for its execution, Russian designers found a ready outlet for their progressive ideas in a new society that demanded a new visual identity and new products. The propaganda displays, clothing and other utility items provided by the designers were stylistically highly avant-garde in that they embraced the modern abstract aesthetic that painters from Cubism onwards had pioneered. They nonetheless succeeded in penetrating to the roots of Russian society. This remained the case until 1932, when Stalin outlawed abstract art and design in Russia and introduced the system of Soviet Realism as the only viable art form.

Top left: *Tatlin's Constructivist tower for the Third International was seen as a monument for the Russian Revolution. Its open forms reflected Tatlin's commitment to the aesthetic of the engineer and it was envisaged as an action centre with a broadcasting area at the top.*

Top right: *A textile design by the Russian designer, Popova, from around 1924. It combines motifs derived from Parisian Orphism with abstract geometric patterns. Textile design was among the most sophisticated areas of design during this period.*

Above left: *El Lissitzky's cover for I. Ehrenburg's 'Six Tales with an Early Ending', showing compositional and colour preoccupations of the post-revolutionary graphic designers in Russia.*

Above right: *An anonymous Russian notice for an 'Atheistic Easter Festival' showing the influence of Malevich's Suprematism on graphic design at this time.*

FRANCE

The 1925 Paris exhibition was noteworthy not simply for its role in popularizing the Art Deco style but also because it was the venue at which the Russian architect Kasimir Melnikov exhibited his futuristic pavilion. This was not the only avant-garde manifestation in 1925, however, as the French architect Pierre Jeanneret (1887-1968), better known simply as Le Corbusier, showed his *Pavillon de l'Esprit Nouveau*.

While one wing of the French decorative arts had been dominated, since the turn of the century, first by Art Nouveau and later by the exclusive work of the *artistes-decorateurs* who were committed to the style that became known as Art Deco, there was an element within French architecture and design in the 1920s that favoured the more purist, Modern Movement approach.

The concept of the 'machine aesthetic' was central to Le Corbusier's contribution to modern style. It was he, in fact, who made that oft-quoted and usually misunderstood statement 'A house is a machine for living in'. What he meant by it was not that people should live mechanical, highly efficient lives, but rather that the principles that govern mechanical mass production should apply to architecture as well. His little 'Domino' house of 1913, basically a cube containing two storeys and with an outside staircase modelled on peasant housing he had seen in Greece, was an early example of a standardized unit made of prefabricated parts and initiated Le Corbusier's interest in the idea that a house could, in many ways, resemble a machine.

In his book *Vers Une Architecture (Towards an Architecture,* 1923) Le Corbusier evoked the mystique of machinery and the beauty of simple type-forms, ending up with an illustration of a simple briar-pipe which, for him, epitomized the idea of a 'universal object'. The belief that type-forms, once achieved, will last for ever was fundamental to the Modern Movement and appeared over and over again as a central theme. Its supporters were convinced that they had finally moved beyond the superficiality of style and achieved ultimate forms.

As well as evolving a highly original architectural aesthetic, both for individual villas and for multi-storey apartment blocks, that was made up essentially of white walls, flat roofs, ribbon windows and a concept of open internal space, Le Corbusier also devoted his energies to the design of furniture. His buildings were fitted out either with built-in furniture or mass-produced 'ready-mades' such as Thonet bent-wood chairs, but the furniture pieces that he designed as independent entities were sumptuous forms in tubular steel and black leather. With Charlotte Perriand, Le Corbusier produced a range of pieces — among them a *chaise-longue*, an arm-chair, and a dining-chair, all made of tubular steel and black leather with just enough upholstery to avoid

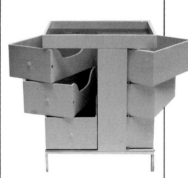

spoiling the architectural line and provide enough comfort for the user. They have since become classics of Modern design.

The French movement was a fairly esoteric affair responsible for the design of private villas and furniture for far-sighted, wealthy clients. Apart from Le Corbusier its main creative forces were Robert Mallet-Stevens (1886-1945) and the Irish-born Eileen Gray (1879-1976). Both Stevens and Gray were committed to the Modern Movement's ideals but at the same time borrowed rich materials from the contemporary French decorative arts. As in Holland the appropriation of the machine, where French Modern style was concerned, took place on a metaphorical rather than a literal level and, in spite of the austere aesthetic evolved in both countries, one cannot talk about a genuine *rapprochement* between art and industry in this context. However democratic its ideals, the Modern Movement remained an exclusive style in these countries, patronized by a wealthy, fashion-conscious clientele.

Top: *Le Corbusier's Villa Savoye of 1929-31 epitomized his ideas about the Machine Aesthetic, with its ribbon windows, 'pilotis' and concrete.*
Above left: *Chaise longue by Robert Mallet-Stevens from the 1920s. The combination of the structural steel frame and the slung canvas seat creates the illusion of a very basic seat.*
Above: *Eileen Gray's little lacquer cabinet from the 1920s attacks the perennial problem of storage in a unique and supremely functional manner.*

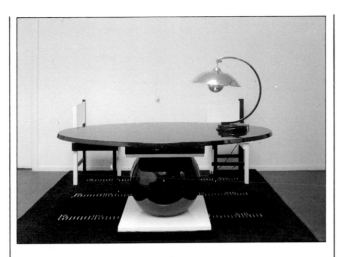

Above: *This assemblage of simple, decorative objects from the 1920s includes a table by J. H. Lartigue, a chrome lamp by Mariano Fortuny and a striking rug by Eileen Gray.*
Right: *Paul Chareau's 'Maison de Verre' is among the most dramatic examples of French* Modern Movement architecture of the 1920s in its total commitment to this new material.
Below: *Le Corbusier's chaise longue in chromed steel and leather is one of the most elegant Modern images from the 1920s.*

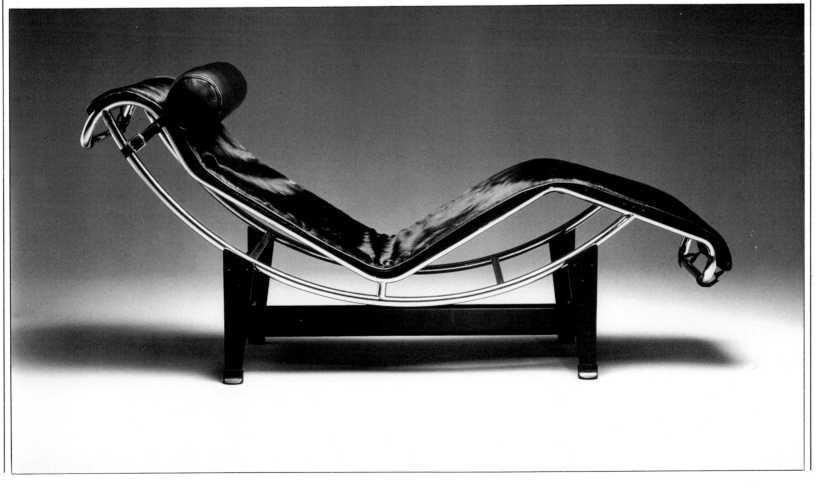

Above: *Joost Schmidt's Elementarist layout for a Bauhaus publication of the mid-1920s.*
Left: *Joost Schmidt's poster for the Bauhaus exhibition, 'Art and Technology', held in Weimar in 1923.*
Below: *Walter Gropius' aluminium waste paper bin of 1935 showing his continued interest in elementary, geometric form.*

THE BAUHAUS

Left: *A design for a folding table from 1924 (now produced by Tecta Möbel) by Erich Brendel, a Bauhaus student. It manifests a typically Bauhaus interest in elementary forms and primary colours.*
Below: *Marcel Breuer's well-known tubular steel and leather 'club' armchair of 1925, known later as the 'Wassily' chair after Kandinsky, for whose house it was designed. Its open forms reflect the Bauhaus interest in spatial manipulation.*

The same accusation of adopting the machine as an idea rather than a reality can be levelled at the achievement of the German design school, the Bauhaus, which opened in Weimar in 1919.

The Bauhaus manifesto, written by the school's founder, the architect Walter Gropius, and illustrated by the Expressionist painter Lyonel Feininger (1871-1956), paid direct homage to the work of the British Arts and Crafts movement, thus establishing a link between William Morris and the Bauhaus.

The main contribution of the Bauhaus to twentieth-century style lay, however, in its promotion of a machine-inspired aesthetic for architecture and the applied arts and in the sophisticated teaching programmes, developed to encourage students to be proficient both in a craft skill and in the manipulation of the language of elementary forms.

The first few years of the Bauhaus' existence were dominated by the presence on the staff of a number of Expressionist painters who tended to encourage students to reduce their aesthetic vocabulary to basic elements but to retain a strongly individualistic and emotive flavour as well. The work of Johannes Itten (1887-1967), for instance, on the Bauhaus foundation course concentrated on exercises such as paper-cutting or working with the contrasts of light and shade. Gropius was unhappy with the way Itten combined this approach with his interest in mystical religion and sacked him from the school in the early twenties.

Itten's sacking marked the beginning of a new phase, initiated by an exhibition 'Art and Technology — A New Unity', organized by Walter Gropius in 1923. Gropius was concerned to take the Bauhaus syllabus away from the emphasis upon subjective experience and towards a more objective definition of form, an approach which was to characterize Bauhaus teaching for the next decade.

After Itten's dismissal the foundation course was taken over by Laszlo Moholy-Nagy (1895-1946) whose background in middle-European Constructivism led him to put more emphasis on the abstract, geometric qualities of materials and on the roles of structure and construction in the design process. From this moment the Bauhaus began a search for universal form which was taken further, in acadamic terms, at this institution than ever before. The teachers responsible for this programme included the painters Paul Klee (1879-1940) and Wassily Kandinsky (1866-1944), who spent their time at the Bauhaus dealing exclusively with the studies of, in Klee's case, line, and in Kandinsky's case, colour. They evolved programmes that encouraged students to rediscover the basic properties of these elements and then to develop highly sophisticated ways of manipulating them.

Bauhaus design

The basic principles behind Bauhaus design focused on the idea of 'learning from scratch'. This was essentially inspired by the idea — derived from the principles of interchangeability and standardization in mass-production — that design for industry means fabrication from basic units. This was combined in Bauhaus teaching with the Morris-inspired notion of 'truth to materials'. In theory at least, therefore, Bauhaus design bridged the gap between craft and industry. This was achieved by educating students both in the principles of basic design and in workshop practice. All the students spent time in the craft workshops — among them wood, metal, ceramic, textile and theatre — and thus became proficient in the use of one particular material.

This division into media and the emphasis on craft meant that the Bauhaus objects all fell within the areas of traditional products — that is, furniture, ceramics, metalwork and so on. Nevertheless, the use of new materials was encouraged and indeed widely exploited. In the wood workshop, for instance, Marcel Breuer (1902-1981) began his time at the Bauhaus designing chairs that resembled Rietveld's famous example and were essentially exercises in construction. It wasn't until a few years later that he made the leap into tubular steel, developing, when he did so, some of this century's most progressive and memorable chair designs.

Breuer's cantilever and 'Club' armchairs were direct results of Bauhaus thinking, as it was their structure that dictated their outward appearance. This was in a direct line of descent from Louis Sullivan's ideas about form following function from forty years earlier. Functionalist theory remained a consistent baseline within Bauhaus thinking right through the period. Like Rietveld, Breuer was convinced that his chairs were styleless and it was generally understood that the same went for all the objects that emerged from the Bauhaus workshops.

Where metalwork was concerned, the two German designers Marianne Brandt and Wilhelm Wagenfeld provided the strongest and most lasting pieces. Again their designs were exercises in the manipulation of basic formal elements with no added surface decoration. The ceramics tended to be simple, white forms and the textile patterns were based on geometric motifs.

A new aesthetic of everyday goods within the traditional art industries emerged, therefore, from the Bauhaus as a result of the rigorous 'deconditioning' process that went on there and the strong beliefs of Gropius, whose idealism pervaded every aspect of the school's theory and practice. While Gropius undertook one project for a car and another for a stove in this period, Bauhaus design remained craft-based, however committed it was to the machine as a motivating symbol. The workshops were equipped with only basic machinery and very few contacts were made with industrial manufacturers outside the school during its lifetime.

The Bauhaus objects and the Bauhaus style were powerful and influential, however. Many were taken up by industry after the school was closed by the Nazis in 1933 and many of them have become familiar appendages of the contemporary environment. The furniture designs by Marcel Breuer and Mies van der Rohe (1886-1969) in tubular steel and black leather, for instance, still epitomize the Modern Movement for many people.

The Bauhaus was never the same after Gropius left it in 1928, although he was followed as director first by Hannes Meyer (1889-1954) and later by Mies van der Rohe. It was never really given a chance in its own lifetime as it was continually mistrusted by local government and starved of funds as a result. Because so many of the Bauhaus protagonists went to the USA — among them Gropius, Albers, Moholy-Nagy and Breuer — to carry out their work on American soil, the Bauhaus name did not sink into oblivion but was given a new lease of life across the Atlantic. It had a strong effect on American design education thinking from the mid-thirties onwards and was acknowledged, in theory if not in practice, as an influence on the ideas of the American pioneer industrial designers.

Walter Gropius (1883-1969) was a German architect who began his professional career in partnership with Adolf Meyer, with whom he built the Fagus factory in 1911. He was a major contributor to the 1914 Werkbund exhibition at Cologne, designing the administrative building and a model factory. In 1919 he was called to Weimar to establish the Bauhaus out of two existing educational institutions. The programme he devised for that school, founded on the principles of what came to be called 'basic design', has influenced design education since the twenties in a major way. As well as the main disciplines of architecture, painting and sculpture, the programme included many areas of hand craftsmanship and design.

When the Bauhaus moved to Dessau in 1925, Gropius was responsible for the design of its new buildings (see students' quarters, *below*) which conformed to the principles of the architectural Modern movement — that is, flat roofs, white walls, metal framed windows and so on.

In 1928 Gropius handed over his post at the Bauhaus to Hannes Meyer and he was subsequently driven from Germany by the Nazis, first to England and, in 1937, to the USA where he took up a position as Professor of Architecture at Harvard.

Gropius remained in the USA until his death in 1969 by which time he had become a major influence on American architectural education. His main contribution has been, therefore, as a teacher, but he will also be remembered for his numerous architectural achievements and for the design, in the 1920s, of a number of products, including a car for Adler and a stove.

REALITY OR SYMBOL?

From the turn of the century onwards the Modern Movement, which had such a major influence on the progress of the decorative arts up to 1930, was dominated by architecture, the so-called 'queen of the arts'. Furniture was seen as a natural extension of this medium, however, and as a consequence all the leading Modern architects of the period had a go at a chair design or two.

In 1932 an exhibition was organized at the Museum of Modern Art in New York entitled 'The International Style'. This consisted of pictures of countless white, flat-roofed buildings from all over the world. It took the USA to admit that this was essentially a 'style', and not the 'ultimate' movement that it had so often been described as. America was more open about the idea of style than Europe, which tended to equate the concept with superficiality, detracting from the real meaning and purpose of architecture and design.

Although architecture determined both the definition and the evolution of the simple, undecorated style in the decorative arts throughout the twenties, this did not in the end help bring design any nearer to industry in real terms. For architecture, the machine implied, in the end, little more than undecorated, geometric form. For the decorative arts, however, it was a much more radical proposition as it meant that, potentially at least, many more objects could be made available to more people. Buildings could not come off the conveyor belt like Ford cars.

While the machine aesthetic depended upon architecture and architects for its formulation in this period and the effects on the decorative arts were a kind of spin-off, it took another thirty or so years for industrial design to be affected by the 'purist' style in a substantial way. It was only the early American manufacturers — Singer and Ford among them — and the German Werkbund that had really tried to come to grips with the idea of machines and mass production actually affecting the look of consumer wares. For them the machine was a reality rather than a symbol: they took their ideas directly from engineering and work organization rather than indirectly through architecture and were therefore more in tune with the real implications of mass production. This was recognized by men such as Tatlin in Russia, who was committed to the engineer rather than the architect or artist as the hero of the modern age and the source of modern style.

Where Modern architecture and design were concerned, however, it was the 'idea' of the machine that inspired the simple, undecorated forms that have become the hallmark of progressive thinking in the 1920s and which have determined the style that we now associate with the idea of the 'Machine Aesthetic'.

Above: *Ludwig Mies van der Rohe's cantilevered tubular steel and leather armchair, designed at the Bauhaus in the 1920s, is probably the best known of the highly formalized objects that emerged from that institution. Reproduced more recently by Knoll International, it has remained the most elegant of the experiments with tubular steel. The harmony of its gentle curves and of the arrangement of the elements has made it one of the 'classic' designs of this century and an example of the Machine Aesthetic at its best.*

Left: *De La Warr Pavilion designed by Serge Chermayeff, an example of the white flat-roofed 'International Style' buildings that were represented at the exhibition of the same name held at the Museum of Modern Art in New York in 1932.*

Poster for the French Line by Cassandre (1901-68).

CHAPTER · FOUR
POPULAR MODERNISM

ART DECO
1925-1939

'Modern simplicities are rich and sumptuous; we are Quakers whose severely cut clothes are made of damask and cloth of silver.'

ALDOUS HUXLEY, 1930

INTRODUCTION

The term 'Art Deco' is derived from the Exposition des Arts Décoratifs, an exhibition held in Paris in 1925 to celebrate the arrival of a new style in the applied arts and architecture. It is remarkable that this simple, abbreviated catchphrase is used today to describe so wide a range of ornaments and presentations — from the profuse and brilliantly coloured 'jazz' patterns of the 1920s to the streamlined metallic modernism of the 1930s. The sheer diversity of these and other interpretations recalls the myriad influences and fashion trends that ran their course in these decades.

Like their predecessors of the Art Nouveau movement, Art Deco's practitioners favoured particular colour schemes and formats which recurred in different countries throughout the period, overriding cultural variations in taste. Brilliant reds, 'shocking' pinks, 'electric' blues, 'siren' yellows, 'tango' oranges and metallic hues of gold, platinum, silver and bronze enjoyed great popularity. Their initial inspirations were Diaghilev's *Ballets Russes*, the fierce colours of Fauvism and Paul Poiret's celebrated fashions. These key shades transformed interior design and dominated decorative accessories — a striking palette that independent designers and manufacturers dipped into enthusiastically. Even under the Modernist banner of the 1930s with its emphasis on cool metallic tones, accents of bright colours were often permitted to trespass over a subdued background. The discovery of Tutankhamun's tomb in 1923 gave rise to the craze for 'antique' shades such as gold, peach and turquoise, employed in striking combinations for room settings and furnishings.

The vogue for Egyptian-style designs that permeated the twenties, was only one of several exotic influences to make its mark on a fashion-conscious public. Negro and 'primitive' art and the American jazz culture were assimilated readily into the novel decorative vocabulary of Art Deco, as were Aztec and Red Indian motifs.

Among this profusion of bizarre patterns and vibrant colours, used to decorate every available surface and space, the understated appeal of Le Corbusier and his followers had considerable impact at the 1925 Paris exhibition. His all-white pavilion, *L'Esprit Nouveau*, heralded a new Modernist alternative that contrasted starkly with the rich and extrovert ornamentation of Art Deco. But even here, in the hands of Art Deco designers, simplicity was infused with elements of glamour and luxury. Writing in the *Studio* magazine of 1930, Aldous Huxley described how 'simplicity of form contrasts at the present time with richness of materials ... Modern simplicities are rich and sumptuous; we are Quakers whose severely cut clothes are made of damask and cloth of silver'.

The progression of the style, from its highly decora-

Left: *'Musik', an Art Deco porcelain group by the Rosenthal factory, designed by Gerhard Schliepstein, 1927.*

Below: *View of the main lounge cabin of the Queen Mary, 1935, decorated in a restrained Modernist style. The sturdy, solidly constructed tables and armchairs put the emphasis on comfort, although the elegant vase-like lamps of glass and chrome, decorative wall friezes and patterned carpet add touches of glamour. The inner curtains and exterior upholstery of the armchairs are of crushed velvet, by Warners.*

tive idiom in the 1920s to the austerely elegant 'functionalism' of the 1930s is traced in the following sections. Highly elaborate and innovative pieces were created in France for luxury markets, while in Britain mass-produced articles gave an illusion of grandeur to those on more limited budgets. In the United States, skyscraper architecture with its spectacular heights and dazzling Hollywood-style interiors encapsulated the more extravagant facet of Art Deco.

INSPIRATIONS

Paul Poiret's revolutionary fashion plates of 1908 and 1911 uncorseted not only the women who wore his creations but the whole of design. His imagination fired by exotic Oriental and Arabian dress, he was the perfect translator of Diaghilev's 'Ballets Russes' into *haute couture*, while his unashamedly luxurious tastes were promulgated through his patronage of artists and craftsmen. Such talents took up the vivid palette of the Fauvists, the angular asymmetry of the Cubists and the geometric motifs of C.R. Mackintosh and the Viennese designers Koloman Moser and Josef Hoffman. The discovery of Tutankhamun's tomb and cross-reference to comparable Aztec and Red Indian motifs stressed the geometric interplay and dramatic colour contrasts. After the catastrophe of the Great War, society wanted to look forwards and designers caught the contemporary urban preoccupations: speed, travel, leisure and luxury. Their patrons were a new breed, self-made people committed to the modern international commercial world.

Ancient and modern

The discovery of Tutankhamun's tomb by Howard Carter in 1922 inspired an Egyptian style that reached its apogee in the 'Odeon' architecture of the 1930s. The 3,300-year-old mask, *above right*, with vibrant blues and reds offsetting shimmering gold, embodies many of the dazzling elements borrowed by Art Deco designers.

Primitive urge

While African wood sculpture such as this ebony figure, *right*, does not readily conjure up the sophisticated modern look of Art Deco, its uninhibited, simplified forms taught contemporary European sculptors to omit inessential detail. Interest in 'primitive' sculpture was linked with the craze for Negro musicians and dancers that characterized the Jazz Age.

Capital ideas

Examples of ancient Egyptian column capitals, *far right*, illustrated in Owen Jones' 'The Grammar of Ornament': capital from the Temple of Luxor, 1250 BC, representing 'the full blown papyrus' with alternating papyri and lotus buds around it;

and capital from the Colonnade of the Island of Philac, 106 BC, representing lotus flowers bound together.

Common motifs

Far right (from top): Geometric fan motifs; sunbursts, often in bronze; interlocking geometrical forms; lightning ziggurats and zig-zags; chevrons; starburst clusters; aztec-shaped plinths and Egyptian pyramid bases; cascading abstract patterns.

Stage-struck

Diaghilev's 'Ballets Russes' astonished Parisian audiences of 1909 with the brilliant colours and bold designs of costumes and sets, captured in the canvas, *above*, 'La Danse du Serpent' by Laurent Lucien Gisell. The 'Ballets Russes', with Leon Bakst as chief designer, were a direct influence on Paul Poiret, the doyen of Paris fashion designers from 1915 to 1925. They also created a popular market for small figures of exotic dancers such as this one, *above left*, by Chiparus.

Fast lane

Art Deco themes and treatment were virtually a metaphor for speed, an obsession that gained momentum after the Great War, and its best expression was perhaps in Art Deco graphics like this Monaco Grand Prix poster by Faltucci, 1930, *left*. Cars were becoming more widely available, flying was in the news and fast, efficient underground train systems were being installed and extended.

Fashionable fancies

'Les Robes de Paul Poiret', 1908, with plates by Paul Iribe, and 'Les Choses de Paul Poiret', 1911, *above right*, illustrated by Georges Lepape, revolutionized not only fashion but also the way it was illustrated. A man of exotic tastes, he started a craze for Persian and Arabian-style costumes. His Atelier Martine, opened in 1911, was the prototype for Art Deco studios.

ABDEGH
ABCDE
Enthusiastic Buyer
GOWNS

While appreciating the argument for the uncluttered geometry of Bauhaus typography, Art Deco adds quirky touches — allowing thicks and thins to meet at an angle as in 'Grock', 1935, *top*, with its 'partial inline'. In A.M. Cassandre's 'Bifur', 1929, *middle*, almost half the letter is omitted, recognition being aided by the shaded background. 'Parisian', 1928, *bottom*, by M.F. Benton, has subtle thick-thin interchanges and exaggerated ascenders in lower case.

FRANCE

Paris in the twenties and thirties was caught in a whirlwind of artistic activity that produced important art movements, avant-garde trends and sophisticated tastes in the world of fashion and interior design. In this exciting milieu, with its rich diversity of moods and temperaments, the Art Deco style emerged as the most popular decorative force, epitomizing the spirit and imagination of the period.

The 1925 Exposition des Arts Décoratifs was an international showcase for the best contemporary designs, presenting a dazzling array of architectural and interior schemes. This celebration of Art Deco was carried out on a vast and monumental scale, and included the works of France's most talented craftsmen.

So all-pervading was the style in France, finding expression across the whole gamut of design disciplines, that in a welter of cross-influences it is convenient to examine the fine and applied arts under specific headings. Each of the sections that follow nevertheless records the transition from the sumptuous exoticism of the early 1920s to the sleek modernism of the thirties.

Paintings, posters and fashion plates

Art Deco stylization in treatment of line and colour affected a wide range of decorative compositions on canvas and paper. Energetic zig-zag lines, angular and abstracted forms and a brilliant palette combined to capture the spirit and sophistication of period tastes, and such devices were employed by many French artists. Apart from the adoption of these stylistic motifs, several outstanding painters and illustrators specialized in the portrayal of contemporary subjects and scenes alluding to the lifestyle and aspirations of their patrons. Events both real and imaginary were the themes of numerous works — borrowed from the world of the theatre and circus or imbued with the sultry night-time atmosphere of casinos, cocktail bars and boudoirs. Unlike the German Expressionists of the period, however, who emphasized the more decadent aspects of real life in an emotive context, the artistic expression of the French painters was charged with vitality and gaiety — theirs was a celebration of life.

The Polish-born artist Tamara de Lempicka (1902-80) was one of the best and most prolific painters of the period who strove to capture the elusive personalities and pastimes of Parisian society. From 1924-1939 she painted numerous portraits, most of them executed in the Art Deco idiom of boldly defined angular forms, gleaming and polished surface effects and juxtaposed planes of patterning. The figures were invariably placed in 'modern' settings, posed dramatically amid skyscrapers and sports cars. These contemporary settings gave tantalizing glimpses of the affluence and cool sophisti-

cation of their subjects. In *Autoportrait* an elegant female figure is seated at the wheel of a car, wrapped in a voluminous steel-grey scarf, with a matching driving hat. The subject assumes a carefree and confident air — as poised and *chic* as a fashion model and a symbol of the new 'progressive' woman.

De Lempicka was awarded the *Prix d'Honneur* at the Bordeaux International Exhibition of 1927, and in this city many other painters cultivated their own ideas of the Art Deco style. Jean Dupas (1882-1964) created highly decorative compositions in which, frequently, stereotyped and elongated figures were posed artificially, like mannequins. In his portrait of a *Woman with*

Above: *'Young Woman in Green', a portrait by Tamara de Lempicka, 1927. Stylish and, frequently, beautiful young women comprise the subject matter of much of de Lempicka's work, posed like mannequins amid juxtaposed planes of patterning, and metallic colour shading.*

a Hat (1926) the smiling subject becomes an attenuated form, echoing the shape of her tall and eccentric hat, and epitomizes the high-spirited and whimsical taste of the period.

René Buthaud (b.1886), another acclaimed Bordeaux artist — he was also a ceramist — created a wide repertoire of Art Deco images through exaggerated mannerisms and a lively technique. In *Femme tenant une fleur* (1924) the figure emerges from a blue-grey background of juxtaposed planes and curves, intercepted by vigorous zig-zag lines and shadows of merging pastel hues. The waving locks of hair and the costume are emphasized by bold black lines — a striking linear interplay which imparts to the whole surface a decorativeness and intensity characteristic of Art Deco compositions.

Other members of the Bordeaux school included Raphaël Delorme (1885-1962), who painted exotic and dramatic scenes derived from ancient and mythological sources, executed in a highly polished style; Jean-Gabriel Domergue (1889-1962), who specialized in portraits of *chic* and sophisticated women, depicted mostly as stylized and elongated forms; and André Lhote (1885-1962), whose Fauve- and Cubist-inspired works influenced a number of contemporary artists, most notable among them his student Tamara de Lempicka.

In Paris, artists such as Robert Delaunay (1885-1941) and Sonia Delaunay (1885-1980) created numerous paintings, graphic works and stage designs in the Art Deco style. Kees van Dongen (1877-1968), who came to Paris from the Netherlands, produced a striking and original series of female portraits that expressed, in an exaggerated manner, the ideals and accentuated tastes of the period. The Japanese artist Tsuguharu Foujita (1886-1968) worked in the city from 1913, where he was commissioned to design decorative frescos for the Paris Cité Universitaire and the Cercle Interallié. He is perhaps better known, however, for his graphic *oeuvre*, in which he made numerous etchings, lithographs and posters of dramatically posed nudes in elegant surroundings. In his poster *Bal de l'A.A.A.A.* a harlequin dressed in blue dances behind a statuesque and erotic female. Her swirling strands of bright yellow hair and orange high-heeled shoes contrast vividly with her bare flesh, creating an effect of playful abandon.

In the commercial field, posters of artistic design were created in the spirit of their Art Nouveau forerunners, the illustrated product and its complementary lettering being subjected to the unyielding stylization of the composition. Images of Paris nightlife flashed across the surface of numerous posters advertising *La Revue de Paris*, the *Revue Nègre* (featuring the American-born entertainer Josephine Baker) and other popular stage productions. Charles Gesmar (1900-28) designed posters and costumes for the actresses Spinelli and Mistinguett. The artist Zig also worked for the Casino de Paris, devising numerous illustrations in an exuberant style. The Russian known by the pseudonym Cassandre

Below: *Watch designed by the French firm Boucheron, of faceted black onyx and gold, c.1925. Watches of the period were sometimes worn as pendants, attached to the lapel by a ribbon or metal fastener, and appeared in various luxurious materials by all the leading French jewellers. Black onyx was favoured for its dramatic appeal.*

Below bottom: *Portrait bust of gilded bronze by the French sculptor Pailagean. The smooth, highly polished surface and simplified features are typical of the period.*

Below: *The haute couturier, Coco Chanel, photographed in Biarritz, 1928. Chanel revolutionized Paris fashions by introducing chic daywear, timeless two-piece suits and flamboyant costume jewellery. She was seen frequently in her own creations, promoting the 'Chanel style' of youth and elegance.*

105

Above: *Pochoir fashion-plate entitled 'Au Clair de la Lune' by Georges Lepape from the 'Gazette du Bon Ton', 1913, featuring a gown by Paul Poiret. Poiret's exotic evening dresses, with their intense Fauve-like colours, had an enormous impact on 1920s fashions and gave rise to new and sophisticated tastes. Lepape's striking illustrations appeared in numerous French journals of the period such as 'Modes et Manières d'Aujourd'hui'.*

Far left: *'Voyagez la Nuit, en Wagon-Lits' by Cassandre, who was awarded the 'Grand Prix' for poster design at the 1925 Paris Exhibition. His simple, direct images elicited comments such as '...here advertising approaches poetry'.*

Left: *Lacquered metal vase by Jean Dunand, on a macassar ebony column designed by Clément Rousseau. The rich, gleaming surfaces and bold geometric motifs are in keeping with French Modernist designs.*

Left: Armchair of anonymous French design, decorated in marquetry with fruitwoods displaying profuse geometric patterns and 'sun ray' motifs, echoed below on the upholstered seat. Orange and peach tones were popular during the period.

Below: Two-fold lacquer screen by the interior decorator Paul Follot (1877-1941), painted by R. Schils and made for the English manufacturers Waring and Gillow, c.1930. The firm's department of 'Modern French Furniture' was co-directed by Follot in Paris. Jungle subjects appealed to numerous artists of the period — Paul Jouve's pacing panthers, tigers and snakes, for example, recall the exoticism of the Art Deco 'animaliers'.

Above: Commode of Modernist design by Louis Süe, of burled ash and anodized aluminium, 1933. The striking decorative veneer, combined here with an industrial metal, was a hallmark of the Functionalist furniture of the period.

(1901-68) came to Paris in 1915, where he was commissioned to create an important series of national advertisement posters, including one for the newspaper *L'Intransigeant* (1925), for the railway *Nord Express* (1927) and the ocean liner *Normandie* (1935). His direct approach, characterized by simplified forms and bold silhouettes, conveyed the period craze for travel, speed and luxury.

Fashion journalism provided another creative outlet for French illustrators through magazines such as *La Gazette du Bon Ton, Modes et Manières d'Aujourd'hui, Art, Goût, Beauté, L'Homme Elégant, Vogue* and numerous others. The artists George Barbier, Georges Lepape, Umberto Brunelleschi, Erté, Charles Martin, Paul Iribe and René Ranson, to mention a few, created a superb and striking range of costume-plates in which the fluctuating whims of a fashion-conscious public were stylishly expressed.

Sculpture

French sculpture of the Art Deco period adopted many of the features found in contemporary paintings — figures were attenuated and forms were angular, and subjects were derived largely from the real, contemporary world. The medium itself, however, permitted greater exploration of surface treatments, where coarse texturing would often be contrasted with smooth and gleaming areas of intense metallic sheen. Art movements such as Cubism and Abstraction influenced numerous sculptors and, in addition, exotic elements such as primitivism contributed to the direct and simplified approach of many period artists. The powerful mask images of African art, for example, served as models on which some of the bolder stylizations of Art Deco were based, and the ancient relief bronzes of Egypt and Assyria provided further inspiration.

Animal subjects figured greatly in Art Deco sculpture, a tradition revived from the *animalier* school of the 19th century. The works of Rembrandt Bugatti, who committed suicide in 1916, influenced many sculptors of this genre, in their combined effects of naturalism and expressiveness. The lively, textured surfaces of his animal pieces in bronze reinforce the vitality and tension suggested by the bold curves and angularities of the modelling. In *A Rooster and Frog*, for example, the broad sweeping tail of the rooster conveys a sensation of power and strength, epitomizing the bizarre and humorous juxtaposition of the two forms. Similarly, the highly polished surface of his bronze *Snake*, with its tightly coiled body and arched head, becomes both a threatening and a decorative force.

Paul Jouve (1880-1973) made numerous animal sculptures and relief plaques, particularly of pacing panthers and tigers whose sleek and muscular bodies conformed readily to the attenuated, streamlined configurations of the Art Deco style. The twin brothers Jan and Jöel Martel (1896-1966) also produced small and intimate animal sculptures in an abstract manner, as exemplified in their bronze *Pigeons* of 1924. Here, the birds are segmented into a series of pronounced curves and jutting points. The images do not depart far from reality but, rather, suggest a directness through their simplified forms. In other collaborations, the Martels combined novel materials such as cement, steel and mirror-glass. In the *Profile Medallion* (1925), of moulded plastic and surface gilding, the hallmarks of their geometrically inspired style are evident. The profile is subjected to the sparse, two-dimensional treatment of the overall design.

Other accomplished animal sculptors of the period included Edouard-Marcel Sandoz (1881-1971), who favoured an exaggerated but realistic approach; François Pompon (1855-1933), whose bronze pieces were simplified and polished; and Armand Petersen and Simone Marie, who both emphasized gently rounded contours, offsetting them by sparkling surface effects.

Interiors and furnishings

Interior designs and furnishings of the period came under the influence of two distinct styles. The first emerged during the early 1920s and embraced a number of exotic and oriental forms, inspired originally by the flamboyant set designs and costumes of the *Ballets Russes*, which had performed in Paris since 1909. The second appeared after 1930 and reflected the Modernist approach of Le Corbusier and his followers. Both trends introduced new forms and materials, and subscribed to their own unique sets of aesthetic values.

The so-called 'boudoir style', with its emphasis on rich and luxurious materials, sumptuous furniture and intimate surroundings, was cultivated by an exclusive set of designers for a wealthy clientele. The fashion for oriental imitations led to the creation of many lavishly decorated interiors, highlighted by contrasting multi-patterned fabrics in bright colours, tassled silk cushions and deeply upholstered day-beds and ottomans. Chairs and sofas were rendered as squat forms and appeared low on the ground, and bedroom furniture was made equally accessible with an overall emphasis on comfort.

A new and complementary range of exotic materials was employed — for those who could afford it — including woods such as emboyna, olive, burr walnut, Cuban mahogany, ebony and macassar ebony, which featured decorative grain effects and beautiful colours. Surfaces were frequently veneered and inlaid with ivory or mother-of-pearl, decorated with floral bouquets, scrolls and simple geometric motifs. Flamboyant tastes also called for the green-dyed sharkskin, known as shagreen, to adorn the panels of furniture and accessories, and lacquer was employed to great effect.

One of the most accomplished and fashionable designers of the period was Emile-Jacques Ruhlmann

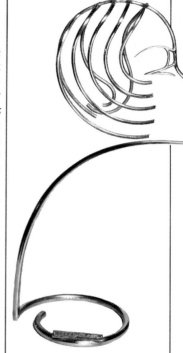

Above: *Polished hat stand of chrome, made for the Italian firm Bazzi, of Milan. The cropped hair and boyish profile recall the popular 'garçonne-look' of the twenties. The stand was probably used to display a cloche hat, an accessory much in vogue c.1925-30.*

Left: *Bedroom interior designed by Emile-Jacques Ruhlmann featuring furniture of macassar ebony, and a hand-made tufted wool carpet of Art Deco design. Macassar ebony was favoured by French designers for its rich, contrasting tones and striking configurations — here the wood is combined with applied strips of polished metal. The low-built bed and dressing table are typical of the period.*

Below: *Art Deco mirror, attributed to Emile-Jacques Ruhlmann, of macassar ebony, inlaid with ivory in a geometric pattern of circles and rectangles. Ruhlmann's furniture was renowned for its superb quality and exquisite detailing — such meticulous attention extended even to areas such as the backs and undersides of pieces.*

Below middle: *Armchair of macassar ebony attributed to Emile-Jacques Ruhlmann. The broad curving back was designed for upholstery on both sides. Here, the rounded shape is echoed below by the addition of large 'bun' feet.*

Below right: *Tubular armchair designed by Eileen Gray, upholstered in aniline leather over a steel and polished chrome-plated frame, 1929.*

(1879-1933), who created many spectacular pieces in the 1920s. In the construction of his cabinets, dining and bedside tables, chairs, desks and day-beds, traditional forms were emphasized throughout by superb surface finishes and rich detail. He made common use of ivory for both decorative inlays and functional accessories such as handles, feet and escutcheons, and sometimes added bronze and silvered plaques to enhance these ornamental schemes. As well as the woods mentioned above, Ruhlmann favoured the speckled patterns of tortoiseshell for his veneers, which he sometimes combined with the linear configurations of macassar ebony, or other woods of contrasting tonal markings. His overall adherence to the refined tastes of the eighteenth century notwithstanding, a number of Art Deco design elements were incorporated into his works: cabinets were sometimes rendered into geometric forms of simple block-like structure; the legs of tables tapered dramatically into thin points, or merged into a massive central support; and sofas and divans were lowered almost to the floor.

The company of Süe et Mare was founded in 1919 by Louis Süe (1875-1968) and André Mare (1887-1932), to design furniture and interiors. Their flamboyant pieces reflected the extravagant tastes of the 1920s, realized in the Ruhlmann style. The work of the craftsman Jules Leleu (1883-1961) also contributed to this highly decorative early manifestation of Art Deco. The *Atelier Martine*, established in 1911 by Paul Poiret, produced at this time oriental-inspired interiors and Cubist-style furniture. Other outstanding period designers included André Groult (1884-1967), who devised co-ordinated room schemes and furnishings of great delicacy in a rich mixture of materials; the illustrator Paul Iribe (1883-1935), who made furniture of superb quality, creating novel effects using shagreen, ebony and slate; Clément Rousseau, whose exotic panelled furniture featured a startling array of surface motifs and complex patterns; Jean Dunand (1877-1942), best known

for his intricate lacquer work; and Pierre Legrain (1889-1929), whose exotic creations of lacquer, bronze, chrome and zebra skin were derived from a diverse range of sources including the arts of Japan and Africa.

The Irish-born designer Eileen Gray (1879-1976) combined the exoticism of early Art Deco with the modernist trends of the 1930s. Her interiors, such as those created in Paris for Suzanne Talbot in 1932, possess a luxurious contemporary appeal highlighted by silvered glass floor tiles and screens and simple lacquered furniture. Zebra and leopard skins were used to accent the subtle colour schemes, draped over tubular steel-framed chairs of pale upholstery. Eileen Gray's designs, elegant and timeless, are as striking today as they were more than 50 years ago.

Lacquer

The oriental technique of lacquering was revived in Paris during the 1920s and became an important artistic medium for leading Art Deco designers and decorators. Interior furnishings such as panelling, doors, screens, furniture and a range of small accessories were adorned with thick coats of shining lacquer, predominantly in shades of black, brown, red and gold. Surfaces were rendered variously with painted or carved scenes, sometimes highlighted with fragments of eggshell on smooth or granular textured grounds.

Jean Dunand (1877-1942) was one of the most accomplished and successful lacquerers of the period. His workshop received numerous commissions to decorate interiors, furniture (for craftsmen such as Legrain and Ruhlmann) and other furnishings, such as those devised for the luxury ocean liners *Atlantique* and *Normandie*. His lacquered wood panels demonstrate a technical virtuosity in their blend of rich colours and exquisite details, capturing the elegance and exoticism of Art Deco at its best. Dunand's subjects were mainly figures — stylized females drawn from ancient Egypt and Japan and fantasy depictions. He also created

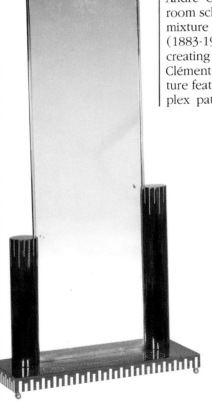

Above: 'Diane', a gilt and lacquered carved wood panel attributed to Paul Véra, who worked for the firm of Süe et Mare, where he designed metalwares and interior furnishings.

Below: *Selection of scent bottles by René Lalique, of clear, frosted and brilliantly coloured glass, c.1920s. Lalique designed scent bottles for numerous French perfumiers including Worth, Coty, and Rogers and Gallet.*

From left to right: Scent bottle of clear glass with slight brown staining, decorated on the sides and stopper with entwined lizards; square-shaped bottle of clear and frosted glass, adorned with female nudes; 'Le Jade', an emerald green bottle moulded with birds and plant stalks, for Rogers and Gallet; frosted glass bottle decorated in the 'antique' taste; 'Poésie d'Orsay', of frosted and brown-stained glass adorned with 'Grecian' dancers; 'Amphytrite', of brilliant emerald-green glass; frosted and brown-stained bottle with relief ornamentations of stylized nudes; frosted and stained bottle with floral decorations.

Above: *Flask by Maurice Marinot of red and turquoise glass, displaying internal decorations of trapped air bubbles, c.1935.*

Above: *Clear glass jar and lid by Maurice Marinot adorned with a trailed collar and internal air bubbles, made in Troyes, c.1935. Marinot wrote, 'I think that a beautiful piece of glass should keep as much as possible the aspect of breath that creates it...its form should be a moment in the life of the glass.'*

abstract compositions, where each plane of patterning introduced a new and complementary colour and texture to the surface. The crushed eggshell technique, in which minute pieces of shell were set into a matrix of transparent lacquer, was his own invention, and he used it to great effect for areas of contrast and shading.

Eileen Gray studied lacquering in London and later in Paris under the great Japanese exponent of the style, Sugawara. In 1922 she opened the shop *Jean Désert*, in which her furniture and lacquerwork were displayed and sold to an exclusive clientele. The Japanese artist Katsu Hamanaka was also introduced to lacquering by Sugawara, and like Dunand (another of the master's students), he worked with many notable furniture designers including Jules, Leleu, André Domin and Maurice Dufrêne. In his screen of *Two Bulls*, in brown and gold lacquer, oriental and Art Deco stylizations combine to create an outstanding work of art. Jacques Nam specialized in lacquer panels, painted or engraved with the pervasive Art Deco motifs of wild and domestic cats. André Margat also favoured animal subjects for his lacquerwork, and exhibited at Ruhlmann's gallery during the late twenties.

Glass

Like the Art Nouveau style before it, Art Deco designs lent themselves admirably to the decorative surface effects of glass, and a diverse range of utilitarian and luxury objects and jewellery were produced throughout the twenties and thirties. French glassmakers of the period achieved unrivalled success in the application of novel techniques to create highly imaginative wares.

René Lalique (1860-1945) manufactured an outstanding collection of moulded domestic wares, including scent bottles for the perfumier François Coty, car mascots, vases, lamps and light-fittings, clock-cases, desk accessories and decorative panels. His mass-produced pieces appeared in brilliant colours such as emerald green and peacock blue or in plain and frosted glass. Most were adorned with repetitive relief designs of animals, fish, female figures, 'sirens', and floral and plant motifs. Often, the rich Art Deco ornamentation was permitted to intrude upon the structure of the objects themselves — for example, bottle stoppers and handles were transformed from merely functional appurtenances into pronounced features of striking decoration.

The *pâte-de-verre* pieces by Francois-Emile Decorchemont (1880-1971) and Alméric Walter (1859-1942) were sculptural in impact, and reflected many of the trends of the period. Their heavy and opaque wares, of crushed glass-paste composition, were moulded into fanciful forms. Vases were adorned with relief patterns of female figures, snakes and geometric motifs, while other pieces were rendered as miniature sculptures depicting animals, fish and reclining nudes.

The continuing and successful collaboration of the Daum brothers gave rise at this time to the production of acid-cut wares of fine Art Deco design. Their luxury

René Jules Lalique (1860-1945) created a magnificent range of glasswares and jewellery in a highly imaginative range of styles. His pieces possess an inventiveness and timelessness, often inspired by 'primitive', 'antique', oriental and contemporary styles, but always demonstrating his supreme individuality as a master craftsman.

Many of Lalique's early works reflect the influence of Art Nouveau, and later, during the 1920s, Art Deco motifs were often permitted to intrude on his designs for scent bottles, vases, car mascots, statuettes and other decorative accessories. These commercial glasswares were sold through fine department stores in Europe and America, and their decorativeness and reasonable prices (by virtue of mass-production) resulted in their immense popularity. Between 1920 and 1930 Lalique created more than 200 different styles for his range of vases, available in clear or coloured glass in vibrant shades of emerald green, 'electric' blue, orange, red, purple, brown and black. Their brilliant surfaces were adorned frequently with bold decorations of stylized plant and animal forms, female nudes and Art Deco geometric patterns.

The superb quality of Lalique's glass was renowned internationally — a rare success achieved through the union of art and industry. The lamp, *above*, entitled *'L'Oiseau de Feu'*, is a flamboyant piece depicting a mythological subject on a base of whimsical insect motifs in the Art Deco style. The moulded emerald-green pendant, *below*, appears like a fossil with its overlapping pattern of dragonflies.

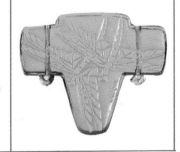

lamps and vases introduced new subtle surface effects, rendered in a bold geometric style. Characteristically, the biting and penetrating lines of the decoration were in contrast to the smoothly polished surface — a striking interplay of textures that recalled the works of many contemporary sculptors.

Maurice Marinot (1882-1960) also strove after a range of novel surface treatments, creating a series of thickly walled scent bottles, goblets and other vessels that were highlighted internally by patterns of trapped air bubbles. André Thuret's glass of the 1920s had a similar abstract decorative content, with speckled coils of clear and coloured glass penetrating the surface. Henri-Edouard Navarre (1885-1970) shared Thuret's interest in the unique qualities of the medium and explored a variety of 'natural' effects which, as the central aesthetic force, he allowed at times to merge haphazardly.

Ceramics

The decorative surfaces of French ceramics displayed the bold figural and geometric designs of the Art Deco style in the twenties and thirties. However, a new and eclectic approach was cultivated concurrently, inspired by the pottery traditions of ancient civilizations in the Near and Far East, focusing significantly on the classic forms and glazing techniques of China. This interest was stimulated by the important discoveries made by numerous archaeological excavations at the time. It resulted not only in a greater appreciation of oriental and ancient prototypes but also in the establishment of new collecting trends and markets in the West.

Emile Decoeur (1876-1953), the Parisian ceramist, created striking stoneware vases and bowls in the Chinese style during the 1920s. His simple and understated vessels were adorned with rich monochrome glazes in shades of yellow, blue, pink, green and white, and sometimes displayed a range of subtle surface effects such as crackling, crazing and tonal mottling. Emile Lenoble (1876-1940) also favoured stoneware for his oriental-inspired wares, which were incised or painted with floral motifs and pronounced swirls in antique shades of pink, turquoise and green, over beige, brown or black coloured grounds.

René Buthaud produced an outstanding series of Art Deco pieces in stoneware, porcelain and glazed faience. His faience pieces were invariably decorated with moulded or hand-painted scenes of statuesque female figures, placed in niches or in architectural or floral settings accented by geometric configurations. His painterly style recalled the works of contemporary artists such as Matisse, Van Dongen and Lepape.

The factories of Sèvres and Limoges produced porcelain statuettes, wall appliqués and vases in the Art Deco style for luxury markets. Numerous freelance ceramists, decorators and artists were employed at various times by these important manufacturers. In addition, painters such as Maurice Vlaminck, Raoul Dufy, Georges Braque and Joan Miró created exclusive ceramics, sometimes in collaboration with the Catalan potter Llorens Artigas.

Above: 'The Starfish' by Demetre Chiparus, of cold-painted bronze and ivory on an onyx base.
Left: 'Dancer with a Turban', a jewelled and cold-painted bronze and ivory figure on an onyx base by the Polish-born artist Paul Philippe. His chryselephantine statuettes, of contemporary fashionable women and exotic dancers, were exhibited at all the Paris salons. This piece, with its silver and gold metallic details, is characteristic of Philippe's work.

Above: *'Fancy Dress' by Demetre Chiparus, of cold-painted bronze and ivory on an onyx base. This Romanian-born artist specialized in chryselephantine statuettes of theatrical dancers, modelled on performers from the 'Ballets Russes' and Paris cabarets.*

Below: *Black and blue ceramic vase by Emile Decoeur. His simple shapes and beautiful monochrome glaze effects were inspired by ancient Chinese prototypes.*

Metalwares and figurines

Decorative metalwork was a speciality of Art Deco craftsmen and an imaginative range of objects and furnishings was created of iron, bronze, silver, copper, pewter and chrome. In keeping with period tastes, surfaces were always highly polished and sometimes additionally ornamented with brightly coloured enamels, contrasting inlaid metals or superimposed pieces of wood, ivory, glass and semi-precious stone.

The figural and floral patterns of early Art Deco and its later modernist manifestation in the 1930s were assimilated readily into the structures and designs of lamps, light-fittings and decorative panels. Craftsmen like Edgar Brandt (1880-1960) created dramatic standard lamps fashioned as cobras in bronze and wrought-iron, with glass shades supplied by the Daum brothers. Armand-Albert Rateau (1882-1938) devised a patinated bronze lamp with long-necked birds and 'claw and ball' feet in the Egyptian style, while Albert Simonet's lamp with its 'oriental' mask friezes and hooved feet recalled the motifs of China and ancient Greece. Such eclecticism was indeed a hallmark of the exotic Art Deco trends of the 1920s.

In contrast, simple and functional silverware was manufactured by firms such as Christofle, Tétard Frères, Chapuis, and Süe et Mare for luxury markets, embodying a greater geometric cohesion. The remarkable designs of Jean Puiforcat (1897-1945) — his novel cutlery canteens, C-shaped candlesticks, angular tea services and table lamps, for example — anticipate later, post-1925 Art Deco formats in their elegantly streamlined efficiency.

The outstanding designer and lacquerer Jean Dunand created superb metalwares using the process known as *dinanderie*. Sheets of copper or other metal were hammered and shaped to the desired form, and afterwards patinated, embossed or chased with contrasting metal inlays to create a variety of surface patterns. This laborious technique was executed by hand, and the juxtaposition of glittering metals that resulted was often spectacular.

Another important branch of metalwork to emerge during the period was the production of chryselephantine statuettes. The term derived from Greek and referred to the combined use of gold and ivory. In the Art Deco context, however, this precious metal was usually replaced with bronze. A diverse range of female characters was portrayed, notably exotic dancers and active contemporary figures in elegant costumes. These statuettes were intended for decorative displays and were immensely popular in the homes of the bourgeoisie.

Ivory was normally reserved for small areas such as the face and hands, while bronze was employed for the bodies and costumes, either patinated or cold-painted in metallic shades.

Numerous firms in Germany, Austria and France specialized in chryselephantine figurines. In Paris, the manufacturers Goldscheider and Etling produced many fine examples, such as those designed by the Rumanian Demetre Chiparus. His extravagant figures catered admirably for exotic period tastes through their lithe forms, dramatic poses and sumptuous costumes. Other Parisian-based artists working in this popular genre included Claire-Jeanne-Roberte Colinet, Marcel Bouraine, Maurice Guiraud-Rivière, Andrée Guerval and Solange Bertrand.

Jewellery and fashion accessories

French jewellers of the period created a magnificent range of pieces in the Art Deco style. Firms such as Cartier, Van Cleef et Arpels, Chaumier, Mauboussin, Fouquet and Boucheron were renowned throughout the world for their extravagant creations in precious metals and stones. Platinum, diamonds and rock crystal were favoured materials, and were often combined with black onyx, richly coloured lapis lazuli, apple-green jade and cabochon gemstones such as emeralds, sapphires and rubies.

Fashions of the twenties called for long and dramatic earrings to offset shorter hairstyles and bobs, dress-clips (which could be worn singly, or interlocked as a large brooch to complement an evening gown or the lapels of a coat), bold 'cocktail' rings, brooches, belt buckles, bangles and long strands of coloured beads and pearls to emphasize lower necklines and waistlines. In some of the finest pieces the basic geometric format was infused with elements of novelty and sheer luxury. Georges Fouquet, for example, created exotic brooches of jade, onyx, diamonds and white gold in the form of oriental masks, and Chaumet and Cartier created bizarre pendant earrings and necklaces adorned with dangling figurines.

Jewellery of more abstract design was created in the late twenties and thirties by craftsmen such as Gerard Sandoz, whose gem-encrusted brooches and pendants imitated the intricate structures and gleaming surfaces of machines; Jean Dunand, who produced lacquered pieces composed of contrasting patterned squares, rectangles and grids; and Raymond Templier and Paul Brandt, both of whom worked in a Modernist idiom, characterized by polished geometric shapes of precious metals, enamels and diamonds. Such simplicity of design and richness of material were typical of Art Deco jewellery, the immense appeal of which gave rise to mass-produced imitations in silver, chrome, paste and Bakelite.

René Lalique produced a series of brilliantly coloured glass pendants, strung onto tassled silk cords, which were moulded in relief with stylized figures and plant motifs. The glass manufacturers Almeric Walter and Gabriel Argy-Rousseau worked in a similar style.

In a less exclusive vein the *couturier* Coco Chanel introduced 'fake' costume jewellery, sometimes of massive proportions, to cater for the extravagant tastes of her clientele. Elsa Schiaparelli featured Surrealist items in her 1930s dress collections, to match amusing creations such as the 'Lobster' gown, and 'Shoe' hat.

Jewel-encrusted fashion accessories were made in the Art Deco style by all the leading Parisian firms. Exquisite beaded handbags with ornamental clasps, enamelled cigarette holders and cases, lacquered compacts, pill boxes, novelty watches and notepads were all created for the luxury market. *Minaudières* were new period accessories for evening use and formal occasions. Their slim box-like forms contained numerous compartments for make-up and money.

Right: *Art Deco paper fan from the Café de la Paix, Paris, c.1930; and a selection of Bakelite buttons adorned with bold geometric motifs, c.1930s.*
Far right: *Pendant by Lacloche Frères in platinum and onyx, encrusted with diamonds and a pearl in the Art Deco style.*
Below left: *'Mystery' clock by Cartier of faceted rock crystal, coral, black enamel and diamonds. All the established*

Parisian jewellers created exclusive pieces for a wealthy clientele — such examples captured instantly a 'look of wealth' by their display of the most precious materials and stylish designs.
Below right: *'Pâte-de-verre' cylindrical vase by Gabriel Argy-Rousseau, decorated in the antique 'Egyptian' taste in characteristic shades of rose, pink and mauve.*

Posters and publicity graphics demanded a bold, uninhibited hand to reduce a message to essentials. The medium found no more apt exponent than the Art Deco graphic artist, whose vivid colours were dramatically contrasted in flat angular shapes. For its part, Art Deco was exhilarated by the pace of modern life and revelled unashamedly in the luxurious and the exotic. Message and manner, then, coalesced in an unprecedented celebration of speed and travel.

The advertisement for the Delahaye motor car, c.1930, *below*, stresses the raking elegance of the vehicle by running it across the monolithic verticals of an opulent setting. The luggage label, *bottom*, c.1930, uses eye-catching contrasts of blue and yellow.

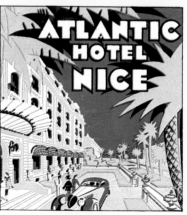

Far left: *Poster published by Hachard et Cie, Paris, for the launch of the Pullman service from Paris to Brussels and Amsterdam.*

Left: *The speed theme finds its way on to a wrapper for a French brand of chocolate, c.1930.*

Below left: *20s leaflet for Air Union's luxury lunchtime London to Paris service, delivers a simple message with dramatic juxtaposition of triangles and colour contrasts.*

Below: *In this poster for Fiat, c.1928, Riccobaldi achieves snob appeal with hard-edged slabs of colour.*

THE USA

If Paris in the twenties and thirties was the international centre of avant-garde art and fashion, then New York was equally important for its blend of creativity and sophistication in literature and the performing arts. An élitist society emerged in the city from about 1925, comprising wealthy patrons and socialites, poets, producers, and actors and actresses from Hollywood and Broadway. This set was typified by the group of writers known as the 'Algonquins', named after the group's favourite meeting place, the Algonquin Hotel. The fast-moving pace of New York was described in the writings of Scott Fitzgerald, Anita Loos, Robert Benchley and Dorothy Parker, and in the lyrics of Cole Porter, whose *Anything Goes* summed up the decade.

Wit, glamour and fantasy were the chief features of the period style, evident in the films of Fred Astaire and Ginger Rogers, the Marx Brothers, Mae West and Jean Harlow, and in the extravagant musical productions of Broadway and Radio City Music Hall. The style found expression through the decorative vocabulary of Art Deco, its patterns of ziggurats, hard-edged geometric forms and gleaming surfaces being potent metaphors for the heady, hectic pace of city life. Exotic trends were also embraced (as they were, concurrently, in Europe) and the craze for Egyptian and Aztec designs penetrated both architecture and the decorative arts. Such inspiration could be noted, for example, in Graumann's Egyptian Theatre on Hollywood Boulevard, with its lavish interiors, and in the pyramidal structures of skyscrapers such as the Empire State Building and Paul Frankl's novel furniture. Jewellery in the Egyptian style and accessories such as scent bottles moulded in the form of 'antique' temples were mass-produced for a fashion-conscious market.

The cocktail set was also well catered for: 'When a girl can sit in a delightful bar and have delicious champagne cocktails ... I think it is divine,' as Anita Loos said in her book *Gentlemen Prefer Blondes*. The latest gowns from Paris were advertised in women's magazines such as *McCalls* (in which patterns based on *couture* creations were illustrated for amateur dressmakers), complemented by evening bags, compacts and glittering jewels. Cocktail bars and cabinets were fitted in the homes of the well-to-do, and with these a host of accessories appeared, including cocktail shakers with matching drinking glasses of polished silver and chrome, and novel cigarette lighters in the form of rockets and skyscrapers. Numerous recipes for exotic and frothy concoctions were also published for those entertaining at home.

Glamour and escapism characterized the 'Hollywood style' of the 1930s, where luxurious Modernist interiors and costumes were conceived on a dazzling scale for huge cinema audiences. Hollywood film sets and

Photograph of the Hollywood film star Jean Harlow. With her platinum-blonde hair, voluptuons curves and figure-hugging gowns, Harlow's soft 'feminine' image was one of instant glamour — a 'look' imitated by women everywhere (and an alternative to the tailored 'hard-hearted' fashions promoted by 'Vogue' and other magazines in the mid-1930s).

clothes designs — for example, those by Adrian and Howard Greer — influenced the latest trends for popular mass consumption. New 'looks' were created for leading actresses such as Greta Garbo, whose *chic* style was to inspire women all over the western world.

In the spirit of Hollywood fantasy and inspired by the cult of Surrealism, Elsa Schiaperelli created bizarre gowns and accessories for her 1930s dress collections in Paris, patronized by an international clientele, and the artist Salvador Dali produced telephone receivers in the form of lobsters, and settees in the shape of Mae West's lips (c.1936). Such whimsical pieces were designed to delight and startle, and were characteristic of Art Deco's pursuit of novelty. The humour and the dream-like delusions of grandeur fostered by the Hollywood style provided light relief for an era haunted by the financial insecurity of the Depression.

City architecture and interior design

'From the chaotic situation arising out of an era of prosperity without precedent for decoration ... a style emerged ... Ornamental syntax consisted almost entirely of a few motifs such as the zig-zag, the triangle, fawnlike curves and designs'. These observations, expressed in 1933 by Donald Deskey, the interior designer of Radio City Music Hall, pinpointed the new, geometric style of decoration that was to dominate American architecture at the beginning of the 1930s. In a frenzy of activity, cities such as New York were transformed by spectacular Art Deco skyscrapers, the sympathetically furnished interiors of which emphasized the glamorous aspects of the style. Radio City Music Hall and the Chrysler and Chanin buildings were among the first to be erected under the banner of 'Modernism', and stood in dazzling contrast to the dingy and outmoded structures beneath them. If America was not represented at the Paris Exhibition of 1925 for the very reason that it had 'no decorative art', as explained by a contemporary critic, the country made up for its absence by quickly establishing an artistic industry. It was making significant contributions to architecture and interior design by the start of the new decade.

Those two outstanding monuments of Art Deco inspiration, the Chrysler and Empire State buildings, appeared on the New York skyline in 1930. The Chrysler building, with semi-circular pinnacles soaring to a height of 319 metres (1,046 feet), was designed by William van Alen and became a captivating exemplar of the new architecture. This structure — which one critic labelled 'a freak ... a stunt' — was suffused throughout with elements of glamour. Its novel white metallic facing gleamed and reflected light like platinum (the jeweller's favourite material of the period), and radiating patterns of overlapping curves and lines played further on the theme of giant sunbeams.

The Empire State building, designed by the firm of Shreve, Lamb and Harmon, was equally striking in its hierarchical structure of towering rectangular blocks, reminiscent of a vast pyramid. Its uncluttered structure

Right: *The top of the Chrysler Building in New York city, a masterpiece of Art Deco architecture designed by William van Alen, 1928-30. The façade is faced in Nircosta metal, its white gleaming surfaces resembling platinum — a material selected by Walter Chrysler for its 'attractive dignified colour'. The building caused considerable public uproar at the time of its completion in 1930, as summarized in an article in 'The American Architect', 'Do you or don't you? That is the question. Some do. Some don't. Some think it's a freak; some think it's a stunt. A few think it is positively ugly; others consider it a great feat, a masterpiece, a "tour de force."'*

was in keeping with the simple geometric tastes of the period. By virtue of its breathtaking heights, however, the building encapsulated the earlier Art Deco predilection for sheer extravagance. Indeed, it remained vacant in the Depression and was aptly referred to as 'the Empty State building'.

Another triumph of Art Deco architecture was the building erected at 570 Lexington Avenue, New York, designed in 1931 by the firm of Cross and Cross for the RCA Corporation. The facade was decorated with rosettes, chevrons and sun motifs (all recurring Art Deco ornamentations), crowned by a profuse network of interlaced struts and pinnacles. Such buildings were described as 'cathedrals of commerce, castles in the sky' by a contemporary writer and, indeed, they bore a striking resemblance to their Gothic predecessors as sym-

bols of affluence, power and optimism.

Decorative friezes and wall plaques in the Art Deco style were added frequently to the facades of buildings, such as the ones created for the second RCA building at Rockefeller Plaza. Monumental cast glass panels with moulded patterns, created by the Steuben Glassworks, were combined on the exterior with stone carvings in low relief by the sculptor Lee Lawrie. Mythological figures emerging out of rippling clouds were portrayed as embodiments of 'Wisdom', 'Light' and 'Sound', the emblems of the RCA Corporation.

Radio City Music Hall opened its doors to the public in 1932, featuring the famous dancing troupe the 'Rockettes'. The exterior of the building was adorned with brightly coloured plaques of metal and enamel, designed by Hildreth Meiers. These circular decorations

Left: *Elevator doors in the Chrysler building, New York city, 1928-30. The decorative graining of the panelling was popular at the time, found also on Ruhlmann-style furniture.*

Above: *Radiator grille in the entrance lobby of the Chanin building, New York city, 1929. The streamlined skyscraper motifs celebrate the new city architecture.*

Above: *Carpet designed for Radio City Music Hall, New York city, c.1925. The 'jazz' pattern of musical instruments highlights the theme of entertainment.*

depicted in an exotic style the various aspects of entertainment, including *Drama*, *Song* and *Dance*. The architectural aims of the building, set out in a contemporary publicity release, were 'to achieve a complete decorative scheme that is an example of sane modern design'.

Such goals were more than fulfilled under the artistic direction of Donald Deskey, who was responsible for the interiors, furnishings and accessories. Deskey was assisted by some of the best freelance craftsmen of the period, and as an advocate of the new, sleek Modernism he selected a range of novel materials such as Bakelite, formica, mirror-glass, aluminium, chrome, cork, leather and luxury skins. He paid particular attention to detail, as noted throughout the spacious complex of men's and women's lounges, public foyers and

private offices. In his *Nicotine* wallpaper design, created for one of the many men's lounges, a marvellous blend of Art Deco motifs was displayed. Printed in dark tobacco brown on an aluminium foil ground, Negro figures appear in a jumbled 'jazz' pattern of yachts, dice, cigarettes, pipes, wine goblets and newspapers — a masculine-inspired theme conveyed in an exuberant style. Deskey also commissioned novel furniture designs, such as vertical weighing machines in the form of skyscrapers, and topical murals such as *Men Without Women* for the men's smoking room, and *A History of Cosmetics* for the women's lounge. Such decorative features, both whimsical and luxurious, were highlighted throughout the building, reflecting an overall effect of 'mock' grandeur.

Other resplendent room settings were to be found in the Chanin building on Lexington Avenue, constructed in 1929 with interior designs by Jacques Delamarre. The executive bathroom on the 52nd floor, for example, was conceived in the manner of a Hollywood film set, with no expense spared. Gold-plated taps and a matching overmantle of glittering sunbeams, engraved glass shower doors, richly glazed tiles and concealed lighting all contributed to the dramatic scheme. The ornamentation of bold triangles and curves was characteristic of the period, and could be found on most of the architectural masterpieces of the 1930s.

In spite of the Wall Street crash of 1929 and the ensuing years of the Depression, the architecture of New York enjoyed a period of renewal under the influence of Art Deco. The Empire State building epitomized the new wave of luxury Modernism, and its grandness drew attention away from its empty interiors.

Above left and right: *Elevator doors of monel (a mixture of nickle and brass) in the lobby of the First National City Trust Co, formerly the City Bank Farmer's Trust Co, in the Wall Street district of New York city, completed in 1931.*
Left: *'Nicotine' wallpaper by Donald Deskey in the men's room of Radio City Music Hall.*
Right: *'Roxy's' private suite in Radio City Music Hall, with interior designs by Donald Deskey. The most up-to-date materials were used throughout the building including aluminium, chrome-plated steel and Bakelite.*
Below: *The Martin Theater on N. Court Street, Talladela, Alabama. The Art Deco façade is boldly decorated with chevrons, zig-zags and a 'key-fret' border.*
Below right: *Decorative frieze*

depicting *'Wisdom'* by Lee Lawrie for the entrance of the R.C.A. building, Rockefeller Centre, New York city. The cast glass wall, below, was made by the Steuben factory.
Far right: *Novel cigarette dispenser and table-lighter by Ronson, c.1920s.*

GREAT BRITAIN

Throughout the 1920s, British interior design was firmly rooted in the traditions of the past and demonstrated an affinity with the antique styles of the seventeenth and eighteenth centuries rather than with the exotic trends of Art Deco. The British pavilion at the 1925 Exposition des Arts Décoratifs in Paris made little impact and was harshly criticized by the French, who described it as 'a fantasy ... created by a retired colonel'. By the end of the decade, however, such historicism became less marked under the influence of Modernism, already heralded in France as the decorative *tour de force* of the 1930s. The preference for antique and reproduction furniture soon gave way to Modernist designs of steel, chrome and leather, in settings rendered more glamorous by the addition of tinted mirror glass and metal foils. Colour schemes for interiors reflected two extremes of taste — either the co-ordination of brilliant shades or the use of subdued white and metallic tones to create an appearance of cool sophistication. On occasion, these approaches were combined imaginatively, as in Raymond McGrath's design of 1930 for the 'Finella' house, Cambridge, which was described in a contemporary account as having a 'mansard ceiling of silvered ribbed cast glass of a jade green colour ... A silver-leafed vault springs from

pilasters of cast glass lit from within, the axial door has a surround of gold mirror, the walls are silver leaf lacquered green, the floor is of black induroleum composition with a border of blue and a line of gold mosaic .

Apart from private commissions, some of the finest Art Deco interiors were created for hotels such as Claridge's in London, decorated in 1929-30 under the direction of Basil Ionides. He employed numerous freelance designers, among them Oswald P. Milne, who transformed the ballroom and spacious lounge. The latter featured a striking geometric carpet in black and beige tones by Marion Dorn, large wall mirrors engraved with exotic plants and curtain ornaments to heighten the effects of space and glamour, and decorative light fixtures of wrought-iron. The hotel's suites were also refurbished on a sumptuous scale in the latest styles. The bathrooms, for example, were fitted with chrome and mirror-glass fixtures against coloured tiles and walls of turquoise and peach. White marbled floors and dramatic ceiling lights on giant zigzag supports of gleaming metal enhanced further the notions of affluence and luxury.

In the foyer of the Strand Palace Hotel in London, designed by Oliver Bernard in 1930, illuminated glass panelling was used throughout — on the balustrade, columns, doors and overmantles — to achieve a dazzling impact. Glamour was also the essence of Basil Ionides' decorations for the Savoy Theatre, executed in 1929. In the foyer, for example, the ceiling was ornamented with a superstructure of undulating curves, and the radiator grilles were fan-patterned and placed in decorative niches, offset by large black urns and Egyptian-style figurines. The auditorium was equally splendid, with walls and panels of silver-leaf, lacquered in metallic shades of gold.

Dramatic interiors were created for the numerous Odeon cinemas scattered around London and its environs. The one at Leicester Square, for example, was designed by Weeden and Mather in 1937 with leopard-skin upholstery and ripple-patterned walls in sparkling gold. In the Richmond Odeon, a Moorish-inspired theme was devised, with balconies transformed by mock architectural settings and pantiled roofs.

Although London in the 1930s was devoid of the skyscraper architecture that transformed cities such as New York, it boasted several outstanding Art Deco buildings. The BBC building at Portland Place, for example, was described in a contemporary issue of *Architectural Review* as 'a victory [for] the Modernists'. The simple curving façade was ornamented with sculptures by Eric Gill and Vernon Hill. Rounded contours also featured on the exterior of the Hoover Factory at Perivale, near London, built in 1932 by Wallis, Gilbert and Partners. Here, an expansive Art Deco

Below left: *Detail of the curved façade of the Daily Express Building, Fleet Street, London, completed in 1931. The black glass and chrome supports create a dramatic Modernist effect.*
Below: *'You Can Be Sure of Shell', a poster designed by the American-born artist E. McKnight-Kauffer, 1931. He worked in England during the 1920s and 30s, creating posters for London Transport and other well-known industries.*

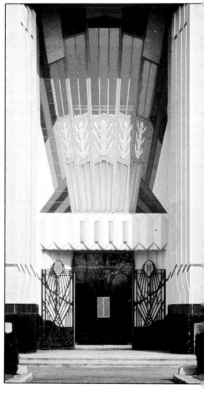

scheme was conceived through its streamlined structures, offset by superimposed curves and semi-circular windows. The white stone was relieved by red, black and blue glazed tiles and accents of bright green paint. The emblematic decoration over the main entrance is of uncertain origin, and has puzzled art historians such as Bevis Hillier, who wondered whether it was 'Ballet Russe, Aztec or Egyptian?' Such a rich mixture, indeed, epitomized the period style.

Decorative arts

During the late twenties and thirties a wide range of luxury and domestic wares was created in the Art Deco style in England. Fine silver was produced by stores such as Asprey's in London, and the manufacturers Waring and Gillow and Heal's sold furniture in the latest designs. Mass-produced articles — for use in the home, or as fashionable accessories — appeared in profusion, and featured the most popular materials of the Modernist era. Tubular chrome frames supported chairs, sofas and tables, the latter combined frequently (and inexpensively) with mirror-glass for a sparkling surface finish. The firm of James Clark Ltd specialized in furniture of this sort, using tinted mirror-glass and tiles in shades of white, peach, grey and electric blue. Chrome and glass were also employed for lamps and light-fittings, and were made more decorative by the addition of bronze or porcelain figurines.

Art Deco dinner, coffee and tea services of pottery and porcelain were produced by all the leading firms — as epitomized by Spode's 'Royal Jasmine' range. Here, simple geometric motifs of curves and squares comprised the only ornamentation, coloured beige, emerald and silver — all highly favoured shades of the period. London department stores such as Harrods and Selfridges supplied home furnishings as well as clothes and accessories. Costume jewellery was readily adapted to the rich array of Art Deco patterns and appeared in a multitude of novelty shapes. Bakelite, ivory, amber, paste, chrome, silver and enamel were all employed imaginatively for day and evening jewellery, and as fashionable accents in the form of belt-buckles, clips, hat-pins, haircombs, handbags and compacts.

The Art Deco style was embraced wholeheartedly by British manufacturers of the 1930s and the works of several of the best period designers are described briefly below.

Clarice Cliff (1900-70) produced striking tablewares and decorative ceramic objects during the twenties and thirties for home and export markets. She worked at the Burslem pottery of A.J. Wilkinson — initially as an apprentice and later as art director for the firm. 'A few well chosen pieces of Miss Clarice Cliff's "Bizarre" ware seem just to add the last touch of distinction to a carefully thought out room,' said an advertisement in the *Illustrated London News* of 1934. Apart from her sensational 'Bizarre' series, Clarice Cliff created other Art Deco patterns of abstract, geometric or figural content such as 'Delecia', 'Patina', 'Crocus' and 'My Garden', in

Below left: *Entrance of the Hoover factory at Perivale, Middlesex, built by Wallis, Gilbert and Partners in 1932. The bright colours of the central design are used to decorate the building's exterior.*

Above: *Relief panel depicting 'Ariel Hearing Celestial Music' by the sculptor Eric Gill, for the exterior of the BBC building in Portland Place, London, completed in 1932. The pronounced curves of the building's façade caused considerable controversy at the time, and were criticized for being 'too modern'.*

Below: *Entrance foyer of the Strand Palace Hotel, London, designed by Oliver Bernard in 1930 and decorated with marble, chrome and illuminated panels of plate glass — a theatrically conceived interior in the Modernist style.*

Top left: 'Actors Prefer Shell', a poster designed by E. McKnight-Kauffer, 1933. The abstracted shapes and planes of flat colour recall the Cubist compositions of Picasso, although the masked subject is in keeping with the new Surrealist style of the 1930s.
Left: Interior panels for the lifts of Selfridges Department Store, London, modelled after Edgar Brandt's wall screens of wrought-iron and bronze, c.1925.

Top right: 'Arc-en-Ciel', a textile design by Eric Bagge, produced by Lucien-Boux, 1926-8. The pronounced 'arc' patterns and Pointillist effects capture the decorative Modernism of the period.
Above: 'Modern' bathroom interior designed by Paul Nash for Miss Tilly Losch (Mrs Edward James), 1932. Panels of plain and textured glass, in shades of pink, purple and black, are arranged like a Cubist composition.

Background: *'Marble' fabric in blue and gold, created by Warner & Sons' in-house designer Bertrand Whittaker, 1923. It was displayed at the 1925 Paris Exhibition, where it was praised as 'frankly modern and original'. The material was woven in cotton and rayon damask, showing an early experimental use of rayon.*
Left: *Four hand-painted pottery figural plaques entitled 'Age of Jazz' by Clarice Cliff. The dancing figures, left and right, appear to tango.*
Below left: *Commercial tin designs, decorated in the geometric Art Deco style. The fashionable female figure, in profile, was a common motif of the period and appeared on compacts, cigarette cases and other accessories.*

Above right: *Silver and enamel lady's cigarette case of English manufacture, hallmarked 1931. The pantaloons worn by the dancers recall the exotic costume designs of Léon Bakst, profusely patterned in the Art Deco style with zig-zags, cubes and stylized flowers.*
Right: *'Tea for Two' service depicting a hand-painted 'Fantasque' pattern by Clarice Cliff, 1931. The novel, triangular-shaped cup handles were popular at the time.*

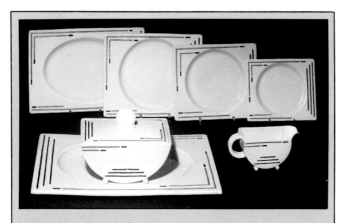

Clarice Cliff (1900-70) created lively and colourful ceramic tablewares and accessories in the Art Deco style. Her pieces were sold through department stores in Britain, and were exported.

After a basic training in pottery techniques, Clarice Cliff joined the Burslem factory of A.J. Wilkinson at the age of 16, where she was encouraged to create her own distinctive designs. She later became Art Director of the firm, and its subsidiary, the Newport Pottery Company.

The forms of her wares followed the bold angularities and geometric constructions of Art Deco, with their triangular-shaped handles, arched lids and pronounced circular contours.

Clarice Cliff also produced a small and exclusive range of ceramics decorated by contemporary artists such as Duncan Grant, Vanessa Bell, Barbara Hepworth, Laura Knight and Ben Nicholson. The black-painted ornamentation of the dessert plate, *below*, was created by the artist Ernest Proctor in 1933, conveyed in an abstract manner. The dinner service, *above*, is from Clarice Cliff's 'Biarritz' range, featuring sparse linear decorations in red and black.

brilliant (and frequently clashing) colours of deep orange, yellow, blue and black. Her dinner and tea services, figurines and wall 'masks' were immensely popular at the time, and were particularly admired for their vivid hand-painted decorations and novel, streamlined shapes. She also produced an exclusive range of ceramics decorated by British artists such as Vanessa Bell, Duncan Grant, Laura Knight, Ben Nicholson, Paul Nash, Barbara Hepworth and Frank Brangwyn.

Another acclaimed studio potter of the period was Susie Cooper, who worked for the Staffordshire firm of A.G. Grey & Co from 1925 to 1932, and later for Wedgwood. One of her elegant designs for Grey was a china coffee service in shades of silver lustre and green, hand-painted in a lively manner with stylized vines and grapes. Her works were sold frequently through department stores such as Peter Jones in London.

Charlotte Rhead worked for the manufacturer Crown Ducal Potteries during the 1930s, creating a series of distinctive tablewares and accessories that featured brightly coloured patterns contained within raised linear borders. This technique of outlining was also found on other pottery of the period, as employed, for example, by Royal Doulton for detailed surface work. Potters such as Vera Huggins and Bessie Newbury worked for this factory, and freelance artists, including Frank Brangwyn, were commissioned to produce exclusive designs.

Wedgwood issued a number of inexpensive Art Deco tablewares in the twenties and thirties, among them those designed by Keith Murray (1893-1981), characterized by their extreme simplicity of shape and matt finishes in pastel tones of grey, buff and celadon. Murray also created thickly walled decorative and utilitarian glassware in clear and muted shades for the firm of Stevens & Williams, engraved and/or cut with restrained geometric or figural patterns. An imaginative piece is his 'Cactus' decanter of 1932, with its square body ornamented by a grid pattern and cactus plant.

During the 1930s Frank Brangwyn (who, in 1895, had painted panels for Bing's L'Art Nouveau shop in Paris) created pottery for Clarice Cliff, Doulton, Foley, and Royal Staffordshire. He also turned his talents to other creative arts, producing furniture designs for the firm of Pollard & Sons, glass for James Powell, and textiles for James Templeton & Co of Glasgow. A carpet of wool and chenille, commissioned by Templeton's, was created by Brangwyn in the Art Deco style. This was ornamented with merging geometric forms, in subdued shades of beige, orange, yellow, olive-green and turquoise. His efforts were praised in an accompanying brochure: 'When an artist of the world-wide eminence of Mr. Brangwyn can collaborate successfully with manufacturers, "Art in Industry" is no longer an aspiration but a reality'.

From 1925 Brangwyn also designed decorative murals for the House of Lords (which, unfortunately, were poorly received and were hung instead at the new

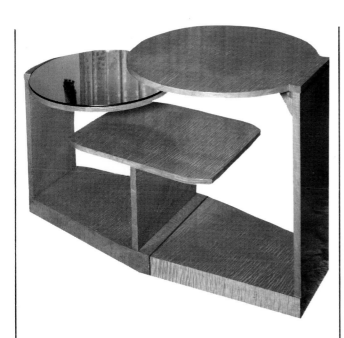

Left: *Nest of tables of Modernist design with mirror-glass inset, by Ray Hille, 1928. Mirrored surfaces of clear and coloured glass appeared commonly on French and English furniture of the period.*

Below: *Unusual silver teapot and accessories made in India, after an English design. The gazelle, with its speed and grace, was a popular Art Deco motif.*

Guildhall in Wales), for the ocean liner *Empress of Britain*, and for the new RCA building at Rockefeller Plaza in New York.

Ornamental panelling was a speciality of Rex Whistler, perhaps best remembered for his wall murals for the Tate Gallery restaurant, London. He was also commissioned to decorate several aristocratic homes and to design stage sets for Covent Garden Opera House and Sadlers Wells theatre. Duncan Grant also devised interior schemes, frequently in collaboration with Vanessa Bell, with painted *trompe l'oeil* murals featuring colourful floral bouquets in recessed niches, curtained effects and other motifs.

Right: *Art Deco lounge interior, recreated from an English suburban home, c.1930. The deeply upholstered armchairs, fan-shaped electric lights, tassled lampshade, circular tables and carpet capture the look of the 1930s — with its emphasis on comfort. The television and radio are a reminder of the increasing affluence of the middle classes.*

SPIRIT OF ART DECO

Solemn Modernist theories of pure, unadorned lines were not to rein in the Art Deco designers. For them brash colours, dynamic geometric juxtapositions and shimmering reflective surfaces matched the exciting contemporary mood, expressing positive action, speed and style. Being life-affirmative, their work abounds with references to nature and natural forces — sunbursts, waterfalls, clouds, flora and fauna, abstracted into geometrical patterns. An exercise in total design, Art Deco mixes exotic materials — figured woods, lacquer, shagreen, bronze, tinted glass — with chrome and plastics, bringing drama to massive architectural schemes and a quirky charm to household wares and fashion accessories.

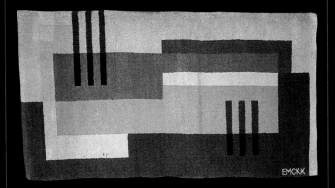

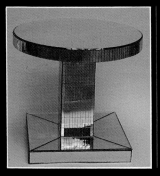

1925 This Axminster rug, *above*, designed by E. McKnight Kauffer, uses strong colours and abstract design like the Cubist paintings of the period to make its immediate impact.

1925 The peach-coloured glass of this coffee table, *left*, literally reflects the preoccupation with metallic surface prevalent in much Art Deco.

1934 Eric Gill grew into his reputation as sculptor and typeface designer during the 30s. This sculpture, *left*, reclines over the portico of the Working Women's Institute, Rockefeller Centre, New York.

1930 Though Bakelite was invented as early as 1910, it realized its potential only in the 30s, when it was used for everything from delicate dressing table sets, such as this English example, *right*, to radios, gramophones and clocks.

1932 The modernist's dream interior, *left*. The dressing table, by Ray Hille, incorporates figured burl wood.

1925 René Lalique's career spanned decades. His first fame came as a jewellery designer. This sapphire, emerald and diamond watch, *right*, demonstrates the fascination with geometric form.

1935 Clarice Cliff has given her name to a style of pottery produced at Burslem, Staffordshire, during the 30s. Her own Bizarre ware, *left*, relied on a garish palette and a kind of abstract naturalism.

1929 E. McKnight Kauffer, who designed the rug on the opposite page, also accepted commissions such as this one, *below*, for Shell Petroleum.

1931 Entrance hall, *left*, 'Daily Express' building, Fleet Street, London, by Ellis & Clarke. Brilliant colour and zig-zags are reflected in shimmering walls of stainless steel – an Aztec temple dedicated to the pace of modern life.

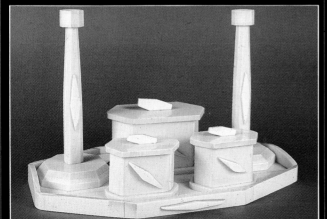

INTERNATIONAL

SHELL

VISIT STAND NO 10 SECTION C

AERO EXHIBITION 1929

HOLLYWOOD STYLE

Hollywood in the twenties and thirties provided millions of people across North America and Europe with the opportunity to escape the stress and humdrum existence of everyday life. Actors and actresses became 'stars' and role-models for adoring cinema audiences, and dictated changing fashions of beauty, style and behaviour. Sets of plush interiors were often impractically lavish and spectacular, but captured the aspirations of an increasingly materialistic public.

Films of romance, melodrama and comedy were produced in their thousands, and toured the newly built cinemas which sprang up in cities and towns everywhere. For these 'dream palaces' a Hollywood-style architecture evolved of striking decorative facades and luxury-designed interiors, in the exotic Art Deco taste. The chain of Odeon cinemas in Britain, for example, were glamorously conceived with their mirrored foyers, auditoriums and *trompe l'oeil* effects. The grand interior of the New Victorian cinema was described in a contemporary account as 'a palace under the sea' with its scallop-shell wall lights and illuminated ceilings. In America, Graumann's Egyptian Theatre on Hollywood Boulevard captured, with typical Hollywood flair, images of the ancient civilization — like a Cecil B. de Mille extravaganza. The dream world of films was, indeed, extended to the architecture and interior design of the cinema.

Right: *The Loyola Theatre, Westchester, California — an extravagant design highlighted by a whimsical concrete 'spire'.*
Below: *The San Marco Theatre, Jacksonville, Florida, with its simple geometric façade of vertical lines and curves.*

Right: *The ticket booth of the Crest Theatre, Sacramento, California, with its 'silver' and 'gold' metal construction of swirling floral motifs.*

Left and below: *Exotic gilded figures at the Rockefeller Centre.*

Left: *Curved façade of the Greystone Hotel, Miami Beach, Florida, white-washed with blue geometric accents.*

English cardboard shop cut-out for Ilford Films, early 1950s

CHAPTER · FIVE

THE AGE OF STREAMLINING

CONSUMERISM AND STYLE 1935-1955

'Just as surely as the artists of the fourteenth century are remembered by their cathedrals, so will those of the twentieth be remembered for their factories and the products of these factories.'

NORMAN BEL GEDDES, 1932

INTRODUCTION

By the mid-1930s the professional designer had had an influence on many of the new products that affected the way the majority of people in the industrialized world lived and worked. It was no longer the prerogative of the rich to own objects that had been considered by an individual with a trained eye. Increasingly, 'style-conscious' goods began to penetrate the mass market and to alter the life-styles of vast numbers of people.

There were many reasons for this dramatic change of scale both in the mass production of goods and in the size of the 'design-conscious' sector of the market, all of them related to the economic, social and technological changes of that period. While one important factor was the increase in the wealth of social groups that had never before had enough money to spend on anything more than the bare essentials, this in turn encouraged manufacturers to increase their output and to find new technological means of achieving this end. Primary among them was the exploitation of new materials, in particular the new metals (and their alloys) and plastics.

Among the numerous mass-manufactured goods to reach a larger audience than ever before was the automobile. Since the demise of Ford's famous dictum — 'It doesn't matter what colour a car is as long as it is black' — styling had become the norm in the American automobile industry and, from the twenties onwards, 'stylists' were employed by the big American corporations to create the 'dream machines' so coveted by the mass market. The people's car, a triumph of 'function' over styling where appearance was concerned, was, however, also a product of this period, and the little European cars — which included, in Italy, Fiat's 'Topolino'; in France, Citroen's 'Deux Chevaux'; and in Germany the Volkswagen 'Beetle' — quickly became familiar appendages of the mass environment in continental Europe. Gone, by the late thirties, where Europe was concerned, were the 'showy', powerful cars of the early years of the decade. They were replaced by a range of small, functional machines which owed their simple aesthetic — or so it seemed — to the engineer rather than the designer.

While the new ideas about 'streamlining' that had grown up in the USA as part of that country's search for an aerodynamic automobile were transferred, in the thirties and forties, into a number of smaller, inanimate domestic machines — particularly those destined for the kitchen like food-mixers and fruit-juicers — the living-room of the popular home was still occupied by products with a more traditional background. The bulbous forms of the 'streamlined moderne' style characterized numerous small products made of metal or plastic, but in sharp contrast most domestic furnishings owed more to the humanistic natural design ideals emerging from

Above and left: *Boulanger's little 'Deux Chevaux', designed for the Citroën company in the 1930s, was among the first of the small, functional, economical cars to emerge in Europe. Its idiosyncratic form echoed its basic construction.* Below: *Danish nursery furniture in beech made by Faellesforeningen. Some of the pieces were exhibited in London in 1951.*

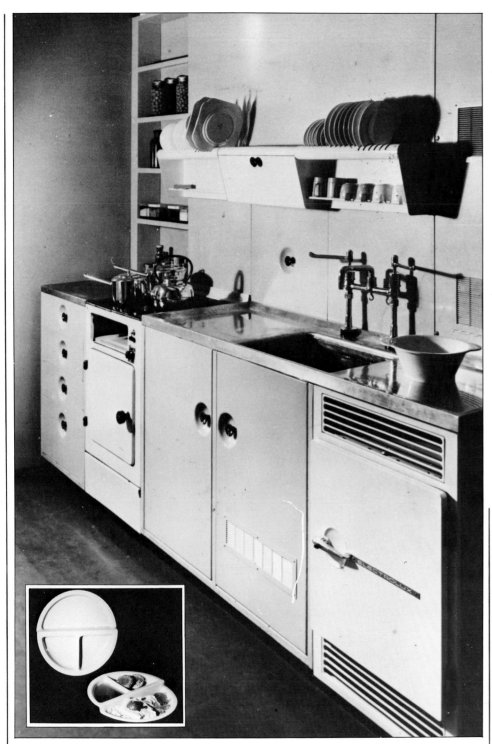

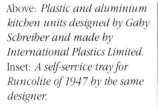

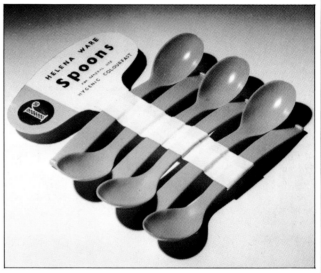

Above: *Plastic and aluminium kitchen units designed by Gaby Schreiber and made by International Plastics Limited.* Inset: *A self-service tray for Runcolite of 1947 by the same designer.*

Above right: *A plastic colander with interchangeable 'snap-in' aluminium inserts for different types of straining, designed by Gaby Schreiber in 1948 for Runcolite.*

Below right: *Gaby Schreiber's plastic spoons designed for Runcolite in 1948 display the same simple aesthetic that she evolved for numerous products made of that material.*

the Scandinavian countries (in particular Sweden and Denmark).

Two distinct cultures emerged — that of the kitchen and that of the living-room — which were conveyed by two completely different design styles and attitudes to living in the mid-century. While the first was a futuristic, pro-technology style that refused to look back over its shoulder, the latter was steeped in traditional values and ideas about comfort. They shared, however, a commitment to the democratic ideal. Design was now no longer the preserve of an exclusive few, but available to almost anybody who wanted it.

Perhaps more than any other aspect of the mass environment the office was, in this period, completely revolutionized by the appearance of the new machines that entered its territory. The streamlined typewriters, adding machines, cash registers and pencil-sharpeners, combined with the new approach towards office organization, meant a completely new environment for this area of daily life. Greater and greater efficiency was encouraged through the use of more and more machines and increasingly intensive time and motion studies. Like the domestic arena, the office of the late thirties bore little resemblance to its predecessor of a decade earlier.

INSPIRATIONS

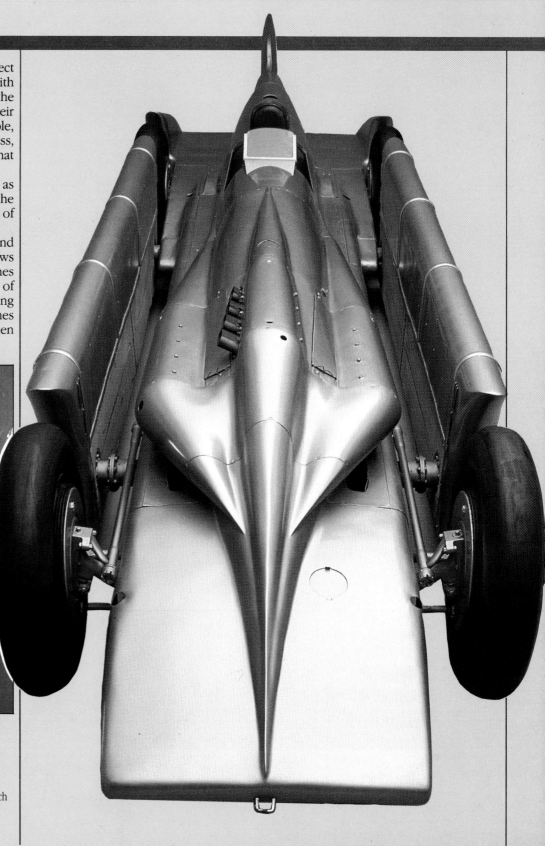

To apply streamlining to a machine or object requires a mental process completely at odds with Modernist Functionalism. Whereas the Functionalists sought to break things down to their essentials and reassemble them as a series of identifiable, connected parts, the streamliners wanted a seamless, integrated whole with moving parts covered, that presented an efficient, sleek outline.

The aim of the streamliners, initially at least, was just as functional. The developments in mass transport made the design of cars, planes, boats and trains an urgent part of the designer's brief.

International competition spurred innovation and daring deeds of aeronautics and driving. With news travelling faster, the torpedo forms of airships, seaplanes and monoplanes became a popular image of technological achievement. So highly did streamlining charge the imagination that its bulbous, tapering outlines caused no amusement when applied to incidental kitchen and office artefacts.

Water source
The earliest inspirations for the aerodynamic aesthetic were nineteenth-century natural history studies, particularly those that illustrated the efficiency with which fish and dolphins, *above*, propelled themselves.

Forward thrust
The javelin form of the 'Golden Arrow', *right*, in which Henry Segrave broke the land speed record in 1929, makes it as much a work of sculptural art as a specialized machine.

Teardrop on wheels

Model of a streamlined bus from 1939, *above*, one of several visionary designs by Norman Bel Geddes intended to exploit the low wind resistance and high fuel economy of the 'teardrop' shape.

Ideas in the air

Detail from a 1912 poster, *right*, advertising the Viktoria Luise, one of a fleet of Zeppelin airships that plied between German cities before the First World War. Ferdinand von Zeppelin gave air balloons aerodynamic form from 1900 by supporting the unwieldy gasbags within a rigid structure of aluminium covered in fabric.

Headliners

The British-built R34, *far right*, made front-page news on 14 July 1919 after the first two-way Atlantic crossing. Before the airship disasters of the 30s, triumphs such as the arrival of the 'Graf Zeppelin' in New York in 1928 kept airships in the news and boosted national prestige.

Built for speed

R.J. Mitchell's 'Supermarine S6B' seaplane, *right*, winner of the Schneider Trophy in 1931. Its streamlined form was later used in the Spitfire. Innovation in metals technology and construction techniques made box-frame fuselages and wing braces obsolete.

Post-war design

It wasn't until the 1950s that the design styles which had originated for machines in the US and for domestic artefacts in Scandinavia began to be replaced by another popular idiom. This one emerged in Italy, where designers played a central role in post-war reconstruction. The Italian style was, however, much more sculptural than its predecessors and much less overtly populist in its appeal.

After 1945 design became one of the important ways in which a number of countries, either defeated or merely deflated by the war, set out to reassert their position within world trade. Conscious that the US had used design as an important means of surviving the economic depression of the 1930s and of making itself a world power to be reckoned with, countries like Britain, Germany, Finland and Japan suddenly became aware of the need to integrate design with industry and develop a national design style that would secure them a place in international trade. The early post-war years were characterized by a 'call for style' in these countries, which made huge efforts to move beyond the

Above: *A view of the Inventory Department in Frank Lloyd Wright's building for S.C. Johnson & Son. The desk was manufactured by Steelcase Inc to a design by Wright and is an excellent example of an early work station. The desk top is cut out for the calculating machine and the typewriter.*

Left: *The great workroom in Wright's Johnson building. This well-lit, open-planned office space was years ahead of its time and influenced countless others that came after it. The office furniture, also designed by Wright and manufactured by Steelcase Inc, is still in use today.*

Below: *Walter Dorwin Teague's simple design for the National Cash Register company.*

limitations of the traditional industrial arts into industrial design proper. This new policy entailed putting less emphasis upon the 'applied arts' and concentrating instead on the design of mass-produced technological goods made from new materials. During this period furniture, for example, ceased to be a craft-based product and became allied instead with experiments with steel rods and the new plastics.

While at one end of the spectrum exclusive goods like hand-made ceramics and glass still entered the lives of a few people, at the other end items such as mass-produced oven-to-table ware aimed at the mass market changed the lives of vast sectors of the population. On another front the world of high technology entered everyday life on a massive scale and the 'consumer society' of the 1950s was presented with machines that could eliminate the burden of almost every manual task imaginable as well as increase leisure options. Design became inextricably linked with the worlds of mass production and mass consumption and style became the means through which the vast majority of the population in the industrialized world defined its social aspirations and its preferred way of life.

Design exhibitions 1935-1955

One of the ways other than through the mass media — which expanded its influence in leaps and bounds in this period — in which design styles became available to a large sector of the population was through design exhibitions. These attracted huge audiences and were received with great enthusiasm. Following the earlier Paris exhibition of 1925 which had introduced Art Deco to the world, the Paris 1937 show was another huge success and presented all the current design styles to its eager audience. One of the surprises of 1937 was the presence of Surrealism, used there as a display style. It was an idiom that was to appear again, after the war, in British and Italian exhibitions.

It was the New York World's Fair of 1939, however, that showed the mass potential of style for the first time. The exhibition was dominated, both in its buildings and in the futuristic products displayed in them, by American 'streamlining'. It was also the first world exhibition at which industrial design was more in evidence than the decorative arts, a fact that represented a triumph for the American industrial design profession, for the new technologies and materials and for design as an aspect of mass marketing. The largest exhibitors were the automobile companies — General Motors, Ford and Chrysler — followed by other mammoth American corporations such as United Steel, Du Pont, Consolidated Edison and National Cash Register.

After the war the large-scale world exhibitions were not immediately revived and their role as disseminators of style was taken on instead by other smaller, specifically design-orientated shows such as the Milan Triennales. It was in Milan that the newly organized nations showed their new products to the rest of the world, demonstrating that design had become part of their economic, social and cultural rebirth.

Below left: *A general aerial view of the New York World's Fair which was held in Flushing Meadow in 1939. The buildings were colour-coded with routes from the white Perisphere and Trylon at the centre radiating out to deep colours at the periphery.*

Below right: *Fitted shelving from the dressing room of the 'House of the Future' designed by the British architects Alison and Peter Smithson in 1956. The projected standardization of the house's components echoed the system of automobile production in Detroit.*

INSPIRATIONS

The age of the atom exploded upon mass consciousness with the bombings of Nagasaki and Hiroshima in 1945 — the shock waves continued to ripple through the design world throughout the 1950s. The molecular model, consisting of primary coloured electron spheres on wires orbiting a nucleus, provided a familiar motif for furniture, light-fittings, coat racks, souvenirs and *objets d'art*. Other bi-products of scientific inquiry included fabric and surface designs based on crystal and molecular structures as observed under the microscope, producing liberated random patterns free from associations with earlier designs. The arbitrary effects produced by the action painters were in keeping with this taste for spontaneity and provided another source of inspiration.

The influence of streamlining had not yet played itself out — witness car design and the Skylon at the Festival of Britain — but it was degenerating from a practical theory to a mannered style. By 1950 a much freer, more sculptural organic inspiration was beginning to produce chairs with curling seats, kidney-shaped tables, ovoid ceramics and elegant trumpet glasses.

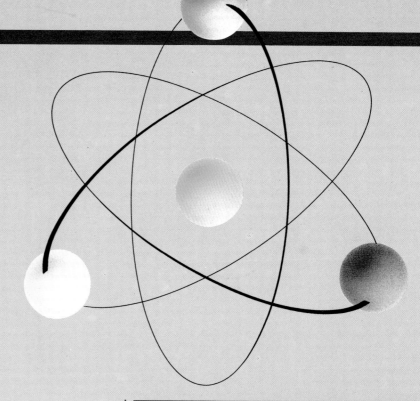

Scooter scoop
Italian designers took up the streamlining ideas from across the Atlantic and used them in a more refined way on various mass-produced lines, including this innovative 'Vespa' motor scooter of 1947, *above*, by Piaggio.

Economic balance
This souvenir from the 1951 Festival of Britain, *above*, depicts the 91-metre (300-foot) cigar-shaped structure, the Skylon, which like Britain's economy at the time had no visible means of support. A symbol of optimism, it demonstrated principles of cantilevering in a way that provided inspiration for the basic design of lamps and light-fittings, *right*.

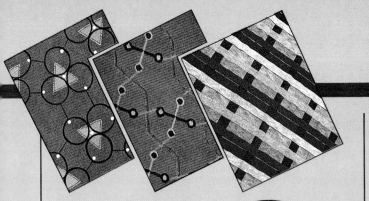

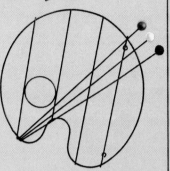

Shapes of the age

Theories about atomic structure, *left*, were propounded in the 1930s. In the 1950s designers found it a rich source to be plundered. This wire and plastic wall ornament, *right*, is a classic example. Scientific research gave impetus to innovations in patterns, too. The molecular structure of boric acid crystals, *above left*, and quartz, *above centre*, inspired these motifs for fabric. This design for curtain fabric, *above right*, was made possible in 1954 by new fibre technology.

Miró reflected

The strange organic and amoebic forms conjured up by Surrealist artists such as Joan Miró — whose 'Personage Throwing a Stone at a Bird' (1926) is inset *above* — were used by the rapidly emerging Italian post-war school. The inspiration for both the sculptural upholstery and steel rod supports of these armchairs, *left*, by the Milan manufacturers Arflex, is evident.

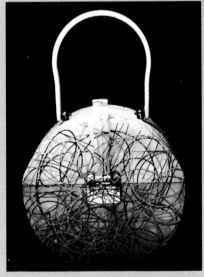

Spillover

'Full Fathom Five', 1947, *left*, one of the boldly experimental drip pieces by the action painter Jackson Pollock (1912-56). His attractively dynamic effects, achieved as a result of a 'creative accident', were borrowed by the designer of this American handbag of the 50s, *above*.

ABCDEFG
ABCDEFGH
abcdefghijk
ABCDEFGHIJK
£123456

Asymmetrical strokes cut at uneven angles give 'Banco', *top*, designed by Roger Excoffon in 1951, a jaunty, uninhibited look that suited the optimistic post-war mood. Script faces were used effectively in the early 50s to brighten magazine pages and advertisements.

'Palette', *middle*, was designed by Martin Wilke in 1951. 'Festival' titling, *bottom*, was conceived specially for Festival of Britain advertising by Phillip Boydell and the London Press Exchange. Its three-dimensional form suited it well to exhibition display.

139

THE USA

In the years between 1935 and 1955 the USA led the way where design was concerned. This was due to that country's advanced attitude towards industrial and business organization and to the presence there of a wealthy mass market eager to consume its exciting new products. Like the films that came out of Hollywood in those years, the new mass-produced goods played the role of fantasy fulfilment for a population for whom the economic depression was a sustained reality.

Streamlining

At the turn of the century the new domestic machines — Singer's sewing machine, Hoover's suction cleaner, Remington's typewriter and countless others — were designed in the same way as all the other 'applied art' products: they were simply covered, for sales purposes, with two-dimensional patterns in the prevailing fashion-

Left: *Walter Dorwin Teague's little Bantam Special camera for the Eastman Kodak company. The aluminium stripes are both functionally justified and visually exciting.*
Above: *An aluminium coffee-pot designed by J. Luck for 'Wear-Ever' in 1947. The simple, undecorated rounded form of the product reflects its manufacturing process and its function.*
Left: *The 'City of Salina', the United States' first streamlined train, designed in 1934. Inspired by experiments in aerodynamics, streamlining became the most popular style of the day, symbolizing speed and the future.*

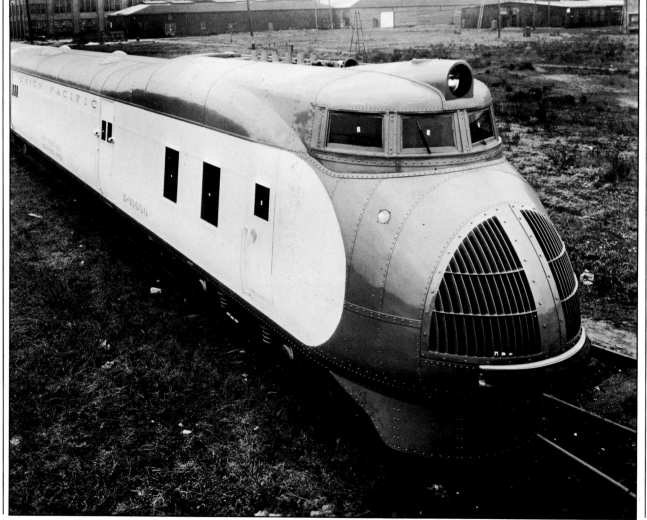

Right: *An American advertisement from 1948 showing the influence of the bulbous forms of Detroit automobile styling on refrigerator design.*
Below: *A cylinder vacuum cleaner of 1946, designed for the Swedish company, Electrolux, showing how, by that date, the style derived from streamlining had become the dominant idiom for electrical products.*

able style, whether Victorian eclecticism or the sumptuous curves of Art Nouveau. In the early years of their mass-production these objects were considered to be 'women's goods' and were therefore decorated to please what were thought to be 'women's tastes'. With the growing success in subsequent decades of the 'machine aesthetic', however, and the repudiation of ornament in avant-garde ideas about style in the decorative arts, even machines themselves gradually began to drop their decorative disguises and to look much more like the pieces of cast, stamped or pressed metal that they actually were, with only enough surface decoration to conceal ugly seams.

This change occurred first in the USA as part of a conscious search for a style for the age, focusing on the design language that came to be called 'streamlining'. This derived originally from aerodynamic experiments, such as wind-tunnel testing, for objects of transport, but it had a number of other visual sources, including Futurist painting, airships, the tapered forms of dolphins and porpoises, and the abstract engineered forms of objects like grain silos, bridges and factory machinery (particularly as portrayed in photographs by people such as Margaret Bourke-White). To these sources were added the futuristic shapes and 'speed whiskers' used by comic-book artists.

These influences all combined to form a particularly American aesthetic characterized by bulbous 'tear-drop' body-shells for mechanical and electrical products and expressive, organic forms for decorative art objects. It was a style that dramatically symbolized the present and the future and took full advantage of the new technologies available for cheap mass-production. It was applied to a vast range of artefacts from locomotives to irons, regardless of their potential for high-speed movement or lack of it.

Where the decorative arts were concerned even the ceramic and aluminium objects of a designer such as Russel Wright (b. 1904) exhibited the same familiar streamlined curves. Only furniture escaped from its impact and even in that category there were notable exceptions like Kem Weber's 'Airline' chair, which translated the smooth curves of streamlining into a chair form, and Frederick Kiesler's aluminium tables, which displayed the same biomorphic shapes that were found in the sculpture of artists like Hans Arp and Joan Miró.

The consultant designers
For design, the major organizational breakthrough in the USA in the thirties was the creation of an independent industrial design profession which set itself up to work, on a freelance basis, with the large manufacturing companies. The pioneer consultants, among them Walter Dorwin Teague, Raymond Loewy, Norman

ONLY DUAL-TEMP GIVES YOU ALL 4 FEATURES!

No defrosting

① **Dual-Temp Home Freezer** really quick-freezes at 15° below zero. Stores up to 70 lbs. of frozen food safely for months. A freezer right in your refrigerator!

② **Dual-Temp Moist Cold Compartment** never requires defrosting! High humidity keeps food fresh and moist without covering dishes. More room for foods!

③ **Dual-Temp Sterilamp** kills germs...helps preserve food longer.

④ **Dual-Temp Moistral** ... the drip tray that automatically empties itself. Many more outstanding features ... see Dual-Temp at your Admiral dealer, today.

Bel Geddes, Henry Dreyfuss and Harold Van Doren, all came from backgrounds in the commercial arts, whether advertising, shop window display or, in a couple of cases, theatre design. They were, therefore, intensely aware of the intimate relationship between design and sales. The first companies to approach them – Eastman Kodak, the Gestetner Company, the Toledo Scale Company and a vast range of others producing such items as shop, kitchen and agricultural machinery – were not only keen to make their goods look more competitive but were also willing to pay huge sums of money to achieve this desired end. The new machines were all given a face-lift, as a result emerging more visually unified, slicker and generally more seductive.

While this group of industrial designers focused its efforts on machinery and produced some of its best designs for objects of transportation – notably Loewy's 'Hupmobile' and his trains for the Pennsylvania Railroad company; Teague's 'Marmon' automobile and Dreyfuss' 'Mercury' locomotive – others such as Lurelle Guild and Russel Wright concentrated on smaller products from the more traditional applied arts sector. They were, however, totally untraditional in their use of materials and their approach towards design. Donald Deskey's Art Deco-inspired interiors and furniture designs for Radio City Music Hall in New York, for instance, combined such materials as cork, aluminium and glass, while Guild's spun aluminium saucepans with wooden handles for the Wear-Ever company exploited this material, as did Wright's huge range of 'hospitality' items, including bun-warmers, sandwich humidors and

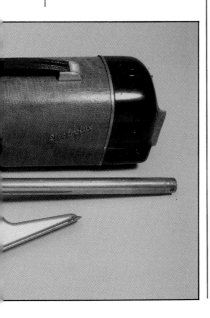

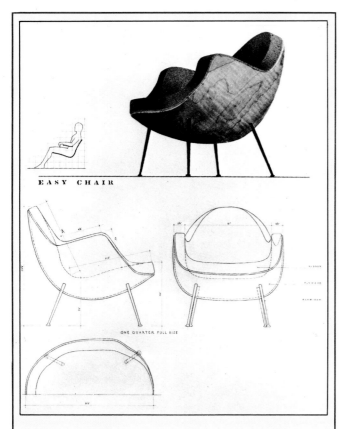

EASY CHAIR

ONE QUARTER FULL SIZE

Charles Eames was born in St. Louis in 1907 and began his training at Washington University's School of Architecture. He continued at the Cranbrook Academy of Art, where he met Eero Saarinen. Together they won the 'Organic Design' competition at the Museum of Modern Art in New York in 1940 with their chairs made of bent plywood. He followed this with a one-man show in 1946 in which his furniture combined plywood and steel rod. In the 1950s and 1960s Eames practised as an architect, designer and film-maker on the West Coast, producing, among other projects, a house for himself and his wife Ray, furniture in wood, plastic and metal and a number of short films. His best-known design was his lounge chair and Ottoman of 1956 covered in black leather. Eames died in 1978. Illustrated here are an early design with Saarinen from 1941, *above*, and a moulded polyester armchair from 1950, *below*.

142

cocktail-shakers. The round, undecorated forms of Wright's wares were a direct visual result of their means of manufacture.

Most of the consultants worked across a vast range of consumer goods and few confined their creativity to the use of a single medium. Because they were a new profession and therefore had no links with the past, and because they saw the US entering a new 'design-conscious' age, the style they promoted was completely modern in inspiration and impact. They took the European Modern Movement as their theoretical starting point and quoted Le Corbusier at length in their various manifestos. Teague (1883-1960), the most eloquent of them, referred, like Le Corbusier before him, to the importance of 'classical' ideals in modern design and illustrated Greek temples to make his point. Their real emotional commitment was, however, to the contemporary world of speed and modern technology.

New materials

The American consultant designers were obsessed with the aesthetic potential of a whole range of new materials from aluminium to a startling range of new types of glass (from 'Vitrolite' to 'Tuf-flex') and to plastics which were still, in the thirties, in a fairly early stage of their development. Loewy (b.1893), for instance, used a Bakelite body for his re-styled Gestetner machine, the body of which covered the exposed Victorian mechanism of the earlier model, and Dreyfuss designed an early telephone in cellulose acetate, which came in a range of bright colours. This provided one of the first visual models for the telephone set that has become familiar in the modern environment.

The furniture designers were more interested in finding new ways of layering, bending and moulding wood than in using new materials at this stage. Inspired by the progress made in Europe by men like the Finn Alvar Aalto (1898-1976), the Americans took their ideas a stage further. By the mid-forties the architect Charles Eames (1907-78) had produced, with the help of the Finn Eero Saarinen (1873-1950), plywood chairs that had three-dimensional as well as two-dimensional curves in them. They were shown at the Museum of Modern Art in New York in the exhibition *Organic Design in Home Furnishings* (1940), which was followed six years later by Charles Eames' one-man show at the same venue. This time he exhibited a range of chairs combining moulded ply seats with steel-rod legs. Their organically curved seats were juxtaposed sharply by their fine, splayed legs.

The 'organic' theme dominated one stream of American design in the fifties, particularly in the area of products for the 'living-room', taking much of its inspiration from the contemporary abstract sculpture of artists such as the late Surrealists Joan Miró (1893-1983) and Hans Arp (1887-1966). Designer-sculptors — Harry Bertoia (1915-78), for instance, who worked with Florence and Hans Knoll in the early fifties — combined sculptural with design concepts. His open 'chicken-

Below: *A West side highway in New York city in the early 1950s showing a preponderance of chromium-plated grilles.*

Left: *The Hardoy sling chair, consisting of a canvas seat suspended on a steel frame. Designed originally in 1938, it has remained a classic. Knoll International manufactures it in the USA.*

Lower left: *The Crosley radio, designed in the USA in the 1950s. Its moulded red plastic forms resemble the extravagant dials on an automobile dashboard from the same period.*

Right: *A gigantic streamlined automobile called the 'Aurora' designed and built in 1957 by an American priest called Alfred Juliano. The bulbous body is made of fibre-glass.*
Below: *Walter Dorwin Teague's giant cash register standing on top of his building for the National Cash Register company at the New York World's Fair of 1939.*

'wire' grid chair was primarily an exercise in abstract form and it rapidly became a familiar appendage of every fashionable American interior in that period. By the mid-fifties the two furniture companies Herman Miller and Knoll Associates had created a new abstract, sculptural furniture style that had more in common with contemporary European attitudes than with the more native American ideas that prevailed in the design of consumer machines and automobiles.

The Museum of Modern Art acted as an arbiter on the question of what was or was not 'good design' and a number of exhibitions with that very title took place there in the early fifties. They emphasized European-inspired furniture and applied art products and tended to neglect the indigenous, streamlined American products which flooded the streets outside the Museum. The American automobile became, in fact, a *bête noire* for the taste-makers of the day, who condemned it as vulgar, ostentatious and superficial. A sizeable gap opened up in American design culture between the ideas of 'styling' and 'design' and the democratic principles that had dominated the thirties began to fade. A more exclusive, European-inspired idea of design emerged in the post-war USA that stood in direct opposition to, and decried the values of, 'styling' and mass culture in general.

The end of the American dream

The consultant designers who had ruled the roost and commanded such high fees in the 1930s had, by the fifties, either died or outpriced themselves and they were replaced by a group of anonymous company men who worked within the large corporation. These men lacked the charisma of their independent predecessors, with the exception of a few individuals such as Eliot Noyes (1910-77), who was then working for IBM. For the most part, however, the excitement of the earlier period was replaced by corporate blandness and it was only on the level of youth 'pop' culture that the USA still had anything to offer the rest of the world where innovative style was concerned.

SCANDINAVIA

The story of Scandinavian design between 1935 and 1955 varies enormously from parallel events in the USA. This is due mainly to the relatively modest scale of industry in the former group of countries, with their continued dependence on tradition and their commitment to the applied arts.

The Scandinavian countries — Sweden, Denmark and Finland in this context — had not long established independent national identities for themselves at the turn of the century but all three considered design a necessary factor within the establishment of their political and economic independence. By 1900 they had all developed their own national variants of the Art Nouveau style and had applied it to their furniture, ceramics, glass, metalwork and textiles, traditional craft areas which had been flourishing for some time in all three countries. With the abolition of their guild systems in the mid-nineteenth century Sweden, Denmark and Finland had all been careful to establish bodies and educational establishments that would safeguard their craft traditions and, by the turn of the century, were all aware of the need to integrate the craft process into industrial production in pursuit of what they called the 'industrial arts'.

Swedish Modern

Sweden was the first of the Scandinavian countries to evolve its own twentieth-century design movement and style. It was encouraged by the activities of its major design organization, the Svenska Sjlödforeningen, which had been putting artists and craftsmen in touch with industry since the 1900s.

The first companies to take advantage of this innovation were the ceramics firms Gustavsberg and Rorstrand and the glass company Orrefors, and the men they employed through the 1920s and 1930s became pioneers of what came to be known internationally by 1940 as 'Swedish Modern'. The style was characterized by simplicity and a use of natural imagery and it incorporated the democratic ideal described by men like Gregor Paulsson. These basic principles illuminated Swedish design well into the post-war period and were the basis of its international popularity in that period.

In 1930 an exhibition in Stockholm created a short hiatus in the development of Swedish Modern as many of the country's architects were temporarily seduced by the harsher functional aesthetic that had developed in Germany. By the mid-thirties, however, Swedish furniture designers like Bruno Mathsson (b. 1907), G.A.

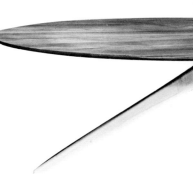

Berg and Josef Frank (1885-1967) had managed to reassert the importance of pattern, human values, tradition and natural imagery in Swedish design. Through their unwavering commitment to natural materials like wood and leather and in their sensitivity to human scale and comfort, these designers were responsible for making Swedish Modern a style to be reckoned with.

William Kåge (1889-1960) continued to work for the Gustavsberg ceramics company through the thirties and, in 1939, designed a ceramic set which, with its white ground and soft grey wavy line pattern, epitomized the simple yet lyrical quality of so much Swedish design of this period. He was succeeded, after the war, by Stig Lindberg who, along with a number of contemporaries, like the textile designer Astrid Sampe, working for the department store Nordiska Kompaniet in these years, took Swedish design confidently into the postwar era.

The Swedish exhibit at the New York World's Fair of 1939 inspired a critic to describe that country's design as 'A Movement towards Sanity' and through its presence there and at other major design venues it quickly became recognized internationally as the dominant domestic style of the mid-century. Shops with such evocative Swedish names as 'Svensk' and 'Form' sprang up in metropolitan centres all over the world and the Swedish style became identified with the idea of democratic yet elegant 'good living' and came to symbolize a world in which tradition, human values and beauty played an important role. Swedish interiors filled the glossy magazines in this period, always resplendent with books and flowers and suggesting that 'Swedish Modern' was a style to live with, not just to look at.

Above left: 'Portex' Danish packet furniture being taken out of its flat packaging and assembled. This inspired much of the 'knock-down' furniture that came after it.
Left: Borge Mogensen's 'Hunting' chair made of oak and leather and manufactured by Erhard Rasmussen in 1950 — a typical Danish product from the period.
Below left: A 'Danish Modern' table, made of ash and teak, designed by Borge Mogensen and manufactured by Ludvig Pontoppodan in 1950.
Far left: The 'Paradiset' Restaurant at the Stockholm Exhibition of 1930, designed by Gunnar Asplund. The circular stairwell had numerous precursors on German soil.

Above: A 'Portex' sideboard assembled from a kit of parts and designed according to strict measurements.

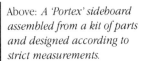

Danish Modern

Although it emerged on the international market a little later than that of its neighbour Sweden, the domestic style of Denmark had by the 1950s become equally popular and available.

While Danish ceramics and glass have established a reputation for themselves in this century that is strongly associated with integrity of workmanship and aesthetic simplicity, it is furniture that most frequently comes to mind in the context of modern Danish design. Names such as Kaare Klint and Mogens Koch, of the next generation, Borge Mogensen, Hans Wegner and Finn Juhl and, more recently, those of Arne Jacobsen, Poul Kjaerholm and Verner Panton are all linked firmly with the popular success of Danish furniture, which dominated the middle years of this century. Between them they established a sense of respect for natural materials — in particular, beech, birch and teak — and

Left: A version of the architect Arne Jacobsen's little 'Ant' chair manufactured by Fritz Hansen from the early 50s up to the present day. Its plywood seat and back are made in a single

mould and attached to a light steel base.

an interest in revived traditional chair-types such as the Windsor, the stick-back, the deck-chair and the Safari chair, their versions of which all affected mass-market furniture in this period.

The typical Danish furniture-designer was a cabinet-maker by training and his approach reflected a concern for craft details as well as a respect for democratic ideals expressed by a search for light yet comfortable pieces that would fit into small dwellings. The tables, chairs, sofas and bookcases created, for instance by Mogensen (1914-72), who worked for the Danish Co-operative Society from 1942 to 1950, were neat, flexible pieces often recalling traditional chair types.

In addition to this socially orientated furniture, however, Mogensen also developed a range of more exclusive chair designs in wood and leather which he named his 'hunting chairs'. The clear African inspiration behind these pieces was also noticeable in the work of his younger colleague, Finn Juhl, who worked in the forties and fifties on a range of chairs that were much more explicitly sculptural than those of the older designers and which depended for their expressive forms on the tribal tools and weapons that Juhl eagerly collected. This strong element of 'primitivism' visible in so much Danish furniture of the period became a major feature of its popular appeal, making it a fashionable interior design style in the fifties. Danish furniture was widely sought after and often emulated — usually badly.

Danish metalwork has also earned a strong reputation, beginning with the work of Georg Jensen in the early century, moving on through that of Kay Bojesen (1886-1958) in the twenties and thirties to that of Henning Koppel in the post-war period. They are all known for simple everyday ware, epitomized by Bojesen's *Grand Prix* cutlery set of 1938. Like the rest of twentieth-century Danish design metalwork has continually displayed a simple elegance which has lent the objects a beauty and usefulness undiminished over several decades. If any quality typifies Danish design in this century it is its ability to create a wide range of timeless objects that are still in production today and remain as fresh as the day they were designed. The 1944 'Chinese' chair of Hans Wegner (b.1914) as well as the even simpler version referred to universally as just 'The Chair', are among the best known Danish objects, designed with posterity in mind.

Finnish flair

Finland was later than both Sweden and Denmark in showing herself as a unified nation with an independent design philosophy. It wasn't until the Milan Triennales of 1951 and 1954 that the Finnish phenomenon became visible, mainly as a result of the wildly expressive glass designs exhibited there by the Iittala company.

In 1947 Iittala had organized a competition that was won by the designers Tapio Wirkkala (1915-85) and Timo Sarpaneva (b. 1926). Neither of them had had previous experience with glass but they both quickly

Above left: *Tapio Wirkkala's elegant 'Kantarelli' vases, designed for the Iittala glass company in the late 1940s.*
Above: *Alvar Aalto's birch stacking stools made from bent plywood and retailed by Artek from the 1930s onwards.*
Left: *Aalto's domestic trolley from the 30s, made of bent plywood and covered with white tiles.*
Below left: *A chaise longue designed by Alvar Aalto in bent plywood and canvas webbing.*
Below: *Timo Sarpaneva's dramatic glass designs for Iittala from 1953.*

developed an expressive, sculptural approach to the material that earned them international reputations in the 1950s. The designs of both men recalled craggy rock forms, a typical Finnish theme of the period, and they quickly became highly desirable objects which appealed particularly to a wealthy international market.

The Arabia ceramics company developed, in contrast, a much more democratic approach to design in the years following the Second World War. The man responsible for creating this company's design policy was its art director, Kay Franck. In the mid-fifties Franck designed a range of simple oven-to-table wares that have since become classics of modern Finnish design. His *Kilta* service, for instance, has been re-introduced and is as successful today as it was in its first incarnation.

The Finnish design style of the 1950s was both bolder and more adventurous than the other Scandinavian manifestations and this is nowhere more apparent than in its textiles and furniture, in which Finnish designers excelled themselves. Finnish textiles, in particular, were remarkable in their use of strong, screen-printed patterns and colours, characterized by an application of bold abstract motifs on monochrome grounds, and the work produced by the Marimmekko company, established in 1951, set the pace in this field. The brightly coloured cotton fabrics that emerged from the factory were mostly intended for upholstery purposes but Armi Ratia, the company's founder, also developed a range of 'pop'-inspired striped cotton fabrics which were made up into simple dress designs that showed the patterns to full advantage.

The Finnish design phenomenon of the post-war years was much less committed to the traditional craft principles that preoccupied her neighbours but relied instead upon stimuli from the contemporary world. At the same time, however, the bent plywood furniture of the great Finnish pioneer, Alvar Aalto, designed in the twenties and thirties, remained in production in the post-war period as 'classic' pieces of modern design.

Left: *Hans Wegner's armchair in bent beechwood with a plaited seat produced by Fritz Hansen. The back and arms are unified to give the chair a sculptural elegance.*
Below left: *Henning Koppel's silver pitcher and bowl from 1945 and 1950 respectively won medals at the Milan Triennale and typified the style known internationally as 'Danish Modern'.*
Below right: *Unlike many of his contemporaries, the architect Poul Kjaerholm moved from wood into metal and designed some of Denmark's most striking post-war furniture pieces.*

ITALY

Italy's design reputation in the mid-century, like that of Finland, was based on the evolution of an exclusive aesthetic which provided sophisticated items for an international élite. In the immediate post-war years Italy underwent an industrial revolution resulting in major social, economic and cultural changes within which design played a fundamental part. Like America and Scandinavia, Italy moved beyond the austere philosophy and forms associated with the pre-war Modern Movement, evolving a much more expressive aesthetic more conscious of the symbolic role of design within modern society.

To this end design in Italy rejected its former dependence upon architecture and became a much more integrated part of contemporary culture.

The Italian line

Writing in 1949 about Italian design, the British designer J.H.K. Henrion remarked that he had observed a 'family likeness' in a number of newly manufactured products. Among those that had come to his attention were Marcello Nizzoli's 'Lexicon 80' typewriter for the Olivetti company; a coffee machine for La Pavoni by Gio Ponti; Pinin Farina's 'Cisitalia' car; and the Piaggio engineering company's 'Vespa' motor-scooter. They all possessed the same organically curved metal forms. What Henrion had in fact noticed was that the Italians had been quick to pick up ideas about product 'streamlining' from across the Atlantic but that they had modified that bulbous aesthetic to create a more elegant Italian version, which they introduced after the war into a wide range of mass-produced goods from buses to coffee machines.

The sudden emergence of this style in Italy was partly attributable to the rapid post-war industrialization that had taken place there, with huge investments in new production machinery. The curves of the objects that Henrion noticed were as much the results of the metalworking machinery that Italy had imported as of the general decision to move away from the geometric forms of Rationalism, which now had uncomfortable political associations.

The new aesthetic also took the organic sculpture of men like Hans Arp, Joan Miró and Alexander Calder (1898-1976) as a stimulus rather than the squares and cubes of Modern architecture.

The combination of these factors led to the emergence of a range of industrially manufactured objects that looked similar. Castiglioni's 'Spalter' vacuum-cleaner for Rem and Nizzoli's 'Mirella' sewing-machine for Necchi, both designed in the mid-fifties, were superb examples of the Italian line at its best and came to symbolize the role of the Italian designer in Italian cultural reconstruction of the period.

Above: Fiat's little 'Model 500' was first produced in the 1930s but was remodelled after the war. Nicknamed 'Topolino' (Mickey Mouse) it was the Italian equivalent of the 'Deux Chevaux'.

Left: Ettore Sottsass' desk design for the Olivetti company from the 1950s shows the typically Italian preoccupation of the time with expressive, sculptural form.

Below: Fornasetti's surface design for this tray from the 1950s shows clearly his debt to Surrealism.

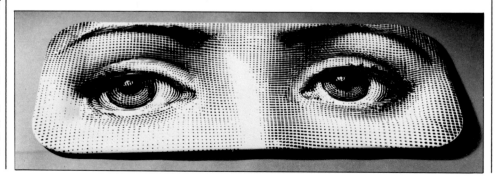

Right: *Osvaldo Borsani's reclining chair, designed for Tecno in the mid-50s shows how Italians saw furniture as technology rather than craft.*
Below: *Hans Coray's aluminium stacking chair was originally produced in Switzerland in 1938 but has been revived by the Italian furniture company Zanotta.*
Bottom: *More than any other Italian object of the period, Piaggio's 'Vespa' motor-cycle of 1947 symbolized the spirit of 'reconstruction'.*

The architect-designers

Another important factor in the sudden upsurge of Italian design after 1945 was the emergence of a new generation of designers — among them well-known names like Vico Magistretti, Ettore Sottsass, Achille and Pier Giacomo Castiglioni, Marco Zanuso and others — who had all been trained as architects in the Rationalist tradition in the 1930s but who found themselves without work after the war. They all took the next most obvious step, which was to set themselves up as interior designers in Milan, working with wealthy clients in that city. They continued this work throughout the forties and early fifties, establishing a name for themselves in the process.

Inevitably most Italian designers made the move from interior design to furniture design easily and they began experimenting with the new materials — bent plywood, steel rod, glass and, a little later, plastics. They were approached by the new furniture companies, which had either industrialized from the basis of a craft workshop or started from scratch, and were encouraged to develop a new furniture aesthetic that echoed the one achieved in technical wares. Soon the same organic aesthetic that had characterized consumer machines began to appear in furniture designs, aided by the new materials, in particular plywood and plastic foam for upholstery. The exaggerated 'streamlined Surreal' forms of the Turinese designer Carlo Mollino

(1905-73) were at one end of the spectrum, while at the other were countless simple little chairs made from bent plywood. Foam fillings were used by Zanuso (b. 1916) in, for instance, his 'Lady' armchair for Arflex and by Oswaldo Borsani (1911-85) in his reclining chair for Tecno. By the end of the fifties numerous desks, tables and chairs had begun to sprout lumpy growths and resemble the amoebic shapes of late Surrealist sculpture.

Lighting designs became pieces of sculpture in their own right, inspired largely by the mobiles of Alexander Calder and the haunting emaciated figures of Alberto Giacometti (1901-66). Companies like Arteluce and, a little later, Flos, concentrated on designs for lighting and acted as patrons to the experts in the field such as Gino Sarfatti and the Castiglioni brothers, who created remarkable pieces in this period. Technology and aesthetics developed hand in hand, resulting in countless innovative, highly expressive designs, all of which clearly reflected the post-Rationalist mood in Italian culture.

By the end of the fifties the youthful enthusiasm of the early years of the decade had died down a little and was replaced by a calmer, more sophisticated fusion of technology and form. This was the era of the plastic moulded chair as a *chic,* sculptural item, and many of the major designers of the day — among them Magistretti (for Cassina); Zanuso (for Kartell); and Jo Colombo — worked on this project, producing a variety of aggressively modern, brightly coloured and subtly curved seating objects.

The third element in the formula for success in post-war Italy was the unerring commitment of a number of manufacturing industries to the concept of design. The most significant ones included the electrical equipment firms, Olivetti and Brionvega; the furniture manufacturers Arflex, Cassina, Tecno and Artemide; and the plastics company, Kartell. Together they provided a complete patronage system without which little innovation could have taken place. Some of them — Arflex, Tecno and Kartell — were led by designers themselves and inevitably saw their contribution to modern design culture as a major responsibility.

The Triennales of the early fifties acted as showcases for Italian design, presenting a highly confident picture of it to the rest of the world. By the middle of the decade an international consensus was emerging that design in Italy had reached a level of sophistication unequalled elsewhere, and had carved out for itself a special role in world trade.

Left: *Marcello Nizzoli's 'Lexicon 80' typewriter, designed for the Olivetti company in 1948. It is made of two pieces of cast metal, the seam line being turned into a visual feature.*
Below: *A range of Italian furniture pieces from the 1950s showing the strong interest in the expressive use of colour and the sculptural potential of wood.*

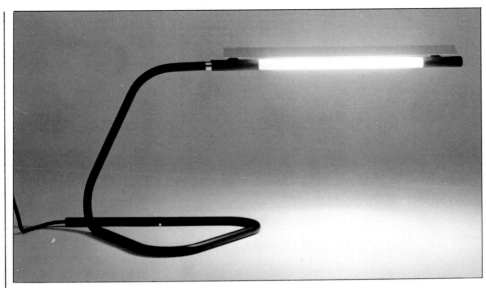

Above: *Gino Sarfatti's light for Arteluce from 1955 demonstrates the Italian interest at that time in combining simple expressive forms with new lighting effects.*

Above left: *The minimal 'Tubino' light, designed by Achille and Pier Giacomo Castiglioni for the Flos company in 1950. Form and function are expressively united.*

Left: *A collection of post-war Italian glass pieces. The use of expressive form and bright colours is a traditional concern in glass made in and around Venice and was much exploited in the years after 1950.*

Above: *A highly expressive Italian glass vase from the 1950s clearly indebted to the work of fine artists like Pablo Picasso.*

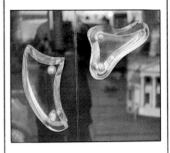

Above: *Glass door handles produced in the 1950s by Fontana Arte and now used to embellish the entrance to a London shop.*

Below: *A silver-plated coffee service from Sabattini in the 1950s shows how that medium was also influenced by the new 'Expressionism'.*

Left: *The Phonola radio, designed in 1939 by the three Castiglioni brothers. It set out to resemble a telephone so that the public would recognize it as a piece of modern equipment.*

GERMANY

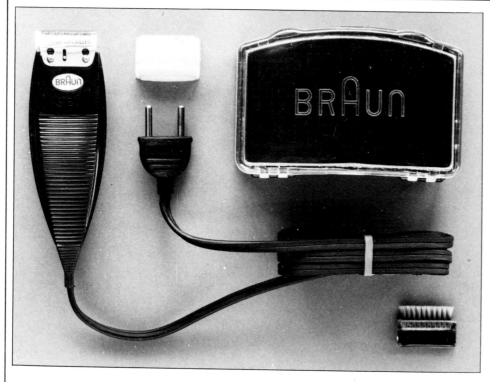

When the Bauhaus was closed in 1933 by the Nazis, avant-garde design activity in Germany virtually came to an end. Members of the staff and students dispersed to other corners of the globe and Hitler outlawed modern design, preferring Neo-Classicism as the style for his regime. A few companies, among them Arzberg Porcelain works, continued to produce simple, monochrome ware in the Modern tradition with the help of designers such as Wilhelm Wagenfeld, Trudi Petri and Hermann Gretsch, but for the most part the period after 1935 was one of isolation for Germany rather than of international Modernism — which was associated with Bolshevism. Ferdinand Porsche's Volkswagen 'Beetle', which was not, in fact, mass-produced until after the war, stands as a solitary German achievement of those years.

It wasn't until the early 1950s that Germany prepared herself for a resurrection of modern design and both the Rat für Formgebung and the Hochschule für Gestaltung in Ulm were formed in 1951. The latter institution was headed by the sculptor Max Bill (b.1908) and took on the brief of carrying on where the Bauhaus had left off. It proposed a highly rationalistic, systematic definition of design and, at first under Bill and later the Argentinian-born Tomas Maldonado, established the basis for the emergence of a 'new Functionalism' in post-war Germany. The products that emerged from the school were highly formalized, geometric, standardized units which carried the machine aesthetic even further than it had already been taken in its first incarnation in the 1920s.

A strict rational aesthetic, which became the basis of what came to be called the 'black box' syndrome in modern product design, typified the post-war German design renaissance. It was also visible in the consumer machines produced by the Braun electrical company through the fifties and sixties. Braun was reorganized in the early fifties and brought in the designer Dieter Rams (b. 1932) in the middle of the decade. It also initiated a design project with students and staff from the Hochschule at Ulm. All the radios, hi-fi sets, food-mixers and razors that Braun manufactured from this period onwards were exercises in pure form which could be analyzed down to their last visual details in terms of abstract formal principles such as harmony and proportion.

The post-war re-emergence of German functionalism was more self-consciously stylistic than the earlier version and it quickly became a major international visual language for technical consumer goods, providing a 'purist' alternative to the more overtly expressive image of the modern machine provided by the Detroit stylists. Japan was quick to emulate the German example, transforming it by the end of the fifties into a highly popular design idiom, synonymous with the world of high-technology products.

Above left: *A 'Model 550' shaver designed by Max Braun in 1951, the year in which his two sons, Erwin and Artur, took over his company. Its simple rational form was to provide the basis for the even more severe 'machine aesthetic' developed by that company in the 50s and 60s.*

Above: *The '2000' coffee-set, manufactured by Rosenthal, was designed by Raymond Loewy and Richard Latham in 1954. Its simple, elegant forms displayed a sense of order that was shared by many other German products in that period.*

Left: *One of the more decorative designs produced by Rosenthal in the 1950s. The form of this piece was designed by Fritz Heidenrich and the surface pattern, which owes much to Surrealism, by Klaus Bendixen.*

Above left: *The Volkswagen 'Beetle' was first conceived in the 1930s by Ferdinand Porsche but went on to become one of Germany's most successful and internationally recognized post-war designs.*

Above: *A photograph taken on the occasion of the opening of the Volkswagen plant in 1938. The 'people's car' had been originally conceived by the Nazis as a piece of military transportation, but its identity was later modified.*

Left: *A poster by Abram Games, produced by the Ministry of Information in 1942. The idiom owes much to the Surrealist work from the pre-war years.*
Middle left: *A convector fire made from chromium-plated steel and designed for HMV by Christian Barman in 1934, one of the more progressive British designs of the 30s.*
Below: *Telephones in moulded plastic designed by the Norwegian, Ericssen, in the 1930s. This model was widely assimilated in the pre-war years and provided an early popular image of a modern machine.*

Above: *Plastic beakers moulded by Streetley for Woolworths in the 1930s. Objects such as these were produced as cheap items for the mass market.*
Above left: *The Utility symbol 'CC1' was attached to all the furniture and fashion items produced as part of the scheme between 1941 and 1951.*
Left: *Marcel Breuer's bent plywood dining table and chairs, produced by Isokon in 1936. They represented the British Modern Movement at its best.*

GREAT BRITAIN

Throughout the 1930s Britain had been well behind a number of other European countries and the USA in applying art to industry, and the examples of British 'design' from that decade are few and far between. Despite a huge expansion in mass consumption Britain didn't move into the mass production of electrical goods on anything like the scale of the USA. British manufacturing was dominated by the traditional industries — furniture, ceramics, textiles and so on — in which design, if it was introduced at all, appeared only in goods aimed at the top end of the market. The modern design work of Keith Murray and Eric Ravilious for Wedgwood, for instance, was far from representative of the mass of production, which remained geared to traditional markets favouring decorative designs and reproduction furniture.

The dominant aesthetic where the decorative arts were concerned was a watered-down mingling together of motifs borrowed from France and Scandinavia but without the philosophical commitment that characterized the design movements of those countries. The few isolated examples of modern design to come out of Britain in the 1930s included Wells Coates' and Serge Chermayeff's radios for the E.K. Cole company (Ekco), both of them stunning exceptions to the general rule.

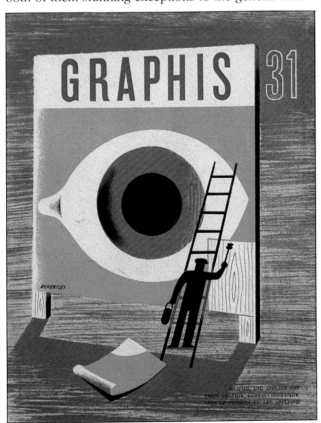

Left: *Jaeger clothing, produced under the Utility scheme, illustrated in 'Vogue' in 1944 and exhibiting primarily utilitarian characteristics.*
Below: *A dressing table designed by Ambrose Heal in 1947 for Heal & Sons. This simple wooden item was in a direct line of descent from the Arts and Crafts Movement, thus consolidating the presence of that particular tendency within British post-war design.*

Above: *Wells Coates' 1945 design in Bakelite for the Ekco radio model A22. Designed first in the mid 30s, this highly original design presented the radio as an item of furniture.*
Left: *Tom Eckersley's cover for 'Graphis' magazine in 1950. The Surrealist tendency was strong in British graphics at this time.*

The Council of Industrial Design and the 'Britain Can Make It' exhibition

Wartime Britain introduced a Utility scheme that limited the design and production of furniture and fashion for a number of years. Headed by the Cotswold-based designer Gordon Russell (1892-1980), the project favoured simple, wooden furniture based on traditional types and practical, hard-wearing clothing.

By the end of the war it had become increasingly apparent that if Britain was to compete in international post-war trade she would have to revise her attitude about the role of design in her mass-produced goods and move beyond her commitment to craft ideals. The Council of Industrial Design was formed in 1944 by the Board of Trade with the brief of raising the design standards of manufactured goods by making both manufacturers and the public aware of its potential. Russell was made director of the Council in 1945 and he brought to it his Arts and Crafts beliefs but also a commitment to the idea that craft principles should somehow be integrated into British industrial mass production.

In 1946 the Council organized a major design exhibition at the Victoria and Albert Museum entitled 'Britain Can Make It'. The press immediately dubbed it 'Britain Can't Have It' because most of the goods displayed there were intended for export. The exhibition design was co-ordinated by James Gardner and was a surprise to many people because of the dominance of an expressive, Surrealist-inspired display style. A whimsical playfulness characterized all the stands and visual references were made throughout to heraldry, pageantry and aspects of the British vernacular such as gypsies and fairgrounds. It created a highly evocative setting for the goods, which were much more mundane in comparison, ranging from kitchen equipment and luggage to sports and leisure goods and furniture, with a few examples of futuristic industrial design, including an air-conditioned bed.

The huge gap between the American influence on the design of the products and the watered-down Scandinavian influence on the decorative arts was all too apparent in 1946. While many of the products were simply modifications of 1930s designs, others were uneasy forays into the future. A handful of truly innovative designs — Ernest Race's aluminium chair, for instance, with its simple forms and splayed, tapered legs — were included but these were exceptions to the general rule which was, on the whole, governed by traditional values. The exhibition was aptly described by one critic as 'a picturesque frame for a mediocre picture'.

The Festival of Britain and the 'Contemporary' style

The Festival of Britain of 1951 was more than just a design show, it was also a tribute to the history of the British people as a whole. Design — in particular architecture — played an important role on the South Bank,

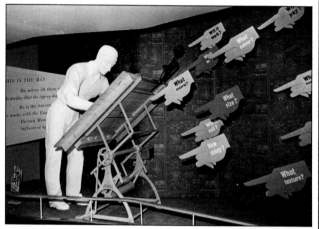

Above: *An air-conditioned bed, one of a number of 'Designs for the Future' exhibited at 'Britain Can Make It' at the Victoria and Albert Museum in 1946.*

Above centre: *A stand from the 'Britain Can Make It' exhibition of 1946 explaining the role of the industrial designer.*
Right: *Marcel Breuer's 'Long Chair' for Isokon, designed in 1936. Breuer's designs showed the strong Scandinavian influence in Britain.*

Above: *A multi-coloured three-dimensional viewer from the 1950s.*
Left: *A glass cocktail set designed for the Festival of Britain by Gaby Schreiber & Associates.*

Above: *Robin Day's 658 chair in plywood for the Festival Hall, 1951.*

Left: *A streamlined battery bicycle, exhibited among the 'Designs for the Future' at 'Britain Can Make It' in 1946.*
Below: *The Festival of Britain's South Bank site, showing a view of the 'Islanders' on the River Walk with the Skylon behind them.*

Ernest Race was born in 1913 and studied architecture at the Bartlett School in London before going on to work in the design department of Troughton & Young, a lighting manufacturer. In 1946 he founded Race Furniture Limited and began working, with a light engineering manufacturer, on a series of chairs that exploited new materials such as aluminium and steel rod.

From the beginning Race was committed to the idea of modern furniture but took many of his ideas — winged chairs and tapered legs, for example — from the eighteenth century. He died in 1964 and is best known for his two little metal rod chairs designed for the Festival of Britain. His 'Antelope' chair, *right*, with its airy structure of a moulded plywood seat on a curvaceous steel rod support — it was designed for outdoor use — typifies the

Contemporary inspirations of amoeba shapes and, in its ball-knob feet, atomic structures. His 'Heron' easy chair of 1948, *above*, combines upholstery with steel rod legs.

SPIRIT OF THE AGE OF STREAMLINING

Two incompatible sets of priorities were abroad in the years straddling World War II. American corporate designers were learned in Modernist theory, but nevertheless found bulbous aerodynamic bodyshells an appropriately slick garb for the wares of a vigorous, efficient society with an aggressive faith in its future. Flashy exaggeration at the hands of the stylists, ever compelled to 'improve' on last year's model, gave streamlining a bad name. A counterpoint, more sympathetic to human scale, was provided by both the cool elegance of Scandinavian 'modern' and the light sculptural forms of furniture and domestic wares from the late 1940s onwards, the bright palette that went with them dissolving post-war gloom.

1935 Plastic radio by Emerson, *left*, is tuned into the streamlining idea, its controls resembling rocket nose-cones.

1953 Two Vogue picture discs, *below* – records in their own right of early 50s American lifestyle.

1944 Plastic record racks from wartime America, *below middle*, moulded with a frieze depicting D-Day landings.

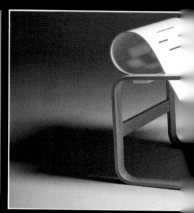

Studebaker State Close Coupled Saloon

Here is two-door safety that's much appreciated by families with small, active children, yet to look at this beautifully styled Studebaker from the outside, you would never guess at the 6-passenger roominess it provides. With the yacht-like lines of a sport coupé, this State Commander Saloon is a popular car in every smart circle—especially with the " young marrieds " and those on the way to be.

1942 Art Deco razzmatazz rounded out into middle age in this Jukes Symphonola Classic juke-box by the Seeburg Corporation, Chicago, *above*.

1950 Charles Eames' stacking chairs on steel-rod legs, *left*, produced with moulded fibreglass seats by Herman Miller. The organic inspiration provided an alternative to aerodynamic design.

1954 Armchair manufactured by Artek, the company founded by the innovative Finnish designer Alvar Aalto, *top centre*. It is based on his pioneer experiments with plywood, conducted in the 1930s.

1939 Clearly aimed at the family motorist, this two-door saloon from the Studebaker catalogue, *top*, is nevertheless consciously styled with 'the yacht-like lines of a sports coupé'.

1955 The advertisement called this new Cadillac, *above*, 'inspiring to behold.' Chrome 'rocket' projections on the fore-end and gleaming lateral trim exaggerate a long aerodynamic profile. Streamlining was clearly a style intended to appeal to aspiring Americans whatever their income bracket.

1942 Swirling stripes echo the timelessly graceful outline of this glass bowl, *top left*, designed by Edward Hald for the Orrefors glass factory.

1946 Condiment set in Melamex melamine, *above*, the innovative design by the Briton A.H. Woodfull giving an early taste of the organic sculptural forms that dominated the fifties.

1952 'Fruit Cup' cotton furnishing fabric manufactured by Warner & Sons to a design by the Paris studio, Leibert — a celebration of Festival style capturing the festive mood of the Coronation. Launched in 1953 and available until 1959, this successful design has an imposing motif — the cups are almost 30cm/12in tall.

1938 Streamlining aesthetic applied by Raymond Loewy to that most immobile of domestic objects, the refrigerator, *above*, for Electrolux.

1947 Post-war Britain rejects streamlining: a kitchen suite of Utility furniture, *centre right*, its 'sensible' shapes and sound construction — albeit from machined parts — echoing Arts and Crafts.

1955 'Contemporary' furniture of typically organic outlines on spindle legs, collected in a re-creation of a 1950s setting, *bottom right*.

1939 Hollywood sci-fi fantasies given three-dimensional expression in Walter Dorwin Teague's DuPont building at the New York World's Fair, *above*.

however, as it provided a new, light and modern environment that was to characterize the Festival and to spread into British everyday life by the end of the decade. The buildings themselves were dominated by the use of steel and aluminium and by their aesthetic qualities of openness and lightness. Industrial design at the Festival was also characterized by a use of light metal structures, epitomized by Ernest Race's 'Springbok' and 'Antelope' chairs which, made of steel rod bent into curved, elegant silhouettes, became symbols of what came to be called the 'Contemporary' style.

Contemporary style replaced 'Modern' in Britain in the 1950s and quickly developed there into the most popular domestic idiom of the mid-century. It borrowed openly from Scandinavia, the USA and Italy and encouraged the use of pattern and colour, providing they were inspired by contemporary rather than traditional sources.

The work of the Festival Pattern Group was an important source of decorative motifs in the fifties as it set out specifically to derive new patterns from science by analysing the formations of crystalline and molecular structures. This search for a new decoration discovered small motifs that were soon found repeated in bright colours on the surfaces of textiles, wallpapers, ceramics and architectural constructions.

'Contemporary' was in essence a complete interior style that combined light furniture — made of wood, metal or both — with patterned wallpapers or carpets and such novel items as room-dividers or plant-stands. Together these elements created a new sense of space which became a hallmark of fashionable fifties interiors. The impact of the Contemporary style was that of an essentially humanistic aesthetic which exploited the expressive potential of colour and pattern and replaced the severity of Modern with a new lightness and optimism. Inevitably, as a popular style it was frequently abused and freely adapted but its essence remained a strong visual symbol of the mass acceptance of design in Britain after the war.

While the model of Scandinavia was welcomed enthusiastically by all levels of society and was highly visible in High Streets all over the country, the American influence was treated, by the design establishment at least, with a great deal of mistrust and fear. For them styling represented the acceptance of a set of excessively commercial and superficial ideals and of an unacceptably vulgar style. *Design* magazine dismissed streamlining as a false doctrine and discouraged designers from looking to the USA for inspiration, unless it was to the furniture of men like Charles Eames or Harry Bertoia.

Although anti-American sentiment was widespread in Britain in the early fifties, by the end of the decade the impact of American mass culture, communicated through the media of movies, advertising and pop music, was a force too strong to be resisted and its influence on the youth of Britain a major agent of social change.

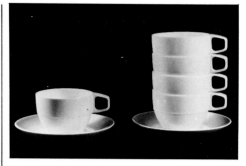

Above left: *A set of stacking cups in plastic designed by Gaby Schreiber in 1946.*
Above right: *Plastic tumblers, designed by Gaby Schreiber in 1958 for use in aircraft.*
Left: *A steel coffee maker, designed in the 1950s but still available today, which exploits the American idiom of 'streamlining'.*
Below: *Rock'n'Roll dancers in a London ballroom in the mid-1950s.*

160

Left: *A cover design for a magazine called 'Everyman' by the Russian-born industrial designer Misha Black.*
Below: *A 1951 photograph from 'Illustrated' depicting a milk bar in Leicester Square. It was part of a camera survey of London undertaken by the magazine.*

Above: *Two pieces of British 'kitsch' from the 1950s which owe much to Surrealism.*

MASS STYLE

By the second half of the fifties the world had become a very different place to live in from that of twenty years earlier. More and more people participated in both the production and consumption of everyday goods, and design had become a prominent feature of many more peoples' lives. It meant buying and using products which were part of contemporary culture and which communicated instant life-style values.

The debate about the meaning of 'good design' raged strongly in the decade after the war in the establishment circles of many countries. Many of them tried hard to stem the tide of the growing concept of 'mass culture' and 'mass taste' and to hold fast to the traditional craft-based values for designed artefacts with which they were all imbued and which meant so much to them. By the mid-fifties there was a sense, however, that they had failed in their attempts and that they were engaged in an essentially pointless task of trying to impose a set of values upon a reluctant public.

Exhibitions at the Museum of Modern Art in New York were just one attempt to restore 'good taste' to the world of American design, while in Britain Gordon Russell wrote extensively on the subject in *Design* magazine, and in Germany the concept of 'good form' was discussed at length. However, in the mass environment, design as a high-minded ideal was being replaced by design seen as style in and for itself, with life-style as its closest ally.

A pluralistic model of design was also beginning to enter the picture as various countries tried to evolve distinct national styles for themselves and different markets within the same country opted for different styles. It was becoming increasingly apparent during this period, however, that design was an essentially international phenomenon, as an object produced in Germany, for instance, was consumed in, say, the USA. The buying and selling of numerous artefacts functioned, therefore, on a completely international basis and events like the Milan Triennales, the annual Aspen design conferences in Colorado, which examined themes that interested the international design community, and the formation of the International Congress of Societies of Industrial Design in these years helped to consolidate this tendency towards internationalism.

Within national boundaries, however, differences in taste were still unresolved and the gap between establishment and mass taste expanded to the point where the designer was presented with a fundamental dilemma about who he was designing for. By the mid-fifties this gap had become, in many cases, an unbridgeable chasm resulting in a major confrontation which threw the questions about design and mass style up into the air once again.

Rear view of a 1959 Cadillac El Dorado.

CHAPTER SIX

MODERNISM GOES POP

THE AGE OF AFFLUENCE
1955-1975

'It'll be a great day when furniture and cutlery design, to name but two, swing like the Supremes.'

MICHAEL WOLFF, 1964

INTRODUCTION

It wasn't until the mid-1950s that the crippling effects of wartime austerity had finally been played out. In Britain, for instance, rationing went on until the early years of the decade and the countries that had been defeated in the war – Italy, Germany and Japan – inevitably took a while to get back on their feet and to establish their post-war presence in the world market. Ironically, when they did so it was these vanquished countries rather than the victorious ones that succeeded in using the idea of design in their economic reconstruction most effectively. By 1955 each of them had evolved a sophisticated design policy and style which was to help restore their national identities and confidence.

The countries that had emerged victorious from World War II – among them Britain, France and the USA – took a back seat in the deliberate economic exploitation of design. France, for instance, so strong an influence on the international decorative arts throughout the nineteenth century and into the twentieth, failed to transfer her energies into the development of an industrial design aesthetic after the war and, as a result, faded from the international picture.

The high period of the USA's influence on international design events had been the interwar years. Its joint achievements of the formation of the consultant design profession and the creation of a new style for mechanical and electrical goods marked out those years as ones of major significance. The high fees charged by the 'superstar' pioneer consultants resulted, however, in their rapid demise after 1945. Increasingly from the 1950s the USA looked to Europe for inspiration, at least where design as a synonym for high culture and 'taste' was concerned. When mass style was in question, however, a very different picture was rapidly emerging.

The Impact of Americana

The design legacy that America passed on to the post-war world was in fact two-fold. On the one hand the professional structure for the practice of industrial design, established by men like Walter Dorwin Teague (1883-1960) and Norman Bel Geddes (1893-1952), was emulated on a world-wide scale and consultant design offices sprang up in many countries all over the world, among them Britain, Sweden, Italy, Germany and Japan. They all focused their attention on the design of goods in the non-traditional sector – what one writer in the thirties dubbed the 'artless industries', that is automobiles and what came to be called, ironically, 'consumer durables'. A designer like Sixten Sason (1912-69), for instance, could emerge at this time in a country like Sweden, which had such strong commitments to the traditional decorative arts. Sason designed vacuum cleaners for Electrolux and cars for the Saab automobile company which had the same streamlined forms as

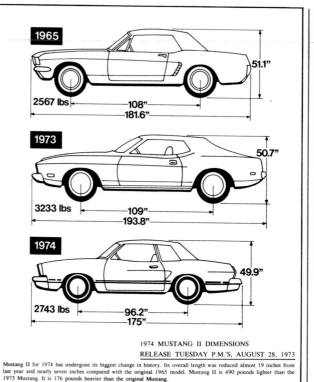

1974 MUSTANG II DIMENSIONS
RELEASE TUESDAY P.M.'S, AUGUST 28, 1973

Mustang II for 1974 has undergone its biggest change in history. Its overall length was reduced almost 19 inches from last year and nearly seven inches compared with the original 1965 model. Mustang II is 490 pounds lighter than the 1973 Mustang. It is 176 pounds heavier than the original Mustang.

FROM: FORD DIVISION PUBLIC RELATIONS, P.O. BOX 1509, DEARBORN, MICH. 48121

Above: *Plastic components of a Herman Miller system designed to store pharmaceutical products.*
Above left: *The dimensions of the 1974 Mustang compared with the larger models of previous years.*

American products. Sason also cooperated with these firms along the same business lines as the Americans with their manufacturing clients. Design consultancies such as the Design Research Unit, headed by Misha Black and Milner Gray, and Gaby Schreiber Associates, working closely with the plastics firm Runcolite, flourished in Britain, modelling themselves on their American counterparts.

The other major contribution of the USA to post-war design lay in the area of mass culture. While the exhibitions at the Museum of Modern Art in New York, held in the early fifties, had put European products — Pinin Farina's 'Cisitalia' sports car and Hans Wegner's elegant wooden furniture among them — on a pedestal captioned 'good design', on the streets outside the tail-finned extravagances from the assembly lines of General Motors, Ford and Chrysler began to arouse a quite different kind of interest. Coupled with the impact of Hollywood movies, advertisements and pop music, an alternative idea of American culture emerged that was soon to invade the homes and streets of industrialized nations all over the world.

The consumer society expanded in leaps and bounds in these years and focused its attention, where material goods were concerned, on the American home, which was illustrated widely, usually in advertisements. The bulging, bulbous fridges, food-mixers, deep-freezes, dish-washers and electric can-openers that dominated the spacious 'open-plan' American kitchen, and the huge finned automobile parked outside in the garage adjoining the suburban house, were American inventions appropriated by an eager European audience the moment it was given the opportunity. These were the 'cocacolonization' years in which, by means of the financial aid that the USA poured into Europe, America spread its culture over the capitalist world. In so doing it affected the lives of millions of people, many of whom had never before even contemplated the possibility of buying a fridge or a car.

The rapid change in life-style experienced by countless people in the industrialized world in the late fifties was a direct result of the influence of the American economy and of that country's approach towards styling and what came to be called 'built-in obsolescence'. Numerous articles were written attacking the evils of styling and object obsolescence but they had little restraining influence on the far-reaching effects of American-style consumer marketing.

The new consumer society

One of the main ideas imported into Europe from America in the late fifties was that of the 'teenager', who quickly became one of the most important consumers of all. A youth market emerged in these years with a considerable disposable income to spend on luxury goods and life-style accompaniments. In Britain the advent of Rock'n'Roll, also imported from America, brought numerous stylistic implications with it for fashion goods and consumer durables. The ready-to-wear clothes industry, for instance, already fairly well established on the American model in pre-war Britain, was revolutionized. It evolved rapidly to meet the expanding needs of the teenage market, which also greedily consumed such necessary life-style accompaniments as motor-bikes, motor scooters, transistor radios, hi-fi equipment and other items suited to its sub-cultural requirements.

With the new wealthier markets well established by the end of the fifties — women, too were financially more independent than ever before and represented a more powerful market where goods for the home were concerned — it was now possible for the first time to talk not only about mass style but mass *styles*. Industrialized society had become both richer and more fragmented and, as a result, design became more pluralistic. This period also represented the death knell of the monolithic pre-war design philosophy of functionalism, which had depended upon a set of hard and fast rules. This was the beginning of a more eclectic, open-ended approach towards design and style, which welcomed both the 'throw-away' ethic and the idea of symbolic appropriateness in objects, seeking to fulfil short-term rather than long-term needs. The commercial appropriation of style was there for all to see and it drew its sources, magpie fashion, from both the contemporary world and the past.

The 1960s were dominated by the explosion of mass culture and by a constant search for stylistic novelty. By the end of the decade, though, the optimism of the early years was replaced by a growing awareness of the economic reality of a looming recession and a feeling that there might be more to design that just style and fun. The oil crisis of the early seventies confirmed these suspicions and, within a couple of years, the fun-loving atmosphere of the previous decade had passed into history. The optimism engendered by, for example, the first space experiments and the expansion of technology, which was seen at first as a cure for all social ills, was replaced by a mistrust of such a naïve view of the future.

Above: *A topless bathing costume design by Rudi Gernrich from the mid-60s, a daring example of what later became a much more familiar sight.*
Left: *The Japanese 'Hikari' bullet train. Although a product of the post-war period this design is highly dependent upon American streamlined trains of the 1930s.*
Right: *An early transistor radio produced in the mid-50s designed for the Radio Corporation of America. Although much smaller than its predecessors this model still depended upon Detroit for its styling details.*

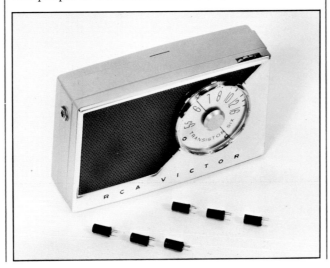

INSPIRATIONS

Consumerism drove a wedge between parents and their young. Identified as 'rebellious', the teenage market was indulged with a new panoply of goods — pop records, Levi's, motorbikes and transistor radios. By 1965 the young had won their independence and were cobbling their own lifestyle from a patchwork of contemporary sources: pop culture, advertising, comics and painting. Warhol's unashamed celebration in paint of commercial culture was picked up, as were Lichtenstein's impactful comic-book imagery and Bridget Riley's dazzling optical tricks. Before long earlier styles — Victoriana, Art Nouveau and Art Deco — were ransacked in the search for style. Resisting the shifting conformity that consumerism can induce, an 'alternative' drug culture dropped out and, barbed in Eastern robes, saw its destiny through a swirl of psychedelic colours. At the sensible end of this rainbow, escapism meant craft revival and rural nostalgia. Meanwhile, technology strived for the moon and futurist fantasies, clothed by Cardin and Courrèges and coiffed by Vidal Sassoon, graced fashion pages.

Portable pop
Transistor technology brought portability to radios. The Sony TR-55, *above*, introduced in 1955, was the world's first all-transistor radio.

Rock rebels
Post-war prosperity created a new consumer group — teenagers — a group which enjoyed vicarious rebellion through sulky-lipped idols like Elvis Presley, *right*, in celebratory gold lamé.

Consumer cult
Richard Hamilton's 1956 collage of American magazine advertisements, *above*, 'Just What Is It That Makes Today's Home So Different, So Appealing?' was virtually the instigator of the British Pop Art movement. Trivial objects from daily life became the material of art, as in Andy Warhol's 'Campbell's Soup, *above right*.

Packaging the past
Designers of the late 60s turned to the packaging ephemera of earlier decades, as in these Chad Valley game box labels, *right*.

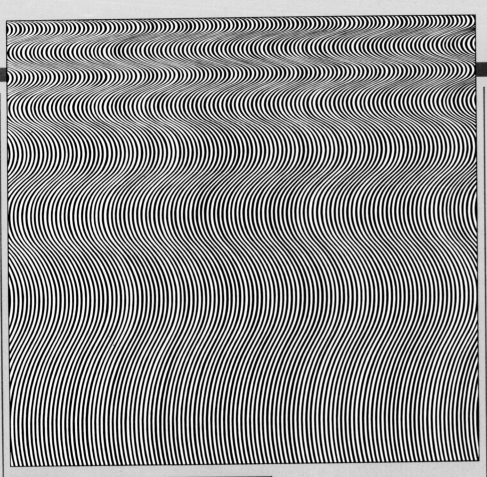

Optical options
Artistic experiments with optical effects, such as this shimmering monochromatic 'Fall' 1963, *left*, by Bridget Riley were easily translated into striking surface designs on fabrics, packaging and cheap household knick-knacks.

Space race
President Kennedy's mission to put a man on the moon before 1970 created an obsession with space, *above*, that fostered consumer gadgetry and, in fashion, futurist fantasies.

Psychedelic protest
Youth self-awareness in a nuclear age brought protest — expressed in the songs of Bob Dylan — and escapism through mystical Eastern cults. By 1965 the Beatles had made the guru, *above*, an essential pop star's accessory. The hippy drug culture introduced lurid 'psychedelic' colours, tidied up into Art Deco swirls in this Milton Glaser poster of Dylan, *left*, produced for Columbia Records.

'Ringlet' *top*, a 60s Letraset face which, with its flamboyant curlicues, is a pastiche of Art Nouveau styles. The alternative lifestyle of the early 70s required an alternative 'typeface': hand-drawn doughnut lettering *middle*, psychedelically coloured and based on the ballooning masthead faces of comics such as the 'Beano'. 'Microgramma' and 'Cooper Black', designed respectively in 1952 and 1921, were in favour among graphic designers of this period.

167

GREAT BRITAIN

Although Britain failed to evolve a consistent, internationally acknowledged design style in the 1950s and seemed to have lost some of its post-war momentum, on the level of domestic mass culture some very interesting developments were taking place that were to affect the rest of the world before too long.

An early manifestation of this was the success of the Contemporary style in providing a popular alternative to the concept of 'good design' that the design establishment was busy promoting and which was based essentially on stale 'Modern' principles inherited from the inter-war period. The outdated concept had little or no relevance for the new consumers, who were desperate to get away from the bland colours and forms which they associated with wartime austerity. The bright colours, curved forms and lively patterns of the furniture and fabrics that made up the Contemporary style provided a much-needed vitality in the mass environment, which took little heed of establishment moralizing and anti-American propaganda.

The acceptance of American mass culture in Britain was an important factor in helping to establish an attitude which, by the early sixties, had come to characterize British design, making it an important centre for anti-Modernist ideas. While the mass market was eager to embrace the new domestic life-style offered by the new 'labour-saving' consumer durables, and the youth of Britain was irredeemably seduced by the images of pop music heroes imported from the USA, at the same time, a number of 'egg-heads', as they described themselves, were also convinced that American ideas about styling and object symbolism were fundamental to a reassessment of design within contemporary society.

The Independent Group

In the early to mid fifties a group of artists, critics and architects — among them Richard Hamilton, Eduardo Paolozzi, Reyner Banham, John McCale, Lawrence Alloway and Alison and Peter Smithson — met at the Institute of Contemporary Arts in London with the explicit intention of analysing the icons of American mass culture, among other ventures. They focused their attention on advertisements, movies and automobile styling and Banham (b.1917), for instance, talked about 'dreams that money can only just buy' and the 'sex and power' symbolism of American car design. Hamilton (b.1922) put together some proto-Pop collages from a number of mass-cultural images cut out from American magazines brought back by McCale. His best-known piece, entitled *Just What is it that makes Today's Home so Different, so Appealing?*, was made in 1956 and with the countless consumer durables and references to ads and movies contained within it, it stands as a lasting monument to Independent Group ideas and attitudes.

Above: *A wall relief by Victor Vasarely for Rosenthal from 1968. The 'Op' patterns that he had pioneered reached their height of popularity in the 1960s and the boundaries between fine art and design became blurred as a result.*
Left: *A chair study by the interior designer, Max Clendenning, from the 1960s. The advances made in the use of plastic foam as an aid for upholstery made possible all sorts of new chair forms.*

Top: *A red moulded plastic chair from 1970. The new materials and techniques created new forms.*
Above: *Robin Day's polypropylene chairs, manufactured by Hille in the early 1960s and still in production.*
Below left: *Peter Murdoch's folded paperboard 'Chair Thing' for children, 1967.*
Below right: *A Finnish moulded plastic chair from the late 60s that owed much to the British Pop movement.*

The group's main contribution lay, however, in the areas of painting and sculpture rather than design for the mass market. It single-handedly inspired the British Pop Art movement which emerged, fully fledged, in the early sixties with the work of artists such as David Hockney, Allen Jones, Derek Boshier and Ron Kitaj. The group was also important, though, as a catalyst in both isolating and making intellectually respectable such notions as bright colours, 'pop' imagery derived from comic books, science-fiction and advertising and other instantly appealing visual qualities such as surface pattern and mixing them with abstract concepts like 'object symbolism' and 'expendability', which were to become such central features of the Pop Design movement a decade later.

Pop design

The Pop design movement emerged first in Britain and moved from there to a number of other international centres. It grew out of the happy conjunction of the ideas of a number of designers, dissatisfied with the antiquated ideas about design that they had inherited from the Modern Movement, with the emergence of a young wealthy market ready to invest in the objects associated with Pop culture, and the presence of a number of retailers, entrepreneurs and manufacturers, ready to employ the former and exploit the latter. The combination of these elements resulted in what was at first a rather makeshift movement, stressing fun, life-style, expendability and symbolism and rejecting austere forms and any emphasis on utility.

Many of the young designers who moved into this area had just graduated from the art schools and were keen to break down the barriers between the areas of fashion, graphics and product design. They were all in search of a new style that they could stamp on the environment as a whole and, to this end, they pillaged any and every visual source that they could find, from painting to popular imagery. The decorative styles that they developed soon covered the surfaces of countless fashion items, furniture, graphics and a whole range of small ephemeral products from clocks and trays to mugs. They were all short-lived and conformed to the formula that Banham described as 'massive initial impact and small sustaining power'.

The most visible surface patterns from the mid-sixties included flags, bullseyes, stripes and other 'Pop' and 'Op' motifs borrowed from the work of painters like Jasper Johns, Victor Vasarely and Bridget Riley. They emphasized surface colour and pattern rather than three-dimensional form and favoured the abstract motif used as an eye-catching signal.

Symbolic themes were widely portrayed, particularly those that emphasized the values upon which Pop culture depended. Among the images most frequently used were those of 'space travel' and the 'child'. These are best demonstrated in products like the capsule kitchen which derived from the space-rocket idea, and in fashion with Courrèges' 'silver-foil' suits and Mary Quant's little girl outfits complete with ankle socks — representing the twin sixties obsession with high technology and spontaneity. They were themes that summed up the optimistic nature of an affluent society, which stressed youthful values and worshipped innovation. 'Youthful' models replaced middle-aged ones in the magazines and anybody over thirty was dismissed as too old.

Pop fashion

The first people to make the Pop design movement a reality came from within the fashion industry and clothing was, predictably, the first area to be revolutionized by the growing emphasis on the youth market. The Scot, John Stephens, was the man behind the formation of Carnaby Street and, for the young female consumer, Mary Quant opened 'Bazaar' first in Knightsbridge and later in the King's Road, London, thereby pioneering the principle of the 'boutique' — the small, personalized shop — which was to dominate female fashion retailing throughout the sixties. She also introduced the miniskirt to Britain and rejected traditional French *haute couture* once and for all by using young, unsophisticated, even gawky models. Her 'play' outfits, which included a plastic mac plus sou'wester set called 'Christopher Robin' and a pin-striped suit called 'The Bank of England', redefined the way young women thought about clothing. For Quant life seemed to be one long fancy dress party and 'dressing-up' was the greatest game of all.

Fashion was the first and most obvious material expression of Pop culture and a number of other young designers, most of them straight out of art school — among them Marion Foale and Sally Tuffin and Ossie Clark — joined Quant in evolving a whole new meaning for clothing as well as a new way of selling it. In France André Courrèges broke away from his native *haute couture* tradition, creating 'space-age' outfits complete with visors, white mini-skirts and ankle boots. Through its naturally close affiliations with 'throw-away' culture and stylistic change, fashion inevitably set the pace and became the model for a number of other design areas in the first half of the sixties.

Above: *A psychedelic wall painting on a building in Carnaby Street in the late 60s.*
Above left: *A range of cardboard boxes by Cliff Richards from the mid-60s exhibiting a range of Pop patterns and colours.*
Far left: *A jacket from the mid 60s sporting one of Pop's favourite and most widely used motifs, the Union Jack.*
Left: *An interior shot of Biba's basement from the 70s with the giant cans that were used to display the food products. Biba interiors designed by Witmore-Thomas.*

Above: *A St Ivel pack for red Leicester cheese with nostalgic overtones.*
Left: *A 1961 fabric showing an early use of bright Pop colours.*
Far left: *A psychedelic Warner's fabric from 1967 called 'Pavlova'.*

Pop furniture

Because of its strong links with tradition and its associations with both physical and symbolic durability furniture was slow to adopt the Pop ethic. When in the mid-sixties it finally did respond, a number of quite radical proposals were put forward which changed the way we think about furniture for ever.

In Britain the new face of furniture was made available to the public largely through the retail medium of Terence Conran's 'Habitat' shop, which, from its first site on the Fulham Road, opened in 1964, expanded to become a major outlet for cheap, brightly coloured furniture and domestic fittings which was aimed at a young, mass market, and which was characterized by simple form and bright colour. Enamel rings accompanied painted furniture and cheap ceramics and bold textiles, many of them Scandinavian in origin.

Individual experiments such as Peter Murdoch's spotted paper chair (made, in fact, from fibre-board) showed that the throw-away principle could be applied to furniture as easily as to more ephemeral items. This chair showed the way for numerous other experiments with cheap materials and expressive forms, notable among them Max Clendenning's 'jig-saw' furniture and Roger Dean's 'blow-up' plastic chair for Hille covered in red 'fun' fur. The message was clear: Functionalism no longer had anything to say in the context of the mass, throw-away culture that was so dominant in this period and many designers were beginning to focus on the consumer and his or her psychological needs in their search for a new aesthetic theory.

In parallel the public — in particular the younger element of it — sought style rather than eternal values as its means of relating to the consumer society it saw around it and which clearly offered so much excitement. The graphic designer Michael Wolff went as far as to claim that 'it will be a great day when furniture and cutlery design ... swing like the Supremes' and even the Design Council, in the words of its director Paul Reilly, had to acknowledge the new Pop values when he wrote: 'We may have to learn to enjoy a completely new palette, for gaudy colours have long been associated with expendable ephemera'.

The style revivals

By the mid-sixties the search for style that was inspired by contemporary phenomena had virtually exhausted itself and the process of raiding the past for inspiration began in earnest. While one sector of fifties society had been preoccupied with Victorian and Arts and Crafts artefacts, mass style had tended to ignore the past in favour of more contemporary stimuli. Now suddenly it turned its head in that direction as well.

Where fashion was concerned paisley shirts suddenly broke in among the Pop and Op patterns of Carnaby Street, and Victorian decoration appeared on the surfaces of furniture, tea-cloths and curtains alongside the Pop Union Jacks and stripes. Once the floodgates had opened it was only a matter of time before the taste-

Above: *A fashion magazine photograph from the mid-60s with a Twiggy-like model wearing hot pants.*
Left: *A fashion shot from the mid-60s. The bright colours, pansticked face with dark eyes and the relaxed pose are typical of 60s' fashion images.*
Below: *A range of brightly coloured disposable paper cups and saucers and plastic cutlery from the 1960s.*

makers went through the whole gamut of revived styles from Victoriana to Edwardiana to Art Nouveau, Art Deco, the 1940s and finally into the 1950s. By the end of the decade mass style had caught up with itself.

Among the many areas affected by stylistic revivals were posters, record-covers, shop-fronts and other items of graphic ephemera touched upon by Pop culture. In Britain designers like Martin Sharp and the couple who called themselves 'Hapshash and the Coloured Coat' drew on a number of past sources for their Pop posters, including Art Nouveau, Alphonse Mucha and Aubrey Beardsley as well as Walt Disney and patterns derived from Islamic art. As a result of these eclectic interests they produced a range of highly complex posters used to promote pop concerts and records. The youth culture that consumed these artefacts was committed to hallucinatory drugs, Eastern religions and the primacy of sensation over the intellect and it sponsored a range of 'alternative' magazines, among them *Oz* and *IT*, which promoted the same visual style as the posters.

By the late sixties the interest in the past had spread beyond the esoteric obsessions of youth culture into a style, or set of styles, that were used widely in advertising graphics, shop interiors and fashion-conscious homes. Barbara Hulanicki's 'Biba' shop in Kensington, for instance, pioneered the revival of the romantic imagery of Hollywood and Art Deco and it was not long before that style became a familiar sight in the mass environment, dominating the visual interests of several social groups. It was available both in its original forms, in junk shops, and repackaged by designers as a style used in a whole range of consumer goods.

This phenomenon was not confined to Britain and the interest in revived styles rapidly turned into a major industry in the USA and in France, where it was instantly dubbed *le style retro*. Nostalgia for style was accompanied, however, by yearnings for the countryside and, in Britain, the early seventies also witnessed a popular interest in the revival of the rural image by stripped pine furniture, both old and new, and by the small flower prints on cotton fabrics produced by Laura Ashley from original Victorian patterns. Past style and contemporary design had by this time become completely synonymous for many people and could be consumed at low prices.

The craft revival

Interest in the past also led to a reassessment of earlier methods of production as well as previous styles and the early seventies saw a sudden rebirth of concern with the craftsman and his objects. The phenomenon emerged almost simultaneously in the USA, Britain and in other European countries, notably Scandinavia, where craftsmanship had never really faded. It was a sign of a reaction against industrialization and high technology.

This reversal of attitudes was characterized by the sudden emergence of small workshops that manu-

factured objects on a one-off or batch-production basis. A more sophisticated, fine-art orientated approach to the production of artefacts from the traditional applied art sector — in furniture, textiles, jewellery, metalwork, ceramics and glass — also developed bringing the concept of the 'artist-craftsman'. Their work was characterized by a mixture of traditional craft, such as thrown pots, with imagery and motifs inherited from the Pop movement of a few years earlier. While the former revivalists like Laura Ashley looked back to tradition where technique and style were concerned, the artist-craftsmen moved on to develop new forms with both new and traditional materials — wood, clay and plastics — inspired by ideas borrowed from the neighbouring areas of minimal and conceptual art. Jewellery, for instance, moved close to the boundaries of performance art, and ceramics in many cases abandoned the wheel in favour of asymmetrical, jagged shapes — as, for instance, in the work of Alison Britton.

Top: *A fashionable, long-haired youth dressed in 'flower power' shirt, walking along the King's Road, London, in the mid-60s.*
Above: *A Minale & Tattersfield grid chair from the 1970s, highly reminiscent of Le Corbusier.*
Left: *A 30s revival interior showing the 60s and 70s obsession with nostalgic styles.*
Bottom left: *The Russell Hobbs Futura 'Forgettle Kettle' from 1973, a rare futuristic design from that period.*
Top right: *Hippie-style body painting from the late 60s.*
Above right: *Cabinets from 1973 by James Gilchrist depicting the dual revivals of craftsmanship and Art Nouveau.*

Above right: *See-through plastic and lace mini-dress designed by Joan Delahaye in 1966.* Below: *A neo-Expressionist chest of drawers by Chris Holmes epitomizes one branch of the Crafts revival.*

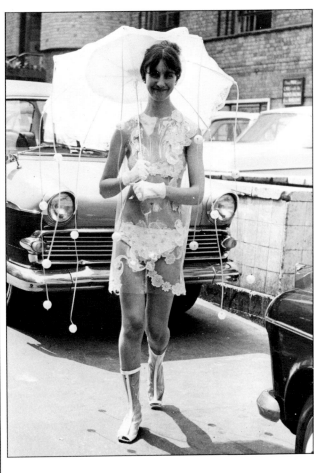

Design for need

While style for style's sake continued to be rampant in the world of mass production and consumption, there were, by the early seventies, signs of growing concern with the question of social responsibility where design was concerned.

Inspired largely by Victor Papanek's book *Design for The Real World*, published at this time, a handful of designers in a number of countries began to think seriously about design for the Third World and for the handicapped and about the question of how to make the most economic use of vanishing natural resources. The Scandinavian countries played a special role in this movement, and design groups such as the Swedish 'Ergonomi' team devoted much energy to developing special cutlery and other pieces of domestic equipment for people with physical handicaps.

Dissatisfaction with both consumerism for consumerism's sake and the aesthetic of Modernism led, in the middle of the decade, to an international crisis of design values from which we are only just now tentatively emerging. While a few grand gestures, such as the Memphis experiment in Italy, have been attempted in recent years, design is, on the whole, still reeling from the shock of its accelerated evolution and its affiliations with mass culture, which had come to a head in the 1960s.

Mary Quant, born in 1934, was responsible in the 1960s for creating a new image for the fashion designer and for fashion design, which stressed youth rather than middle age and offered fun, inexpensive clothing in place of sophisticated *haute couture*.

In 1955 Quant opened her shop, Bazaar, first in Knightsbridge and later in the King's Road, London. It offered complete 'play' outfits to a group of young people tired of the drab fashion items available to their parents' generation. Two years later she married Alexander Plunkett-Green and their business expanded through the years of 'Swinging London' to become a huge financial success, diversifying later into bed linen and cosmetics.

Quant, pictured *below* in a photograph of the time, became a symbol of London in the sixties, transforming the way that fashion is retailed to the consumer with the invention of the boutique. Two models from the sixties *above* are pictured wearing Mary Quant Ginger Group outfits.

THE USA

This baby can flick its tail at anything on the road!

Take the wheel of a new De Soto, and pilot her out through traffic toward the open road. Before you turn your second corner, you'll know you're driving the most exciting car in the world today. Here are some of the reasons why:

New Torsion-Aire ride! You get an amazingly level ride with De Soto's new suspension—Torsion-Aire. You take corners without sway . . . stop without "dive."

New TorqueFlite transmission! Most advanced ever built. Gives a smooth flow of power, exciting getaway!

New Triple-Range push-button control! Simply touch a button and *go!* Positive mechanical control.

New Flight Sweep styling! The new shape of motion—upswept tail fins, low lines, and 32% more glass area.

New super-powered V-8 engines! De Soto engine designs are efficient and powerful! (Up to 295 hp.)

Drive a new De Soto before you decide. You'll be glad you did. De Soto Division, Chrysler Corporation.

Wide new price range . . . starts close to the lowest!

FIRESWEEP—big-value newcomer—priced just above the lowest. 245 hp   **FIREDOME**—medium-priced pacemaker—exciting performance. 270 hp   **FIREFLITE**—high-powered luxury—the last word in design and power. 295 hp

DE SOTO

. . . the most exciting car in the world today!

De Soto dealers present Groucho Marx in "You Bet Your Life" on NBC radio and TV

Left: *A 1950s advertisement for the 'De Soto', emphasizing its dramatic tail-fins and chromed details.*   Above: *An open-plan office, the components of which were produced by Steelcase Inc.*   Below: *Charles Eames' plastic moulded shell chairs shown here for use in an auditorium.*

Style in the USA remained, throughout this period, divided into two separate strains. On the one hand it was under the patronage of the big corporations and, through them, spread internationally to become the dominant 'executive' style of the period. American ideas and design style determined the appearance of large internationally orientated spaces, such as airports and the office environments of large multi-national companies. The American furniture manufacturers — Knoll, Herman Miller and, on a larger scale, Steelcase — provided the office systems and furnishings for these interiors. The style was characterized by the use of black leather, chrome and glass and Charles Eames' public seating from the period provided one of the models that was widely emulated — usually badly.

In many ways the style resembled the earlier 'Modern' idiom, but this time round it was much more obviously linked to the ideology and practice of big business. The late buildings of the Modern Movement team, of Mies van der Rohe, Marcel Breuer and Le Corbusier, provided many of the American settings for

1959 EDSEL

Half its beauty is its new, low price!

Makes history by making sense

Exciting new kind of car! Plenty of room for six. Plenty of power without hogging gas. Soundly engineered. Solidly built. And priced with the most popular three!

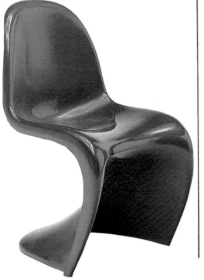

Above left: *A cover of the Saturday Evening Post depicting Eero Saarinen's Womb chair, produced by Knoll International.*
Above right: *A 1959 advertisement for the Ford Edsel automobile, a marketing exercise that proved disastrous.*
Left: *The Dane, Verner Panton's one-piece cantilevered plastic chair from the 60s, manufactured by Herman Miller.*
Below: *Charles Eames' tandem seating, a familiar sight in countless international airports through the 60s and 70s.*

Above: *A piece of American 'art glass' from 1970, made by Dominick Labino. The glass movement was one of the strongest elements of the American Crafts Revival.*

Eliot Noyes (1910-77) was the son of a Harvard professor of English and trained at Harvard's School of Architecture, where he came into contact with Walter Gropius and Marcel Breuer. His first important post was as Curator of Design at New York's Museum of Modern Art. Noyes' role at MOMA was to develop criteria for 'good design', which remained the basis of his own work for IBM executed from the late 1940s onwards.

Highly influenced by the work of Marcello Nizzoli for the Olivetti company in Italy, Noyes was employed by Thomas Watson, the son of the founder of IBM, to transform the company's identity and the appearance of its business machines. He brought in Paul Rand to tackle the company's graphics and Breuer to design buildings for it. Noyes took on product design himself and worked on a range of office equipment which have since become classics of their kind. His large electronic office typewriters were exercises in both advanced technology and sophisticated form.

In 1956 Noyes was formally appointed as Corporate Design Director of IBM and he remained in this role until his death. He was a very different kind of American industrial designer from his 'consultant' predecessors of the 1930s, who favoured streamlining and high commercialism. Noyes owed much more to the ideals of the European Modern Movement. His portable dictating machine of 1964 *below* typifies the sophisticated and elegant solutions that he achieved for IBM. His brushed aluminium petrol pump cylinders for Mobil, *above*, part of a garage forecourt scheme, suggests uncluttered efficiency in a style that survives today.

Above: *A mock-up of the interior of the Boeing 707 aeroplane designed by Walter Dorwin Teague Associates in 1956.*

Below left: *A photograph by Charles Eames of a poster, also designed by him, which depicts a range of his furniture from the 1940s onwards.*

Below right: *Marilyn Monroe at an airport in 1954, illustrated in the New York 'Daily News' of 10 September of that year.*

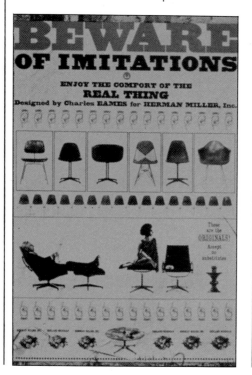

Top: *A Herman Miller factory line showing the production of the Charles Eames moulded fibre-glass shell chair. The rubber shock mounts that cushion the junction of the steel legs and the plastic seat are shown on the left of the picture.*

Above: *Children clambering over a rocket-shaped playground device in Los Arboles Park in Torrance, California. It was built as a means of getting children off the streets and into the playgrounds.*

this corporate style, which stressed efficiency and anonymity.

The consultant design teams that survived into this period moved increasingly into corporate design as well, developing what were called 'corporate identity' schemes for the big organizations. Teague Associates, for instance, continued, after the death of its founder Walter Dorwin Teague in 1960 to work with the Boeing company, designing plane interiors that were respectable but unadventurous as well as advertising brochures and graphics that were representative of the American advertising style of that period.

Probably the best known industrial designer of these years was Eliot Noyes (1910-77) who worked with IBM from the late fifties, designing a range of 'golf-ball' typewriters that have since become familiar in the modern office. Noyes was also employed as a consultant by Mobil and his no-nonsense petrol pumps which were simple, functional products with a strong corporate image for that company epitomize the corporate style of the sixties and seventies.

It was also in these years that the days of the large American automobile — that object which had inspired so many eulogies as the 'Gothic cathedral' of mass culture in the fifties — drew to a close. Following the publication of Ralph Nader's book *Unsafe at any Speed* in 1965 the huge finned monsters were finally considered to be little more than death-traps and were replaced by the 'compact' car, a concept that could never outdo its predecessor where popular symbolism was concerned.

Throughout the 1960s the USA felt the impact of the same youth styles that had characterized British mass culture. The neo-Art Nouveau graphic movement, for instance, found its American equivalent on the West Coast and became the visual accompaniment to the 'Hippie' movement of the late sixties. From that moment onwards a rapid succession of popular styles emerged in the USA, stemming both from revivals and new experiments.

While America continued, and still continues, to be highly style-conscious there were, however, relatively few signs of native innovation, as most of its fashionable styles were imported either from Europe or from Japan. It was not until the emergence of the Post-Modern movement in the late seventies that America could be said to have given birth to a new design aesthetic that was all its own.

Top: *An advertisement for two ranges of Charles Eames seating, including his famous lounge chair of 1956.*
Above left: *A Mickey Mouse telephone produced by the American Telecommunications Corporation.*

Above right: *A picture phone produced by the American Telecommunications Corporation.*
Left: *A photograph from an American fashion magazine of the mid-1960s showing Pop-inspired underwear.*

ITALY

After 1955 design in Italy continued to play a strong role within that country's cultural life and its position in world trade. By the end of the decade the naïve exuberance of the early post-war period had been replaced by an increasing sophistication in its manufactured goods. The foray into plastics, for instance, which was accompanied by the development of a *chic* aesthetic smacking of the 'good life', engendered a range of objects which communicated Italian design values to the rest of the world. Unlike the Scandinavian style, which was centred around the human being and was based on natural materials, Italian objects of this period — notably furniture and electrical products — were isolated exercises in sculptural form, usually presented in catalogues without a backcloth, as if suspended in space and indicating, through their slick aesthetic, exclusiveness and luxury. Black leather, chrome and highly finished plastics were the materials of the domestic furnishings of the period, accompanied by lighting forms which recalled abstract sculpture. Together these elements made up what came to be called the 'techno-chic' style. By the middle of the sixties it filled the pages of glossy interior magazines all round the world.

'Techno-chic' made no concessions to the past. It stood for an essentially contemporary society dominated by conspicuous consumption and rapidly became the international hallmark of sophistication and affluence. It succeeded in providing an international, wealthy, taste-conscious market with the appropriate material symbols with which to create their personalized environments and express exclusive life-styles.

The main protagonists of this Italian style were the same names that had dominated the previous decade, many of them indeed still working with the companies that had offered them employment in the immediate post-war years. Vico Magistretti, for instance (b.1920) worked with Cassina from 1960, creating many of its most memorable pieces in those years, among them his plastic dining chair of the early sixties and, more recently, his 'Sindbad' sofa. Marco Zanuso (b.1917) and Richard Sapper (b.1932) provided Brionvega with many of its *chic* electrical products; and the Castiglioni brothers, Achille and Pier Giacomo, worked with, among other companies, Flos and Zanotta. Jo Colombo emerged as one of the heroes of the decade providing, before he died prematurely in the early seventies, some of its most memorable icons, among them his minimally elegant 'Spider' lamp and his 'Elda' armchair, with its white moulded plastic shell and rich upholstered leather infill. Lighting stands out as a high achievement of this period and no sophisticated interior was complete without a piece of Italian 'illuminated sculpture'. Castiglioni's 'Arco' light for Flos is probably the ultimate 1960s Italian design object.

Above: *Achille and Pier Giacomo Castiglioni's little tractor seat for Zanotta. Designed originally in 1957, it has remained in production since then.*
Left: *The Dandolo chair from 1970, one of the most remarkable and expressive of the plastic moulded chairs to come out of Italy.*

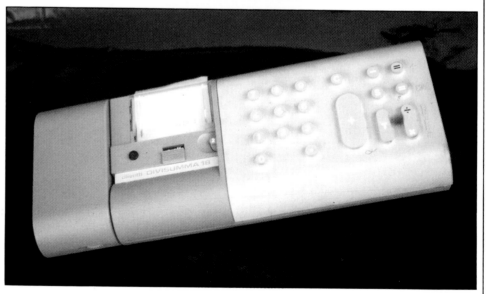

Radical Italian design

While mainstream Italian design grew increasingly sumptuous and expensive-looking in these years and finally severed its links with the democratic idealism that had characterized the early years of national post-war reconstruction, the 1960s also witnessed the birth of an 'alternative' design movement in Italy that debated the role of design within manufacturing industry and its unquestioned alliance with advanced capitalism and consumption. Dubbed 'Radical Design', 'Anti-Design' or 'Counter-Design', this movement provided — theoreti-

Above: *Mario Bellini's little calculator for the Olivetti company, designed in 1972. The sensuous curved surfaces and light colours made it a product that was to inspire many others.*

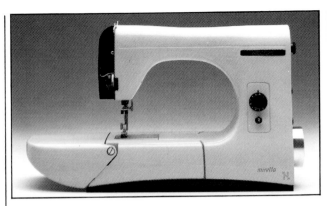

Left: *Marcello Nizzoli's elegant 'Mirella' sewing machine designed for the Necchi company in the mid 1950s.*

Left: *Ettore Sottsass' playful yellow secretary's chair for Olivetti from the early 70s.*
Far left: *Brionvega stereo radiogram of 1966, designed by A. and P.G. Castiglioni in a chic 'dice' casing inspired by Op art.*
Below : *Poltronova's 'Joe Sofa', a familar Pop icon which owed much to Claes Oldenburg.*

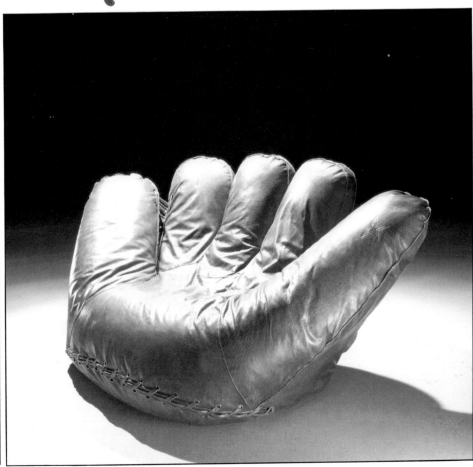

Born in Milan in 1920, Vico Magistretti trained as an architect in the polytechnic of his home city, graduating in 1945 and subsequently becoming one of the leading Italian architect designers of the post-war period.

Like so many of his colleagues, he turned from architecture to furniture design in the 1950s because of the lack of available work in architecture. He co-operated with a number of the newly formed furniture manufacturing companies of those years. For Arflex, for instance, established in the early fifties, Magistretti designed one of the first brightly coloured plastic moulded dining chairs to come out of Italy. His concern was to become intimately acquainted with the technological possibilities of the material and to design elegant sculptural forms reflecting the moulding techniques involved.

He began working with Cassina in 1960, providing numerous chair designs for the company. 'Sindbad', *above*, produced in 1982, was inspired by a horse blanket that Magistretti came across in a London shop. The little red wooden chair with the rush seat, *below*, is a Cassina design from the early sixties showing his continued commitment to furniture traditions.

Magistretti's work for Cassina from 1960 to the present is all characterized by a restrained elegance, an understanding of the materials involved and a strong sense that the object is going to be used by human beings who require comfort and practicality from their furniture.

cally at least — an antidote to the status quo that was inextricably linked with capitalism and conspicuous consumption. It proposed a more environmental, humanistic design philosophy that embraced the notion of popular taste as an essential element.

The unchallenged father of this movement was the architect-designer Ettore Sottsass (b.1917) who, from 1958 onwards, worked as Olivetti's chief consultant designer in the areas of computers and typewriters. While Sottsass integrated some of his 'alternative' ideas into his work for the company — visible, for instance, in his famous Pop-inspired red 'Valentine' typewriter and in his bright yellow secretary's chair — it was primarily in his more private work, in his designs for furniture and ceramics, that he brought his radical ideas to full maturity in the sixties.

Two major influences determined Sottsass' thought processes and design activity in this decade. The first was American Pop art and culture and the second was Indian mysticism and primitive cultures. Both sources provided Sottsass with an alternative definition of objects. He saw them as visual symbols which were integrated into the culture that created them but which allowed their users freedom of operation at the same time. The objects he saw around him, and which inspired his ideas at this time, were defined by him as 'aids to liberation', providing potential paths of freedom for the individual who either used or contemplated them.

The British Pop Art movement was a strong influence on Radical Italian design in this period. The Florentine architectural group Archizoom, for instance, openly acknowledged its debt to Britain's Archigram and that team's comic-book style visualizations of future cities. From 1966 a number of Italian architectural groups — among them Superstudio, Gruppo NNNN and Gruppo Strum — chose the 'alternative' path and devoted their energies to working on Utopian visions of the future, which appeared in the forms of sketches or photographic collages rather than built constructions. They all openly embraced the concepts of 'bad taste' and stylistic revivalism as crucial ways of bypassing the 'techno-chic' aesthetic and debated at length means of working outside the mediation of mass manufacturing industry.

Radical design reached its apogee in the late sixties, when it coincided with the student revolutions and found an eager audience in all those disillusioned by the consumer society they saw around them. The visionary work produced as proposals for an alternative environment appeared in exhibitions and radical periodicals, predominantly *IN* and *Casabella*, but few projects were actually realized. Superstudio's 'Dream Beds', for instance, appeared only in prototype form.

The line between mainstream and radical design remained clearly drawn, although a few companies tried to break into the latter area and exploit it commercially. Zanotta, for instance, produced its 'Sacco' and 'Blow' chairs in this period, the first a shapeless bag with

Above: *Gae Aulenti's chair, sofa and coffee-table suite, 'Stringa', designed for Poltronova, demonstrates the Italian obsession with chrome and leather.*
Left: *Joe Colombo's bar stool 'Birillo' for Zanotta of 1972 reveals his sense of formal innovation and visual elegance.*

Below left: *The inflatable 'Blow' chair, designed by d'Urbino, Lomazzi and de Pas for Zanotta in the mid-60s characterized the Italian Pop movement of that decade.*
Below right: *The Castiglioni brothers' table lamp for Flos which exploited the effects achieved by indirect lighting and became a classic Italian design of the 1960s.*

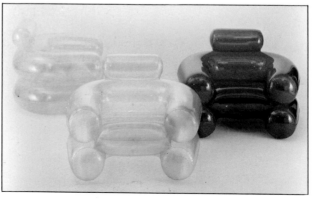

polystyrene balls inside it and the second a transparent inflatable plastic chair. These were followed soon afterwards by 'Joe Sofa' a huge stuffed leather base-ball glove which owed a strong debt to the American pop sculptor Claes Oldenburg. For the most part, though, the paths between the two areas remained uncrossed and Italian Radicalism had little influence on mainstream furniture production.

The unrelentingly Utopian nature of radical design proved, in the end, its undoing and by the early seventies most of its exponents had faded from view. Sottsass continued to work for Olivetti but became increasingly disillusioned about design's radical function within contemporary society. Italian mainstream design continued to dominate the international market, although its message became increasingly muted and its forms less remarkable. A few individuals came to the fore in this period, among them Mario Bellini (b.1935) with his wedge-shaped typewriters for Olivetti. They created a new style for high technology consumer goods that was quickly picked up and copied, particularly in Japan.

Italy was still the country on everybody's lips where 'high style' was concerned, however, and by this time it had completely eliminated the last vestiges of Scandinavian humanism. This latter style had lingered into the early sixties on the international scene but was eventually replaced by Italian *chic*.

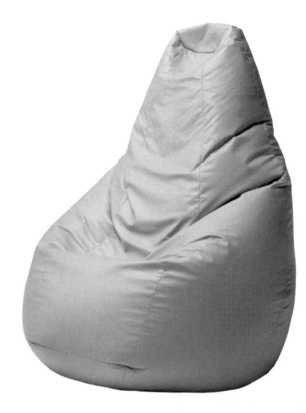

Above: *A piece of 'Pallandro' wallpaper from the 1960s confirms the 60s obsession with effects of Op art.*
Left: *The 'Sacco' chair of 1968, designed by Gatti, Paolini and Teodoro for Zanotta, was an exercise in anti-form.*
Below *Ettore Sottsass' Pop Valentine portable typewriter, designed for the Olivetti company in 1969.*

FINLAND

Although we usually think of the Scandinavian contribution to modern international design as dominating the 1950s, Finland, due to its late arrival on the scene was less committed to the craft ideal and welcomed the new materials and the Pop style with open arms. This was most noticeable in the areas of textiles and furniture, where brightly coloured stripes and highly finished plastic products gave Finnish design a brand-new look in the 1960s, thanks to the work of the Marimmekko and Vuokko companies in the area of textiles and the Asko furniture firm.

Finland's lack of craft traditions meant that its designers were not, on the whole, restricted to working within a single medium. This gave rise, in the sixties, to a strong Finnish industrial design movement in which the heroes of the previous decade, Tapio Wirkkala and Timo Sarpaneva, abandoned their preoccupations with glass and moved into the creation of a range of simple domestic products, such as saucepans, all of them imbued with the elegant expressive Finnish aesthetic of those years which combined functional purpose with sculptural curves. They were joined by another name, that of Antti Nurmesniemi (b.1927) who became one of the best-known Finnish industrial designers of the sixties and seventies, representing his country abroad at numerous exhibitions and conferences. He excelled, as did his colleagues, in the design of products for the kitchen which possessed the same fine qualities that characterized the other manifestations of 'Finnish Flair'. Like the textiles and furniture, his pieces were often brightly coloured and suggested a new modern aesthetic combining high quality with new materials and modern forms.

Above: *A design from 1951 by the sculptor Tapio Wirkkala for the Iittala glass company. The decorative engraving on this highly stylized religious piece reflects Wirkkala's essentially fine art approach towards the design of modern artefacts.*

Above: *A cutlery set designed by Tapio Wirkkala for the German company Rosenthal in 1961. The aggressively modern and highly expressive silhouettes of these pieces reflect Wirkkala's background as a sculptor in the modern tradition.*

Above right: *Kay Franck's 'Kilta' oven-to-table ware, first manufactured by Arabia in the mid-1950s, has recently been put back into production. After the war it provided young married Finnish couples with functional ware they could afford. Franck was head of Arabia's art department until 1973.*

Right: *A chair by Esko Pajamies for the Finnish furniture company, Asko from 1974. Part of the 'Koivutaru' range which returned to bent birch after the plastics of the 1960s, this piece recalled the work of Alvar Aalto from the early century.*

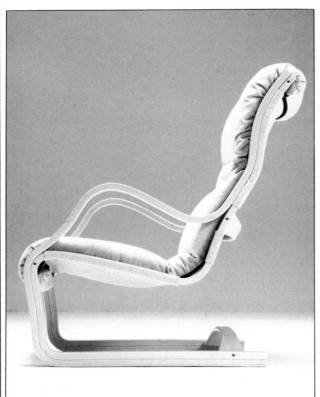

Antti and Vuokko Nurmesniemi (formerly Vuokko Eskolin) are two of Finland's leading contemporary designers, the former best known for his work in the fields of interior and industrial design and the latter for her stunning textile designs. Antti Nurmesniemi set up his own studio in 1956 while his wife began her professional career within the Marimekko company. She broke away in the early 1960s to form her own textile firm and, with Marimekko, produced the brightly-coloured printed cotton Finnish textiles, inspired by 'Pop' and 'Op', which made such a dramatic impact in the 1960s. She is committed to natural materials and goes so far as to wrap her textiles in recycled paper rather than in plastic bags. The chair from the early 1980s, *above*, was designed by Antti and covered in a textile by Vuokko. The clothing items, *right*, are made from Vuokko's fabrics showing her strong feeling for basic patterns and simple lines.

JAPAN

The progress of Japan after 1945 parallels in a number of way those of Italy and Germany. As in those countries, it was on the basis of American aid that Japan made a bid to become a major industrial power. In that effort she focused her attentions less on heavy industry than on manufactured technical goods such as cars and electronic equipment.

The story of modern Japanese design goes back to the second half of the nineteenth century, when Japan opened herself to the West and began to participate in international trade. In the early days she concentrated on heavy industries and exported only such traditional items as ceramics, fans and kimonos. In that period Japan developed a policy of watching carefully what was going on in other countries and of emulating what she saw. This continued into the next century.

Before the Second World War Japan kept herself informed about design developments in the West and went so far as to set up a design education system based on Western principles. Manufacturing was based, however, where small consumer goods were concerned, on the workshop principle right up until the 1930s, when the Americans took automobile production to Japan. The country responded quickly by expanding its own industry in competition with the Americans. Toyota, for instance, emerged in this period from an earlier loom manufacturing company and Sharp, initially set up in 1915 to manufacture propelling pencils, moved into the production of radios and gramophones.

Until 1945 these developments took place in a piecemeal manner. After its defeat in the war, however, Japan began an intensive and rapid programme of industrial expansion. By the sixties she had developed a wide range of manufacturing companies in the areas of cars and motor-bikes (such as Honda, Datsun and Yahama); cameras (such as Pentax, Nikon and Olympus); and electronic equipment, including Sharp, Sony and National Panasonic.

Post-war design

In the early post-war years Japan's products were crudely made and expressed no particular design policy. The main aim at that time was to produce cheap, technically advanced products that could be sold all over the world in great numbers. To this end vast sums of money were invested in research and development and the companies concentrated on keeping ahead of the field on a technological level.

In the fifties Japanese products emulated their American counterparts for the most part, as the greatest need was to penetrate the USA market. As a result many products looked as if they had come straight out of Detroit with their exaggerated forms and chrome details. How-

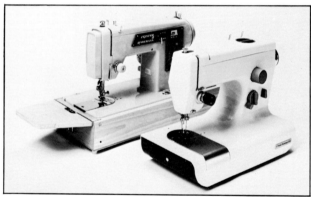

Above: *Sharp's QT-12 stereo radio cassette recorder in silver, yellow, red and blue meant the death of the black box.*
Left: *Frister and Rossman sewing machines designed to suit American (left) and European (right) tastes by Pentagram.*
Below: *Honda's 246cc 'Dream' motor bike of 1960, a visually complex machine.*

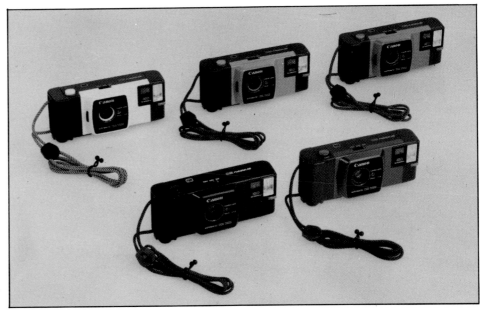

Above: *Sony's TC-777 open reel tape recorder of 1961 symbolizes a world of advanced technology.*
Above right: *Canon's little 'Snappy 20' camera of the early 80s has turned the camera into a toy.*

Above: *Sony's ICR-90 integrated circuit radio of 1969 exploits the possibilities of miniaturization to the full.*
Below: *Sony's SL-7300 Betamax video cassette recorder of 1975 became a world-wide market leader.*

ever, the Honda company set an example of how to sell Japanese goods to the USA with its little 'Honda 50' step-through motor-cycle. It was developed in a form most appropriate for the Japanese market: it was small and with an open frame (unlike the Italian Vespa, for instance, which was much bulkier), given that it had to be ridden through rice fields and narrow alleys in Japanese cities. Honda needed to sell his bike to the USA if it was to be a financially viable proposition and he had therefore to compete there with the heavy American motor-bikes and the Marlon Brando/James Dean image that went with them. He promoted it as a 'fun' bike for all age groups, appropriate for use on short outings such as shopping or going to the beach, and the idea quickly caught on. Honda broke into the American market on a massive scale.

It was clear that Japan not merely had to find a style for her products but she also had to market them aggressively if she was to find the much needed international outlets for them. From the late fifties onwards, therefore, design became an intrinsic aspect of both the mass-production and mass-marketing of Japanese products.

By the sixties and seventies Japan had found her own style and Japanese goods were all given a complex 'high-technology' look. The plethora of knobs, controls and complicated graphic details on the surfaces of its hi-fi equipment, cameras and other consumer durables was matched by the bewildering chrome details on its automobiles. The emphasis was on low-cost, technological sophistication and value for money, and Japanese goods began to flood the market, both in the USA and in Europe, on the basis of these criteria. For the mass market Japanese style stood for space-age luxury even if it wasn't always clear how the products worked or how they would fit in with the other objects in the domestic environment.

The 'Japanese miracle' of these years was the combined result of a number of different factors, not least the closely integrated role of design within production and sales. Japanese designers are anonymous team-members whose commitment to the company parallels that of the factory workers. In Japan the relationship of an employee with his company is very different from its parallel in the West. This partly accounts for the way that Japanese industry managed to integrate design into its formula for success so effectively.

The Japanese company that emphasizes design most strongly is the electronic equipment firm Sony, whose products are aimed at a slightly higher sector of the market than those of its competitors. Within the Sony organization the design department has a higher profile than in most Japanese firms and it plays a more sophisticated role in the development and sale of its products. The model for the Sony style was less that of Detroit symbolism than of German 'good form'. Through the sixties and seventies Sony paid increasing attention to visual details in its products, to features such as the harmonious placing of knobs and controls. This was in marked contrast to the more *ad hoc* styling of goods emerging from more down-market companies such as Sharp and Sanyo.

Since Sony's venture into 'good design', however, other Japanese companies have become aware of the importance of the aesthetic appeal of their goods, and have made them more 'quality-conscious' than before. Japanese goods are in most cases no longer the poor relations of their German or Italian equivalents but are often both more technically advanced and more visually sophisticated. Through its huge successes of the last two decades Japanese manufacturing industry has become much more confident about the design of its goods and includes design in its brief not simply as a marketing ploy but as a quality with its own merit.

SPIRIT OF THE AGE OF AFFLUENCE

With post-war austerity a thing of the past and the oil crisis an unforeseen hazard, the mood was one of optimism and expansionism — a time, in short, for entrepreneurs. To catch the attention of a newly prosperous young market, their watchword was novelty. This demanded jokey shapes, lurid colours and rampant surface decoration. The impetus came from a kaleidoscope of shifting contemporary obsessions — rock music, psychedelia, and escapism through oriental mysticism, Hollywood nostalgia or rural revivalism. A parallel preoccupation with gadgetry and advanced technology converted functionalism into sleek 'techno-chic', characterized by black hi-fi and crane-angled lamps.

1968 Mini-dress from Wallis, *far left*, the British High Sreet chain, one of a series of shirt dresses that, according to a fashion writer of the time, brought the expensive jersey material to the 'post classic' mass market.

1971 Fashion model, *left*, with 'mystical' eastern face make-up and bedecked in Islamic jewellery marketed by Adrian Mann at Harrods and Yves St Laurent.

1967 Bernard Rancillac's 'Elephant' armchair in plastic, *below*, produced by Galerie Lacloche in various primary colours — furniture forsakes functionalism for fun.

1957 These glass vases by Nils Landberg, *above*, are typical of the delicately fluid forms mass-produced by Orrefors. They gained world-wide popularity in the late 50s.

1972 'Lip' brand plastic-cased watch by the French designer Roger Tallon, *left*, anticipate Post Modernist colour accents on watch hands and winder.

1973 Felix Dennis, Underground Press baron, *right*, surrounded by 'alternative' magazines. Comic strip and text overprinted with psychedelic colours predominate.

1970 Toiletry and cosmetics packaging, *right*, with a touch of Hollywood glamour, from Barbara Hulanicki's Biba store, London. The Biba logo is in revivalist Art Nouveau style.

1969 'Lunar Rocket' pattern, *below far left*, by Eddie Squires for Warner's. The space race was a source of inspiration for designers.

1966 The 30-storey Federal Central Court house, *below left*. In a booming, optimistic economy, Modernist architecture such as this late design by Mies van der Rohe suggested an appropriate anonymity and efficiency.

1969 A Victorian terraced house, *below*, gets the Swinging London treatment, with psychedelic decoration sweeping across the building regardless of angles and textures.

FREE-FOR-ALL

The period between 1955 and 1975 witnessed many changes in the area of mass style, with the result that both the environment and the popular understanding of the concept have been radically transformed. This has encouraged the development of pluralism and eclecticism — that is, the possibility of many styles co-existing together and influencing each other. Thus 'high style' may be generated by an up-market élite or it may emerge from subcultures that have developed their own style on the street.

The period since 1955 has also seen the final destruction of Modernism, both as a single style and as a philosophy which maintains that people can be told by a design élite what they should like. Commercial manipulation and the mass media now perform the function of disseminating styles and of making them widely visible. Mass style can be generated by films — as was the case with *Bonnie and Clyde*, *The Boyfriend* and *The Great Gatsby* — or it can be sold through colour supplements, mass publications in general or through High Street stores.

It is easier to promote style in fashion items and cheap life-style accompaniments than it is in more expensive goods, but by the mid-seventies it was clear that even furniture and electronic equipment had strong 'fashion' or 'stylistic' elements built into them and that they were not intended to last for all time.

The demise of 'upward emulation' as the only means of disseminating style has meant that the design profession is no longer always in total stylistic control and that 'street style' is now a strong force within contemporary culture. Style can move upwards, downwards, or even sideways and the 'style-makers' have had to become increasingly open to sources coming from all over the place.

Although the affluence of the sixties gave way to a more austere period in the early seventies, design and style had by then become such popular concepts that there was no going back. By the mid-seventies design was being sold as a named concept to a larger than ever sector of the consuming public and had become one of the most clearly visible and influential aspects of contemporary mass culture.

Right — top, middle and bottom: *'Klikits', the new press fastener which took fashion fastenings into the space-age, demonstrated in action on this leather mini-skirt by Miss Liesbeth London in 1967.*

Above far right: *Suburbia in the 21st century. An illustration by Ford Motor Company's advanced stylist suggests that transportation and fashion will move forward together.*

Right: *A girl dressed in typical Hippie dress of the late 1960s. It is predominantly Indian inspired, indicating the importance of Indian culture to the late 1960s.*
Centre right: *A 1970s interior features Le Corbusier chairs and a gigantic 'Hyper-real' image on the wall behind them.*

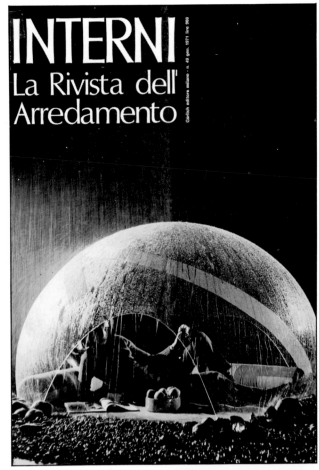

INTERNI
La Rivista dell' Arredamento

Gierlich editore milano · n. 49 gen. 1971 lire 900

Top left: *Cover of 'Interni' magazine from 1971 depicting a one-man environment capsule.*

Top right: *'nostalgic' packet design by Witmore-Thomas for the Biba store from the 70s.*

Above right: *Cubes'n'Tubes by Aberglen Holdings.*

Above: *The 'Slimstyle' Lambretta motor scooter from 1962, the first model to have disc brakes as standard equipment.*

'Casablanca' sideboard, 1981, by Ettore Sottsass.

CHAPTER SEVEN

'LESS IS A BORE!'

STYLE NOW
1975 – TODAY

'Every journalist reacted by saying that the furniture we designed was bad taste. I think it's super taste. It is Buckingham Palace that is bad taste. Memphis relates to the actual world; we are quoting the present, and the future.'

ETTORE SOTTSASS ON THE LAUNCH OF THE MEMPHIS FURNITURE GROUP IN 1981

INTRODUCTION

The sixties had been years of high consumerism, with new techniques in moulding leading to cheap, bright, even throw-away furniture and clothing. Huge box-like buildings with vast expanses of plate glass, difficult to heat in winter or ventilate in summer, were being thrown up in the fever of a building boom. Many of them have since had to be demolished or partly rebuilt because their prefabricated 'clip-together' structure proved unsound. At the same time, voices representing the 'alternative' hippie lifestyle were warning the world about the destruction of natural resources and the pollution of the environment. In some ways the prophecies seemed to be fulfilled: the oil crisis of the early seventies had worldwide repercussions and forced society to think seriously about energy conservation and economy of performance. The ideas of the designer and commentator Victor Papanek (b.1925) on the relationship of design to the real needs of consumers became influential. For the first time international design awards began to go to projects that incorporated energy-saving techniques and more serious consideration was being given to everyday human requirements in terms of physical comfort and convenience, adequate lighting and isolation from noise. 'Green Design' was born.

Consumers began to demand an uncompromising functionalism and simplicity of their domestic products, exemplified by Manhattan loft-livers who moved in to former industrial buildings and made use of industrial objects for domestic purposes. The industrial aesthetic — high tech — was born, and eventually extended across all manifestations of design, including architecture. The first exposed structure buildings were erected in Britain in the mid-seventies.

Clive Sinclair (b.1940) had given us our first pocket calculator in 1972, and a pocket television set in 1975. The first personal computer became available in 1977, and the first personal stereo, the Sony Walkman was launched in 1978. By the beginning of the nineties, computers had become so much part of our everyday lives that parents began to express concern over their children's addiction to computer games such as the Nintendo Gameboy.

The Bauhaus sparseness was supplemented by the aesthetic of clean Scandinavian interiors throughout Europe and the USA. Then, under influences as varied as pop culture, high tech and ancient classical sources, designers began to look beyond the 'less is more' formula. The first revolutionary was US architect Robert Venturi (b.1925), who declared abruptly in the early seventies: 'Less is a bore'. New decorative styles evolved, often taking advantage of new manufacturing techniques. They included a sometimes outrageous ornamentalism and the revival and further development of decorative painting and crafts, with strange cultural cocktails deliberately clashing. This Post Modern movement affected architecture, furniture,

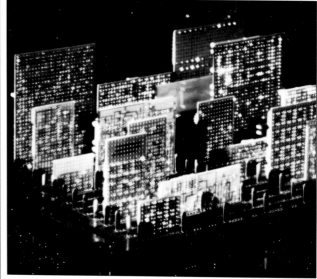

Top: *Richard Seifert's pristine and monolithic NatWest Tower in the City of London, 1981. The ground plan relates to the Bank's motif; a gleaming exterior finish exaggerates its 183-metre height.*

Above left: *Neo-Bauhaus black leather and chrome chair, the Ibis, by Boss Design. The pure lines and simple form are still popular after 60 years.*

Left: *Clive Sinclair's first pocket calculator, 1972, for the larger pocket. Later versions were the size of a credit card, and electronic gadgets of this size could incorporate circuits providing complex computer games with basic graphics. This rather bland early design has no memory.*

Above: *New York at night? No, an IBM circuit board of the mid 80s.*

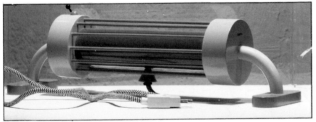

Above: *The Mazda Miata is representative of the global design business. Designed in a California studio and made in Japan, it recalls post-war British and Italian sports cars.*
Right: *Purist and functional Perpetua battery-operated table lamp, by Tobia Scarpa for the Italian company Flos, 1982.*

Below: *Prototype Post Modern radiant heater for Studio Alchymia by Michele de Lucchi.*
Bottom left: *SITE architects' Best Products showroom, Virginia, USA, its peeling façade contrasts with its functional box shape.*
Bottom right: *Branson Coates' Caffe Bongo in Tokyo, 1986; Mad Max aesthetic meets classical frescoes.*

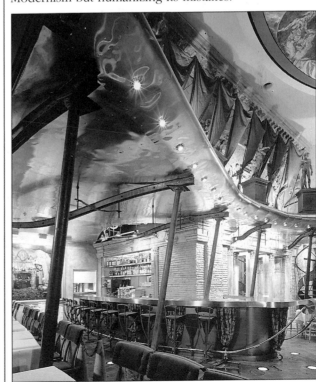

textiles and consumer products, and with a sophisticated clientèle to cater for, it had to meet high specifications of quality. The new styles added colour and humour to a bleak city landscape where Modernism had been festering and where bland computer hardware took its place at work and encroached on the home environment.

The retail boom of the mid-eighties accelerated this tendency, with new shops and stores adopting the latest fashions for interiors like so many new suits. In product design, new manufacturing techniques meant that more interesting organic shapes could supplant the black box. The use of tactile qualities and metaphor could be incorporated in objects with which the user could have a 'relationship'. 'User-friendliness' became a selling point. But as the Post Modern aesthetic was absorbed and popularized into everyday culture, it was inevitably devalued and often reduced to a meaningless confection of pastel colours and playbrick shapes.

The deep recession of the late eighties and early nineties forced people once again to take more seriously the depletion of natural resources and environmental pollution. The consumer boom was over, there had been massive redundancies in the design consultancies, and a time of reflection was called for. The term Green Design was coined and applied to anything that considered longevity, protection of rare species of plants or animals, recycling or the exclusion of non-biodegradable products in its design and use. In the domestic interior, one-off or limited-edition pieces of furniture and accessories began to replace the homogeneity of mass-produced objects, as individualism and quality took over from expendability. Neo-Modernism began to emerge, taking the rationality of Modernism but humanizing its mistakes.

INSPIRATIONS

Not content with number-crunching and filing, the computer has turned its digital hand to designing – previously one of the bastions of creative genius. Designers have tamed the beast, however, and computer-assisted work no longer always betrays its origins. Products combat the new technology with sensuous new shapes and textures and touches of humour. Even the most functional artefacts, long since slickened into sculptural techno-chic, now sport charming, even absurd dashes of colour. Bauhaus has been humanized.

The hollow ringing pipes, clanking footplates and twanging wires of warehouse, hospital and factory make sweet music in a few high-tech homes. Elsewhere, the clean breeze of white neo-Modernism is beginning to blow away the short-lived pastels of Post Modernism. Office interiors dance to the environmentalists' and humanists' tune, with manual opening windows and informal layouts. Memphis furniture, all plastic laminates in tarty colours and meaningless patterns, has yielded to the rough trade of the New Primitives.

Unrefined taste

An oil refinery, *right*, has a terrible beauty in its counterparts of silver tubes and red inspection platforms. A frugal arrangement of service tubes, *far right*, adorns the outside of the Pompidou Centre, Paris. Having all servicing elements exteriorized frees the interior space, and adds layers of visual complexity to the exterior.

Left: Despite early resistance from traditionalists, the Apple Macintosh has become a universal tool and has broadened the visual vocabulary for graphic designers, with new type designs such as this from Emigré Graphics.

194

Above right: An uncompromising functionalism is the essence of this London kitchen, designed by Eva Jiricna, 1985, using professional catering equipment and industrial electricity points. Stainless steel, glass and reconstituted stone give the design a permanence that might outlive its aesthetic lifetime.

Light music

Laser technology furthered the progress of miniaturization in sound reproduction from compact discs, *right*.

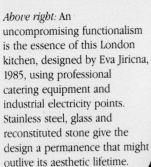

Shapes of the age

'The special qualities of Memphis' decorations are their inert, aphonic neutrality, their deliberate lack of learned references ... and their brutal figurative indifference'. This typical motif, *middle right*, recalling the molecular and crystal structures of early 50s patterns, is like an enlarged Letraset graphic tint pattern. A positive virtue is made of the non-slip pattern of a cast-iron stair tread, *top right*. Coiled cabling, formerly manufactured only in tight coils of white, black or grey plastic, *right*, was made available in vibrant colours.

During the eighties, increasingly sophisticated graphic capabilities and user access threatened to make every Mac owner a potential designer. Traditionalists like Neville Brody at *The Face* and dissenters like 8vo, designers of *Octavo* magazine, have been won over by the Apple Macintosh's versatility, flexibility and the visual approach to inputting commands.

Above: *Apple Macintosh Quadra 900 with 21-inch colour monitor.*

THE USA

The seventies brought the death of three US design pioneers. Henry Dreyfuss, the father of 'human scale', who for more than 50 years designed all kinds of objects from coffee cups to aeroplanes, died in 1972. Eliot Noyes, who trained under Walter Gropius and Marcel Breuer and was responsible for the Museum of Modern Art exhibition in 1940 which launched the careers of Charles Eames and Eero Saarinen, died in 1977. Noyes had designed for various companies including Mobil, for whom he created the classic Mobil petrol pump and mushroom filling-station canopies, and was consultant director of design at IBM from 1956 until his death. Eames, who died in 1978, was best known for his development of new materials culminating in ranges of moulded plywood and fibreglass chairs made by Herman Miller. A decade later, the death of Raymond Loewy, arguably the most charismatic of this generation of American designers, concluded the first chapter in the life of this new profession.

The place of these founding fathers has been taken by a continent-wide generation of new independent design firms. At first struggling to win the respect of industry, these designers are now hailed in magazines such as *Business Week* as the new heroes of American industry. Typical of these consultancies, usually with the word 'design' in their titles rather than the name of a founder, are Smart Design in New York, Design Logic in Chicago, and Lunar Design in Palo Alto, California. In many cases, the principals of these firms are first- or second-generation immigrants who are bringing a more European look to American design. The effect is at its most pronounced in California in part because so many Europeans have settled there, and in part because it does not have the ties to the previous era of American design leadership, the Machine Age. Here, firms such as Frogdesign and IDEO have brought sophistication to the products of Apple Computer and other high-tech companies.

Away from the West Coast, however, there is a break from Bauhaus ideals exemplified in the New York Museum of Modern Art's Design Collection. Design on the East Coast, and perhaps more significantly in the Midwest, the former 'rust-belt', is notable for its exploration of new concepts such as 'product semantics' which aim to restore some of the lost distinctiveness to American products.

Such trends are not completely new, however. American pragmatism has always softened lines and compromised good taste in the name of fun. Even the purist New York product designer Morison Cousins has created humorous objects such as a car vacuum cleaner with a 'face' and 'moustache' for Dynamic Classics, and an anthropomorphic convection oven for Maxim, combining innovative design features with a friendly appeal.

These designers have succeeded despite the demise of the former economy of abundance, in which 'new' meant this year's model and 'old' meant last year's. The oil crisis

Above: *SITE Architects' design for Best Products Showrooms, Houston, USA, 1975. Deliberate imperfection and decay, executed immaculately, with good taste and humour.*
Left: *The San Francisco based clothes chain, Esprit, has recognized the importance of design in merchandising as much as in its products. This Paris store is by Antonio Citterio.*

of the seventies changed attitudes, although not enough for some such as Victor Papanek, author of *Design for the Real World.* As the 1990s dawned after the wanton Reagan years, these crises were repeated, but now as then not all designers heed the warnings.

Furniture manufacturers such as Knoll use the best designers in the USA to execute corporate and functional Bauhaus-inspired works as they have since the thirties. Gradually, a more informal spirit has come into play, reflecting changing ideas of the workplace. Herman Miller's loosely related 'Relay' range of furniture is an example of the new thinking, while its rival Steelcase has set up a high-profile New York subsidiary, Details, which aims to commission top designers from around the world.

Another design area in which the USA has made a contribution in recent years is that of *haute couture.* For years US fashion houses went to Paris or Milan and bought or copied European designs, which continue to confer social status and respectability. But there is now a solid core of excellent US designers, including Calvin Klein (b.1942) and Ralph Lauren (b.1939), who have the same feel for immaculate cut and fabrics as the Italians. A number of more original figures have emerged, notably Donna Karan (b.1948) who has feminized workclothes while still retaining their all-American comfort and practicality.

The same continental divide that is seen in product design is also seen in graphic design. Fresh, colourful and more European-feeling work comes from the West Coast; whereas witty rather than pretty is the rule on the East Coast, with Tibor Kalman's M & Co., Drenttel Doyle Partners and others continuing in the word-centred tradition of Herb Lubalin (1919-81), Bradbury Thompson (b.1911) and Paul Rand (b.1914).

The new generation of architects was characterized by a talent for 'lateral thinking'. The SITE architects, for example, had built their controversial Best Products showroom in Richmond, Virginia, in 1972; the front of an otherwise ordinary building appears to be peeling off. Michael Graves (b.1934) emerged in the mid-seventies as a powerful force.

The vein of ironic humour running through Post-Modern design defies the years of over-serious functionalism. One side-effect of the trend is that it has restored the idea of the architect as the creator of a complete environment. Chairs for Knoll by Venturi, stained glass by Meier, and tableware for the New York company Swid Powell by almost everybody are a reminder not only of classical architectural tradition but also, paradoxically, of the holistic approach of the American modernist.

The USA continues to carry a torch for Post Modernism as the rest of the world tires of it. The style perhaps found its natural habitat in designs for overblown hotels for Disneyworld. Graves' controversial proposed Whitney Museum addition, which does violence to the original by arch-Modernist Marcel Breuer, may provide the movement's epitaph. Through all these stylistic shifts, Philip Johnson (b.1906) remained at the centre of American architectural controversy while Venturi (b.1925) is likely to be remembered more for his key writings in celebration of the vernacular, *Complexity and Contradiction in Architecture* (1966) and *Learning from Las Vegas* (1972) than for his buildings.

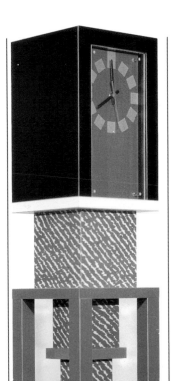

Above: *George J Sowden's fiercely Post-Modern Metropole clock for the Italian company Memphis, 1982. Grey and white paint effects are contrasted with black, bright yellow and red on the face, and touches of green and lilac.*

Far left: *Working in Los Angeles, April Greiman has fused her rigid Swiss graphics training with Californian colour and new technology to produce a distinctive new style for the region.*

Left: *Milton Glaser's work typifies the New York school with its ever-present wit and frequent allusions to art of the past.*

Born in 1934, Michael Graves studied design and architecture at Harvard, and is also a practising painter, sculptor and furniture designer. Having taught architecture for many years, he joined a group of New York architects in the 1970s, devising together a new International Style of architecture. Today, some of his furniture is being manufactured, including designs for Memphis and US Sunar company. The Public Services Building in Oregon clearly shows his richly eclectic and colourful decorative style.

Left and above: *Façade of Michael Graves' Public Services Building in Portland, Oregon, whose monumental style echoes the 2,000-year-old alabaster canopic shrine from Tutankhamun's tomb.*

JAPAN

Since 1975 Japan has consolidated its marketing lead in the consumer electronics, car and motorcycle manufacturing industries and in some cases has recently taken a design lead. Motorcycle manufacturers Honda, Yamaha and Suzuki continue to produce reliable ranges whose low cost is reflected in a spare design that for some Western enthusiasts lacks macho chunkiness. Car-makers Toyota, Honda, Mazda and Nissan once produced vehicles noted more for their reliability and economy than for any breakthrough in design. Compared with their European counterparts they seemed too American, overdressed in chrome and with fussy, uncertain bodylines.

This has now changed and Japan's designers, mainly in-house with these major corporations but with important stimuli from independent outside groups, are producing some of the most exciting products in the world. Consultancy-based design is still an exception to the rule in Japan, but this is slowly changing. An extreme example of the trend are the 'concept houses' such as Water Studio, responsible for limited-edition 'retro-styled' cameras for Olympus, cars for Nissan, and motorcycles for Suzuki.

The increasing understanding of the importance of design for the Japanese is reflected in the setting up in 1981 of the Japan Design Foundation, which benefits from strong government funding. Evidence of the new design awareness comes in the celebrity treatment accorded to certain Western designers such as Philippe Starck (b.1949) and Nigel Coates (b.1949) who have built prominent and individualistic works in Tokyo, and Luigi Colani who advised Canon on its camera designs.

As Japan becomes increasingly style-conscious its designers have been influenced by Post Modernism. As a result the 'black box' or 'silver box' concept of design that characterized the electronic consumer goods of the seventies has given way to more subtle effects. The 'red' Canon camera and pink Sharp radio are merely the tips of an iceberg. In contrast to these confectionery-coloured

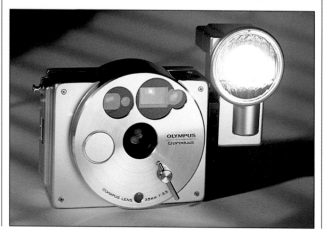

Below: *Colour exerts its presence. The Sharp QT-50 stereo radio cassette recorder of 1985. Rounded and 'streamlined' in form, prettier and wittier than its predecessors, less of a noise box, more of a fashion accessory.*

Right: *Kawasaki continue to remain a market leader in motorcycle design. This model, somewhat lighter in styling than the macho designs of previous decades, still expresses speed and functionality.*

Far left: *The brainchild of Naoki Sakai's Water Studio, a radical alternative to the Japanese norm of in-house design, the Olympus O Product camera bucks the national trend for ergonomically shaped black boxes.*

Above left: *Issey Miyake's extraordinary sculptural clothing, much of which takes its shape from the wearer's body. This subtly toned ribbed knit coat of 1985 could be worn in the street, but is perhaps more of a high art form.*

Right: *An early Sony Walkman, with its clean industrial look. From 1978, Sony opened up a new era in personal entertainment.*

Left: *Easy-to-operate camcorders like the Sony Handyman — the amateur videographer's dream — have become regular intruders into social occasions in the nineties.*

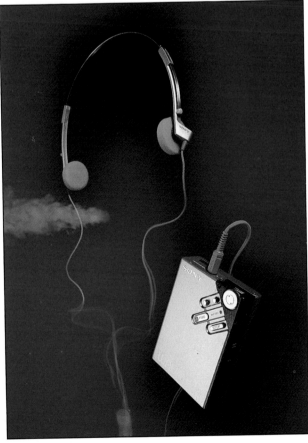

objects, there are also a number of sophisticated dark grey hi-fi ranges, notably by Yamaha, whose enigmatic appearance recalls the look of pebbles in a Japanese garden.

In an inspired combination of high technology and design flair, Sony invented a whole new field of private recreation with its Walkman personal stereo system. Its sporty, outdoor aesthetic is in tune with the self-image of the roller-skating teenager and yet also at one with the Japanese wish to achieve isolation within a crowd.

Despite the fact that its industry is based on innovation, Japan continues to support the old traditions, crafts and arts. In his posters Ikko Tanaka shows a respect for traditional calligraphy and makes heavy use of line to divide large areas of coolly uniform colours. Graphic designer Tadanori Yokoo and stage designer Eiko Ishioka exemplify other aspects of the Japanese tradition that are less easily assimilated abroad. One of the few Japanese fashion designers to continue working from Tokyo is Issey Miyake (b.1935), whose sculptural concept of clothing, with fabric draped around the body to form unusual shapes, is very much of the moment and yet strongly reminiscent of traditional Japanese styles.

Having equalled the West in design, there is growing awareness within Japan now of a need to bring together success in product design with Japanese decorative traditions. While the work of fashion designers such as Miyake, Yohji Yamamoto (b.1943), and Rei Kawakubo (b.1942) of Comme des Garçons already display ample evidence of their nationality, it is now likely that design in other fields will begin to pursue the same direction.

FRANCE

The leadership of France has always taken active steps to promote the national culture as well as technological advance. These preoccupations continue as strong as ever.

The choice of the British Richard Rogers (b.1933) and the Italian Renzo Piano to design the Pompidou Centre in Paris in the seventies was an inspired one at a time when France had no obvious architectural heir to Le Corbusier and Jean Prouvé. This building, a temple to the high-tech aesthetic, with its exposed structure and servicing elements, enjoyed a period as the most talked about and visited building in the Western world. Its long-term benefit has been to promote a renaissance of technology-led French architecture whose champion today is Jean Nouvel. He and others have added more outspoken buildings to Paris and other French cities.

Also at the behest of the government, furniture design has witnessed an upsurge of activity, led by the ebullient figure of Philippe Starck who has become well known as a designer of chairs, café and hotel interiors, as well as for bringing unexpected and fantastical shapes to such mundane objects as ashtrays and juicers. Where Starck leads, others now follow, many helped on their way by the government-sponsored Valorisation et Innovation dans l'Ammeublement, a body that exists to promote better furniture design.

The same happy tale cannot in general be told in product and graphic design. The French have gained a certain reputation in graphic design, with groups such as the controversial Grapus leading the way, making political statements through parodies of popular styles. This group went mainstream with graphic schemes for such prominent locations as the La Villette park and the Louvre museum and has had a broad influence. But in general, the standard is low.

A few French manufacturers have always been good at commissioning the right designer, with car manufacturers such as Renault and Citroën and domestic appliance manufacturers Moulinex and Terraillon quite happy to buy in the best industrial designers from around the world if, as is frequently the case, there is insufficient local talent. Larger enterprises such as the TGV and the aircraft of Aerospatiale continue to express national technological prowess in their design.

In the mid seventies France had passed its peak as leader of the world fashion market. Paris had coped brilliantly with the pop-culture sixties, with the likes of Courrèges translating the zany spaceman styles into *haute couture*, but the rather more romantic fashions of the seventies were beyond the comprehension of many designers. The tailored look at which the French excelled was out, and following the inclinations of the rapidly maturing ex-hippies, loosely fitting Eastern prints were in vogue. However, Yves Saint Laurent's use of lush exotic

Right: *Model for I.M. Pei's controversial glass pyramid for the Louvre, now built, and an accepted part of the everyday visual culture of Paris.*
Below right: *Young blood in the forms of Jean-Paul Gaultier (whose Spring 1992 collection is pictured) and Christian Lacroix, brought a new lease of life for Paris at the centre of the fashion world.*

Above: *Philippe Starck became the design celebrity of the 1980s. His Royalton Hotel in New York shows a continuing* preoccupation with opulent decorative arts.

Right and below: *Richard Rogers' extraordinary Centre Georges Pompidou in Paris, opened in 1978. The original inside-out building, with everything architects strive to hide on bold display. High-tech at its best — or worst, according to some Parisians at the time. Many have now warmed to it, and it is said to be the most visited building in the world.*
Below left: *Oblique room setting designed by Marc Chaimowicz for an exhibition at Liberty of London in 1984.*

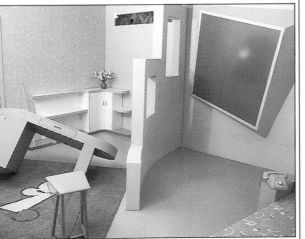

fabrics such as velvet, brocade and gold-threaded chiffon, cut generously to create voluminous shapes, caught the mood precisely. His Eastern-influenced styles were a welcome relief from the tailored mini-skirt suit of a few years before. Thierry Mugler (b.1946) and Claude Montana (b.1951) took up this more liberal treatment of fabric, and their designs with wide shoulders and baggy cut are still popular. The rise of Christian Lacroix (b.1951) and Jean-Paul Gaultier (b.1952) and the arrival of Karl Lagerfeld (b.1938) at Chanel has ensured Paris's survival at the centre of the world of fashion. But the age of couture houses is pretty well over, the diehards surviving on franchised perfumes, accessories and make-up, and the newer ones surviving almost entirely on off-the-peg sales.

Right: *The Grapus cooperative was founded in the heady days of the '68 événements. In the 1980s they won establishment work such as signage for the Louvre and La Villette, but then disbanded.*

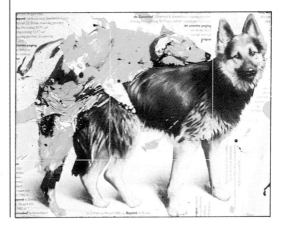

ITALY

The sixties had taken Italy to fever pitch with new production methods made possible by technological advancement. Plastic moulded furniture, blow-up chairs, veneered and moulded plywood pieces were being produced by the thousand. Italy's manufacturing base largely consisted of comparatively small factories and workshops, which meant that it was well-placed to withstand the harsh economic climate that came in the wake of the 1973 oil crisis. The exhibition 'Italy; the new domestic landscape', which took place at New York's Museum of Modern Art in 1972, confirmed Italy's pre-eminence in industrial design. In the ensuing mini-boom the Italian government did everything in its power, with tax concessions and grants, to encourage companies to use these smaller design-orientated and self-supporting production units, which by their nature were able to adapt quickly to the new requirements of a changing market-place.

The Italians have kept alive the Renaissance appreciation of a good training in fine art or drawing for designers of all kinds. Some consultancies employ fine artists alongside designers to stimulate their work. Giorgetto Giugiaro (b.1938) is founder of the renowned ItalDesign company, which specializes in car design. He has been responsible over the years for models ranging from the immaculate Ferrari and Maserati sports cars to the sensible Golf, Passat and Scirocco, the Lancia Delta, and the innovative 'fridge on wheels' Fiat Panda.

The Memphis Group was set up in 1981 by Ettore Sottsass (b.1917), an architect with a fear of conventional design. He decided to abandon the architectural discipline, and built up a relationship with Adriano Olivetti. By the early eighties he had been designing almost all Olivetti's electronic products for more than 15 years. If it had not been for his success in the conventional arena of corporate design, his launch of the Memphis Group in 1981 would not perhaps have had so much impact.

Sottsass's colleague Alessandro Mendini (b.1931) had been studying provincial Italian bourgeois taste, and argued that as padded and laminated cocktail bars and plastic-bobble decorated chairs represented the most prevalent style, that was the reality of what was happening. At the time Mendini was collaborating with Andrea Branzi of Studio Alchymia, and Mendini and Sottsass put on an exhibition at Alchymia in 1978. They took elements of different cultures and put them together in a new way, to make a new alternative. For the decoration of objects, they borrowed from 'bad taste', calling the results 'quoting the present'. Memphis continued until 1988, when Sottsass officially declared the movement over, having made its point. The seven years of its existence, during which it hired foreign designers, such as George Sowden from Britain, to produce furniture in response to its ideals, radically changed the face of design in the eighties.

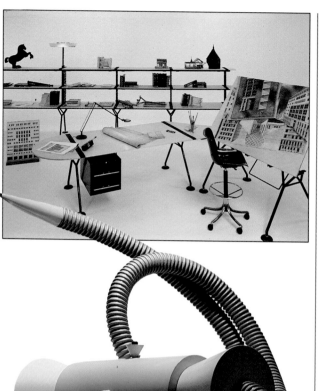

Left: *Norman Foster's purposeful-looking Nomos office furniture system for Tecno, 1986.*
Below left: *Michele de Lucchi's decorative vacuum cleaner prototype for Studio Alchymia, 1984.*
Below: *Knitwear from Krizia, 1985, in luxurious cashmere.*
Bottom: *Comfortable, good-looking and lighthearted, this is the Tramonto, a New York skyline sofa. Designed by Gaetano Pesce for Cassina, 1983.*

The work of Vico Magistretti (b.1920) contrasted greatly. There is a strong, almost severe simplicity in his work. Many of his designs hark back to the stark functionalism of Bauhaus, but they are more yielding, giving greater consideration to human comfort. This is obvious in his classic 'Maralinga' sofa, with its soft, spongy leather. Magistretti is a great technician, incorporating ingenious hingeing systems in his pieces and finishing them off in immaculate lacquers.

The network of small specialist workshops also stands Italy's fashion industry in good stead, making it an obvious source for short runs of high-quality special-order cloth. Fashion designers such as Romeo Gigli, Giorgio Armani (b.1935), Gianni Versace (b.1946), Gianfranco Ferré and knitwear designers such as Krizia and Missoni would be unable to survive without the backup of the specialist workshops, where hand finishing and perfection in detail are the norm and the respectful use of exclusive and expensive fabrics is a matter of pride. Some foreign designers, such as Jean-Paul Gaultier of France and Spain's Sybilla have sought Italian financial backing and manufacturing skills.

Architects such as Cesar Pelli, Gae Aulenti and Mario Bellini (b.1935) have international standing and undertake important commissions both inside and outside the country. The manufacturer Alessi makes constant news commissioning designers worldwide to create high-quality domestic products. Michael Graves, Philippe Starck and Oscar Tusquets have designed kettles and colanders for the international design *cognoscenti*. But, with these exceptions, the Italian design world in general has lost some of its impetus and pre-eminence to the French, Spanish and certain young German designers.

Above: *Stool by Anna Castelli Ferrieri for Kartell, 1982. Circular shapes make the hard metal more attractive, but is it for sitting on or posing on? That low back looks excruciating.*

Ettore Sottsass Jr was born in 1917, and studied architecture, graduating in 1939 and going straight into the army to fight. He left in 1945, having survived as a prisoner of war, with no money and little hope, but started making models and small craft objects.

In 1956 he met and struck up a relationship with Adriano Olivetti, who employed him to develop the design of Olivetti's new electronics division. The pioneering and sympathetic work he did then, and continues to do for the company, gave him the experience he needed to experiment with his contemporaries in Milan in other fields. They were all looking for something completely new, but no one was sure what it was. Months and years of discussion slowly but surely led them to producing a collection of prototype furniture designs for the 1981 Milan Furniture Fair. They were controversial, to some shocking, but proved to be commercially successful. Memphis entered the field of product design, and sold around the world. The Carlton sideboard *above*, in wood and laminate, is from Sottsass' first Memphis collection of furniture and is typical of its joyously uninhibited use of bright colour and strange disposition of surfaces, turning it into a startling piece of sculpture.

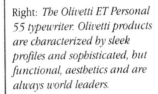

Right: *The Olivetti ET Personal 55 typewriter. Olivetti products are characterized by sleek profiles and sophisticated, but functional, aesthetics and are always world leaders.*

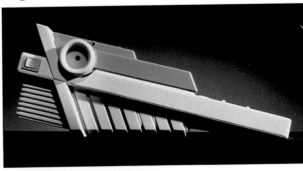

Below right: *Ferrari Mondial QV, designed by Pinin Farina, and in production from 1982. Along with Giorgetto Giugiaro, Farina is one of the cult figures of Italian car design, which started early this century, producing coachwork for the first horseless carriages.*

GERMANY

Despite the closure of the Hochschule für Gestaltung in Ulm in 1968, the spirit of austerity, purity and functionalism that this school carried over from the Bauhaus is still championed today by design-conscious companies all over the world but nowhere more than in Germany itself. The most notable example is the Braun company, which has set a world precedent for domestic products, with its look, style and technical innovations being widely imitated. The classic Braun matt black has become synonymous with quality; its very severity is its beauty. Recently, Braun has made tentative concessions to the Post-Modern movement, with the use of small touches of colour and a more human feel in its products, but as Post Modernism wanes, these departures already look like aberrations. The person who gives Braun its design leadership is Dieter Rams, an Ulm-influenced industrial designer. He and Ulm alumni in consultancies and teaching positions around the country ensure the continued survival of the school's values.

One small note of dissent comes from the short-lived New German Design movement coordinated by Christian Borngräber. Centred on Berlin — always a city for renegades — designers such as Andreas Brondolini and others created disturbing furniture and other articles that ques-

Below: *Use of typography is conservative in the extreme with many leading corporations using Berthold Helvetica as their house typeface.*

Above: *Room setting by Levy. This simplistic architectural interior is in a converted German warehouse. The glass table is supported by white geometric shapes; the sofa looks unforgiving.*

Below: *The clinically clean lines of the world famous Bulthaup kitchen. The industrial aesthetic executed in top quality steel to the highest standards; the ultimate designer kitchen.*

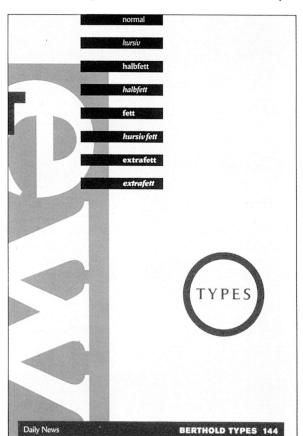

normal

kursiv

halbfett

halbfett

fett

kursiv fett

extrafett

extrafett

TYPES

Daily News   **BERTHOLD TYPES 144**

tioned the norms so rigidly adhered to. Elsewhere in Germany, it seems that each city can tolerate just one radical – lighting designer Ingo Maurer (b.1932) in Munich, Kunstflug in Düsseldorf and Ginbande in Frankfurt. A more subtle shift away from old dogmas is seen in the work of consultancies such as Frogdesign and Phoenix Design whose products are characterized by a freer handling of form and a readiness to embrace bright colours.

Many German designers work for manufacturers who generally have a deep understanding of the role of design within the company culture. This is one reason for the endurance of a certain conservatism in design, but it also explains the continued excellence and success in competitive markets of BMW and Mercedes cars and many other products. Other companies benefit from enlightened patrons of design in high positions who employ good designers from around the world. Klaus-Jürgen Maack at the Erco lighting company, Rolf Fehlbaum at furniture manufacturer Vitra and Philip Rosenthal at the Rosenthal china and glass company are cases in point.

It is difficult to know how the unification of West and East will affect the future of design in Germany. The fact that the Bauhaus was based in the East and the lasting fondness there for certain socialist values together with exigencies forced by Germany's leading role in promoting environmental protection legislation would suggest that the philosophies of the Ulm school are set to endure into the next century.

Right: *Not so much Bauhaus revival – it never went away – the Tecta range from Möbel. Op art red laminate table, with lamp incorporated by Stefan Wewerka, 1980. Bauhaus cubic red and grey chair by Peter Keler, 1925. Black lacquer storage table by Stefan Wewerka, 1980. Original Marcel Breuer chrome and leather chair, 1925, still looks modern and stylish.*

Below: *Ingo Maurer's innovative lighting designs represent the acceptable face of radicalism in Germany, where the values of the Bauhaus and Ulm schools still hold.*

Above: *Tecta Möbel. Strangely the original 1930 El Lissitsky acrylic armchair design looks more modern than Wewerka's table and chrome chairs, designed 50 years later.*

Below: *Tecta Möbel range, by Stefan Wewerka, 1979. The slightly awkward asymmetrical chairs, perhaps more for looking at than for sitting on, are covered with original black and white Bauhaus design fabric. The table is designed so that further identical units can be added, making more obscure shapes.*

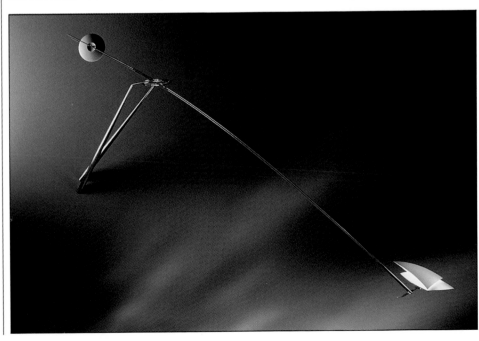

SPAIN

The years since Franco's death in 1975 have seen dramatic changes wrought by Spain's bloodless revolution. A spirit of hope swept through the country, giving new aspirations to the world of the creative arts.

The early and mid eighties in Madrid saw La Movida, a music, arts and fashion movement which first attracted the world's press to the capital. Barcelona entered a period of feverish activity in art, design and architecture which did not slow down until completing its preparations to host the Olympic Games in 1992. Architects such as Oscar Tusquets and Oriol Bohigas were old enough to write knowledgeably and analytically on Spain's immediate past, but young enough to benefit from the vast amount of work available in Barcelona. The socialist government's solid financial commitment to the promotion and development of Spanish design meant that there could be an investment in talent. Within five years, Spain was on the international art and design circuit, setting itself up to rival Italy.

Fashion and furniture, as the most immediate, consumable and lively areas of design, were heavily promoted, and both areas benefited greatly, beginning to export to other European countries as well as consolidating its home market. The home market was very buoyant, appearance being high on the Spanish list of priorities. When living at home — which many still do into adulthood — spare cash is spent on clothes and entertainment. When the Spanish set up home, choosing the right style and the right furniture is enough of a priority to necessitate some 300 design shops around Spain. Furniture designers such as Pedro Miralles, Jorge Pensi, Alberto Lievore, Vicent Martínez and Jaume Tressera have produced refreshingly different work for small manufacturers. While product design is generally behind, the work of Josep Lluscá and Quod Design have gained a good reputation.

In Barcelona, Javier Mariscal (b.1951) is the undisputed king of design, with his work reaching — like a favourite Mariscal icon — octopus-like, into the everyday visual culture of the city. Since Barcelona was chosen as the site of the 1992 Olympics, his graphics, illustrations, interiors, ceramics and accessories — not to mention the Olympic mascot, Cobi — symbolize the pluralism and energy of the city. Money invested in improving the infrastructure of Barcelona set off a major refurbishment of important buildings and derelict areas, which gave the city a huge boost in many related areas, especially leisure. Clubs and the design of clubs and bars are a major preoccupation in the nightlife-loving city, the lead being taken by designers Alfredo Arribas and Eduard Samsó with clubs such as Network and Las Torres de Avila.

While naturally there is cross-fertilization, regional differences can be marked in Spain. The city of Gaudí, with its centuries of influences from trading partners from all around the Mediterranean, has spawned a number of highly individualistic designers and architects, such as

Right: *Ricardo Bofill's Theatre of the Palace of Abraxas at Marne la Vallée outside Paris, 1978-82. Bofill's pre-cast concrete classicism provides 10 storeys of flats disguised as an amphitheatre, a good example of metaphor in Spanish architecture.*

Below: *Fashion designer Sybilla's work inspires striking photographic images, this one a Dali-esque landscape by Javier Vallhonrat. The white wired wool coat and olive dress are vintage 1987.*

Below right: *Jordi Garces and Enric Soria designed this house outside Barcelona consisting of a series of cubes set on a wide terrace. Use of low-tech materials and traditional techniques in this sophisticated design places it within the Reductionist tradition.*

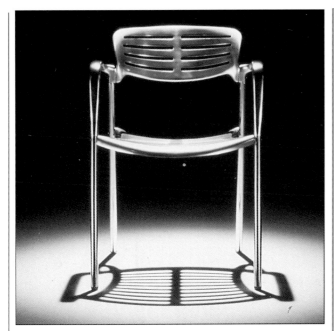

Above: *The Toledo chair by Jorge Pensi, 1988. Manufactured in cast aluminium, this outdoor café chair is intended to be indestructible.*

Below right: *Javier Mariscal's Hilton trolley for the Memphis Group, 1981. The dynamic shape is ironically intended to denote speed — the last feature necessary in a drinks trolley.*

B orn in Valencia in 1951, Javier Mariscal moved to Barcelona to study graphic design. The city in the early seventies was still repressive but enjoyed a lively sub-culture, which Mariscal joined as a cartoonist for underground magazines. In 1978 he staged a one-man exhibition in Barcelona called Gran Hotel, in which he expanded his eccentric, immediate creative style into interiors, print, paintings, upholstery, T-shirts and ceramics. After ten years of prolific output, he won the contract for Cobi, his design for the Olympic mascot, and for all his manifestations for the Games. He set up a large multidisciplinary studio where he began to take commissions from all over the world, especially Japan. His easy, hedonistic, disrespectful style belies his output. Mariscal designs as often and as compulsively as most people breathe.

Above: *Javier Mariscal's Cobi Troupe television cartoon based on the life of the 1992 Olympic mascot, Cobi. Mariscal's lively representation of Barcelona in the background is a recurrent theme.*

Alfredo Arribas, or graphic designers Peret and Pati Nuñez. Even the Modernism of José-Luís Sert is expressive and responsive to its context and culture. Madrid, with a more egocentric and introspective viewpoint, has bred a new generation of neo-rationalists, at whose extreme is the work of Alberto Campo Baeza. His Casa Turegano represents the summit of his achievements, with its cubic shape and overlapping interior spaces like a Chinese puzzle, severe in its geometry. Former Harvard professor Rafael Moneo has produced a number of public buildings. His Mérida Museum uses vernacular small red brick and high arches typical of his style, both sensual and monumental. His Madrid Atocha railway station was finished in time for the 1992 Madrid European Cultural Capital celebrations. Dramatically curving walls of red brick lead to a large spherical tower, and walkways over the platforms and escalators give a constant sense of movement. From here departs the high-speed train to Seville, where Expo '92 was also responsible for a major rebuilding and refurbishment programme involving top international and Spanish architects. The roads and railway connections were also improved to encourage long-term business investment as well as tourism in Andalusia.

Fashion designers such as Antonio Miró, Sybilla, Roser Marcé and Adolfo Dominguez enjoyed huge success throughout the eighties. When the tempo slowed to a more manageable pace in the early nineties, they were able to concentrate on serious and long-term business links, particularly in exporting to Germany and Japan.

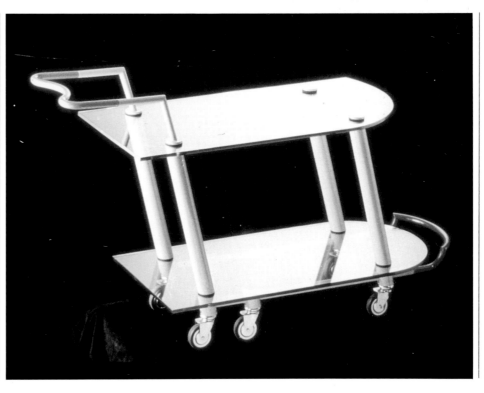

GREAT BRITAIN

After the boom years of the swinging sixties and the 'I'm backing Britain' campaign, when London had been the heart of the pop scene culturally and socially, the beat was perhaps slowed down by the hippie movement, which was less susceptible to media-inspired fads. The war babies had grown up and were setting up home, and they formed a huge market for home goods. The mid seventies saw the start of Terence Conran's most influential period, with 12 Habitat stores around the country, and several abroad. The Habitat look, promoted through well-designed mail-order catalogues, was aimed squarely at these affluent homemakers. The wares were bright, clean in line, unpretentious and a little bland. Conran's version of the French farmhouse kitchen with fittings in plain wood and traditional chairs, and pots and pans and utensils on display, had an influence in homes across the country.

Textile and fashion designer Laura Ashley (1926-88) commercialized flower power, making pretty patterned fabrics and wallpapers, as well as romantic Victorian and Edwardian-style dresses. Victorian countryside nostalgia took off, starting with printed cotton frocks, and, through to today, reaching food packaging, where the adoption of Victorian or country themes lends a little 'home-made-ness' to mass-produced preserves.

In architecture and product design, a strong feeling for

Above: *Bodymap, 1985, distinguished by body-aware lines and anarchic detailing.*

Born in 1931, Terence Conran went to public school and then took a textile design degree at Central School of Art and Design, London. His degree show was wildly successful, and he received commissions straight from college. Also experimenting with making furniture, he set up a little workshop and produced a collection to show at the Festival of Britain in 1951, which brought in further commissions. Soon afterwards he went to France for a period to work in a restaurant, and was there inspired by the whole ambience of the French kitchen and café life. This inspiration was eventually to influence virtually every British kitchen through his Habitat shops. He opened his first Soup Kitchen in 1954, the first place where young people could eat cheaply in a relaxed atmosphere, and, soon after, his first shop. Thirty years later, his extraordinary vision and business sense brought the worldwide expansion of Habitat shops, selling good-quality kitchen equipment and his own well-designed furniture, and sufficient funds for serious property investment, including the development of the world's first Design Museum.

Below left: *Craftsmanship by Ron Carter for Peter Miles Furniture. Haarlem stained ash dining chairs, 1984.*

Below: *Interior of Terry Farrell's coolly colourful Post Modern Water Treatment Works at Reading, Berkshire.*

Above: *Daniel Weil designed his Bag Radio in 1981, questioning the idea that electronics should be hidden inside cabinets.*

Below: *Packaging for Liquid Geometry game, by Loncraine Broxton & Partners, where the design reflects the product.*

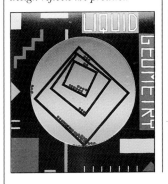

Above: *Ron Arad's wacky concrete sound system, ghetto chic for £1,500 in 1983.*

Left: *Post Modern graphic design studio in a converted chapel in London by Roger Mann, 1984.*

Above: *China Wharf aroused much controversy when built in 1986, but now is sufficiently accepted to feature on the covers of London telephone directories. By Campbell Zogolovitch Wilkinson Gough.*

Below: *Norman Foster's Renault Centre in Swindon, Wiltshire, 1983, whose tension wires and dainty girders inspired a generation of emulative work. The slight pitch of the roof adds visual interest.*

conservation began to be felt. Houses were being sold as 'energy-conscious' for the first time, and interest was expressed in alternative energy sources such as solar panels. With the onset of recession in the early nineties, advertising of products centred on durability and economy rather than newness.

The leaders in British furniture design continued to work as craftsmen rather than for industry, apart from certain contract manufacturers such as Hille and Scott Howard. At the schools of crafts and wood-working, such as John Makepeace's Parnham House in Dorset, furniture was more sculptural than practical. Designer Ron Carter (b.1926) displays an Arts and Crafts appreciation for the grain of the wood and his designs are of an almost Shaker purity in their restraint.

In 1976, the first serious exposed-structure office building was completed – Bush Lane House in the City of London – by Arup Associates. With its exterior lattice forming a tubular 'exo-skeleton' it looks extraordinary and functions beautifully today. As Modernism continued to flag, new forms of expression emerged. In the Lloyds Building, Richard Rogers created a highly conceptual building with strict functional requirements. Its heavily articulated surface and striking lift shafts loom over the mainly neo-Classical City of London.

For years Britain led the field in graphics and advertising. The adamant refusal by most advertisers to sell cheap products in a cheap manner allowed this art to flower in Britain. A rich eclecticism showed itself over the years in the elegant mystery of the Benson and Hedges campaigns, and the English pub humour of the John Smith television commercials for beer. Increasing competition between High Street supermarkets led them to employ top graphic designers, illustrators and packaging designers to update the look of their merchandise and stores. Out-of-town shopping centres and malls also relied heavily on signage graphics to set the right mood and attract custom.

In the late sixties and early seventies fashion designers such as Bill Gibb, Ossie Clarke, Jeff Banks and Mary Quant were in their element, riding on the crest of a buoyant economy. Economic recession hit by the late seventies but the early and mid eighties boom saw a major revitalization in London fashion coinciding with the emergence of designers such as Vivienne Westwood (b.1941), Katharine Hamnett (b.1948) and Jasper Conran (b.1959). Jeff Banks made a comeback with high-fashion off-the-peg clothes made for the middle market of office working women. But as recession hit more deeply in the late eighties, many fashion companies went bankrupt and those that survived began to depend more heavily on export business.

For vast numbers of young unemployed who lived in squats or undeveloped industrial buildings, making the most of rubbish found around the streets became a way of life, and from this hard necessity a kind of style emerged. Ironically this ghetto chic reached the consumer market, with shops such as One Off in London's Covent Garden selling sofas made of car seats and chrome tubing, and furniture made from rough driftwood. Art made from 'found

Above: *Ron Arad took advantage of the springiness of steel in this group of chairs, Strict Family, 1991, characterizing different family personalities.*
Above right: *Jasper Morrison's best-selling Sofa, marketed around the world and made by the British manufacturer – retailer Sheridan Coakley Partnership (SCP).*
Right: *Zig-Zag bookcase with laminated shelves in dark blue, white and lilac, by Arc Design Partnership, 1984. The unlikely shape is highly practical, ensuring that books lie against each other and do not fall over.*

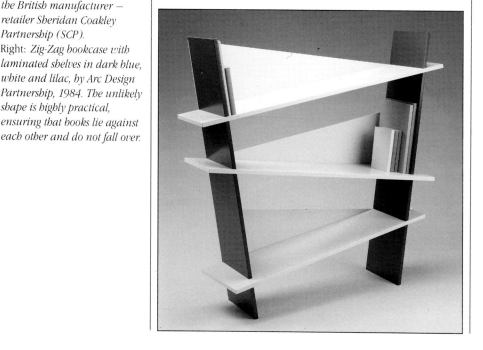

1992 The fashionably rumpled look of green cotton in this shirt for a Japanese retailer, Every Kind of People, a London-based company, is a classic case of global design, *above*.

1985 Memory-joggers, *above*, even training shoes joined the computer age. One shoe of these Micropacers by Adidas is fitted with a microcomputer which records performance.

1983 'City' table, 'Carlton' sideboard, 'Tahiti' table lamp and 'Treetops' standard lamp by Ettore Sottsass for Memphis, *below left*.

1984 Arc Design's 'Tilt' tables, *below*.

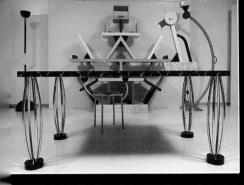

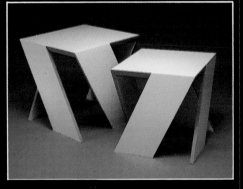

1988 Din Associates' Department X fashion store, *above*, part of the Next group. The industrial aesthetic tempered with wood and terracotta walls in London's Oxford Street. Everything, including the stock room, is moveable and on show.

1990 Borek Sipek has achieved stardom in the frenzied world of design with his preference for historicism, with this ceramic design, Albertine, drawing on his Czech heritage, *below*.

1982 Exterior staircase and Milan sky reflected in the Fiera exhibition building, *left*, a shimmering example of Post Modernism meeting the high-tech aesthetic in architecture.

NETHERLANDS

The most significant contribution to design development from The Netherlands has been in the field of graphics. Studio Dumbar run by Gert Dumbar (b.1940) in The Hague, leads with corporate identities, posters and exhibitions that are famous for questioning every step in producing a design solution. Much of Dumbar's work is for public services such as the PTT (Dutch Post Office), the railways, museums and government ministries. Dumbar's complex but sophisticated corporate identity for the recently privatized PTT shows his approach at its best. The rectilinear design has obvious connections with Dutch art and design. Its elements may be used flexibly to provide subtle clues of PTT identity rather than in the monolithic way of IBM or British Telecom. This allows for other design groups to use the Dumbar work as a starting point in future PTT projects.

Dumbar took over where Total Design, an Amsterdam consultancy founded by Friso Kramer in 1962, left off. Total was among the first design groups to revolutionize the use of graphics, going for clean, sans serif faces instead of the expressive letterforms widely in use at the time. Younger graphic design groups such as Hard Werken, Anthon Beeke, Una Design Consultancy, and Samenwerkende Ontwerpers make graphic design more lively now than in Total Design's day while still holding to the Modernist tradition.

Similar values hold true in product design where Leiden-based Ninaber Peters Krouwel best exemplify a precision in the handling of linear and planar form and an uncommon sensitivity for materials. Like many Dutch designers, these figures emerged from an excellent industrial design programme at Delft Technical University. Philips has maintained a high profile, but its product range is confused and does not as a whole share these Dutch values, preferring to pursue a 'global' look.

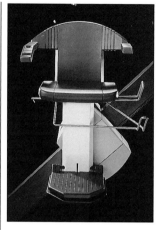

Above: *Ninaber Peters Krouwel, Holland's largest product consultancy, designed this dental chair whose elegant functionalism is typical of the best in Dutch design.*
Below: *Design groups such as Studio Dumbar, which designed this Holland Festival poster, have used new photographic and typographic tricks to inject life into the Modernism espoused by older groups, such as Total Design.*

Above: *The cover of this design manual for the Dutch Ministry of Education and Science, 1984, by Total Design, is an excellent example of an image constructed from typography, using different type sizes and colours. Total Design was also responsible for the Dutch Post Office (PTT) logo shown on the Studio Dumbar handbook (left). The logo was part of a complete corporate identity scheme undertaken for the PTT in 1978/9.*

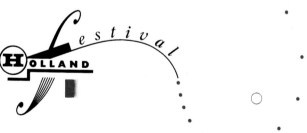

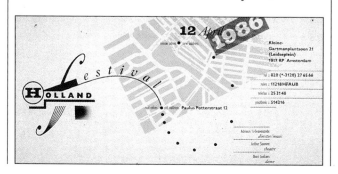

COMPUTER AGE

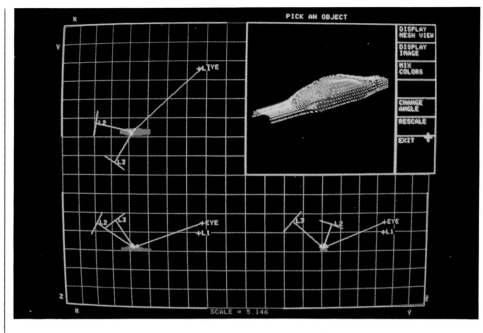

The uptake of computers by the design professions continues unabated. In graphics, many designers — including some who swore they would never be won over to the new technology — now use the Apple Macintosh and other computers. The improved ability of such hardware to combine type, graphics and images captured from print or video sources is being exploited to great effect. Having passed through a phase where everything computer-generated had to boast of the fact with a technocratic appearance, designers are settling down to use computers in the way they are meant to be used — as tools. The possibilities are extraordinary: a typeface may be changed and distorted and moved around the layout — to the consternation of purists but to the delight of many others. Computers are increasingly finding their way into colleges, a further indication that they are indispensable tools for designers rather than gimmicky devices used only to produce a particular look.

For the architect and industrial designer the tedious task of drawing perspectives can be done more quickly and accurately by computer. Images can be transmitted by telephone, checked, altered and returned in minutes. Renderings produced by this means can be a convincing presentation tool, conveying more to a client about a project than is possible by conventional means.

A computer can be programmed first to 'draw' an object in 3D, and then to rotate the wire-frame image so that it can be checked from every angle. This image may then be shaded to produce the appearance of a solid object. This saves hours, even days, and of course outlay at the modelmaking stage. New technology called stereolithography will shortly allow a real three-dimensional solid model of a product to be generated solely from computer data without the need for a modelmaker.

Above: *Said to be the most powerful computer of the mid-eighties, the Cray supercomputer at General Motors, USA, handled car design with graphics, analysing aerodynamic performance.*
Below: *Peter Greenaway's film,* Prospero's Books, *made spectacular use of the Quantel Paintbox and showed that computer-generated graphics need not look garish or technocratic.*

Below: *In architecture as in industrial design, CAD is an important tool for designing and visualizing.*

Bottom: *The design of a vehicle as complex as a space shuttle using 'wireframe' images, which can be rotated and viewed from all angles.*

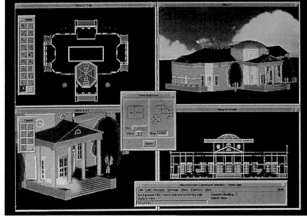

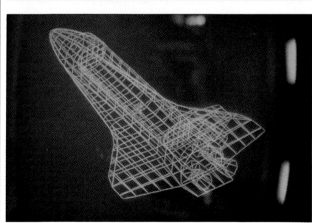

INDEX

BIBLIOGRAPHY

CHAPTER · ONE

THE ARTS & CRAFTS MOVEMENT 1850-1900

Adburgham, A. *Liberty's: A Biography of a Shop* (London, Allen & Unwin, 1975)

Agnius, P. *British Furniture 1880-1915* (London, Antique Collector's Club, 1978)

Anscombe, I. & Gere, C. *Arts and Crafts in Britain and America* (London, Academy Editions, 1978)

Art Workers' Guild. Pamphlet (revised 1975)

Arwas, V. *The Liberty Style* (London, Academy Editions, 1979)

Aslin, E. *The Aesthetic Movement: Prelude to Art Nouveau* (London, Ferndale Editions, 1969) *The Furniture Designs of E.W. Godwin* (Victoria & Albert Museum, 1970, reprinted from the Bulletin Vol III No 4 pp 145-54, London, October 1967)

Bock, J. Thesis on Voysey's Wallpaper Designs (unpublished)

Charlish, A. *The History of Furniture* (London, Orbis, 1976)

Cheltenham Art Gallery and Museum Exhibition. C.R. Ashbee and the Guild of Handicraft, 1981

Clark, K. *The Gothic Revival: An Essay in the History of Taste* (London, John Murray, 1962)

Cobden-Sanderson, T.J. *The Arts and Crafts Movement* (Hammersmith Publishing Society, 1906)

Comino, M. *Gimson and the Barnsleys 'Wonderful Furniture of a Commonplace Kind'* (London, Evans, 1980)

Crystal Palace Exhibition. Illustrated Catalogue, London, 1851. Unabridged republication of The Art Journal, Special Issue (Dover Publications, 1970)

Denvir, B. *The Early 19th Century: Art, Design and Society 1789-1852* (London, Longman, 1984)

Fairbanks, J.L. & Bates, E.B. *American Furniture 1620 to the Present* (London, Richard Marck Publishers, 1981)

Fine Arts Society. Morris & Company Exhibition in association with Haslam and Whiteway Ltd, 1979

Pugin to Mackintosh Exhibition in association with Haslam & W. Arch Designers, 1981

Garner, P. *20th Century Furniture* (London, Phaidon Press, 1980)

Gibbs-Smith, C.H. *The Great Exhibition of 1851* (Victoria & Albert Museum Catalogue, HMSO, 1981)

Girouard, M. *The Victorian Country House* (New Haven, Yale University Press, 1979)

Haslam, M. *English Art Pottery 1865-1915* (Antique Collector's Club, 1975)

Hayward, H (ed). *World Furniture* (London, Hamlyn, 1969)

Leicestershire Museums. Ernest Gimson and the Cotswold Group of Craftsmen, 1978.

MacCarthy, F. *The Simple Life. C.R. Ashbee in the Cotswolds* (London, Lund Humphries, 1981)

National Museum of Wales. The Strange Genius of William Burges 'Art-Architect' 1827-81 (ed J. Mordaunt Crook, 1981)

Naylor, G. *The Arts and Crafts Movement: A Study of its Sources, Ideals and Influences on Design Theory.* (London, Studio Vista, 1971)

Pevsner, N. *Pioneers of Modern Design from William Morris to Walter Gropius* (London, Penguin, 1968)

The Sources of Modern Architecture and Design (London, Thames & Hudson, 1981)

Rees, W. (ed). Cardiff Castle: Illustrated Handbook, 1978

Savage, G. *Dictionary of 19th Century Antiques and Later Objets d'Art* (London, Barrie & Jenkins, 1978)

Tames, R. *William Morris. An Illustrated Life of William Morris 1834-96* (London, Shire Publications, 1979)

Tate Gallery Exhibition. The Pre-Raphaelites, 1984

Watkinson, R. *William Morris as Designer* (London, Trefoil Books, 1983)

Wedgwood, A. *A.W.N. Pugin and the Pugin Family* (Catalogue of Architectural Drawings in the Victoria & Albert Museum, 1985)

CHAPTER · TWO

ART NOUVEAU 1890-1905

Billcliffe, R. *Mackintosh Watercolours* (London, Carter Nash Cameron, 1978)

Bloch-Dermant, J. *The Art of French Glass 1860-1914* (London, Thames & Hudson, 1980)

Champigneulle, B. *Art Nouveau: Art 1900, Modern Style, Jugendstil* (New York, Barron's, 1976)

Mackay, J. *Dictionary of Turn of the Century Antiques* (London, Ward Lock, 1974)

Madsen, S.T. *Sources of Art Nouveau* (London, Da Capo Press, 1975)

Masini, L-V. *Art Nouveau* (London, Thames & Hudson, 1984)

Museum of Modern Art, New York Exhibition. Art Nouveau. Revised catalogue, ed P. Selz and M. Constantine, 1975

Powell, N. *The Sacred Spring: The Arts in Vienna 1898-1918* (London, Studio Vista, 1974)

Revi, A.C. *American Art Nouveau Glass* (London, Thomas Nelson & Sons, 1968)

Schmutzler, R. *Art Nouveau* (London, Thames & Hudson, 1964)

CHAPTER · THREE

THE MACHINE AESTHETIC 1900-1930

Giedion, S. *Mechanization Takes Command* (New York, Norton, 1969)

Heskett, J. *Industrial Design* (London, Thames & Hudson, 1980)

Lodder, C. *Russian Constructivism* (New Haven, Yale University Press, 1983)

Naylor, G. *The Bauhaus* (London, Studio Vista, 1968)

Overy, P. *De Stijl* (London, Studio Vista, 1968)

Pulos, A. *American Design Ethic* (Massachusetts, M.I.T. Press, 1982)

Buddensieg, T. and Rogge, H. *Industriekultur: Peter Behrens and the AEG 1907-1914* (Massachusetts, M.I.T. Press, 1984)

CHAPTER · FOUR

ART DECO 1925-1939

Arwas, V. *Art Deco* (London, Academy Editions, 1980)

Battersby, M. *The Decorative Twenties* (London, Studio Vista, 1976)

The Decorative Thirties (Studio Vista, 1976)

Bloch-Dermant, J. *The Art of French Glass 1860-1914* (London, Thames & Hudson, 1980)

Keats, J. *You might as well live: The Life and Times of Dorothy Parker* (London, Secker & Warburg, 1970)

Klein, D. *Art Deco* (Octopus Books, 1974)

Lesieutre, A. *The Spirit and Splendour of Art Deco* (London, Paddington Press, 1974)

Newman, H. *An Illustrated Dictionary of Glass* (London, Thames & Hudson, 1977)

Robinson, J. *The Golden Age of Style: Art Deco Fashion Illustration* (London, Orbis, 1976)

Walters, T. *Art Deco* (London, Academy Editions, 1973)

CHAPTER · FIVE

CONSUMERISM AND STYLE 1935-1955

Ambasz, E. (ed). *The New Domestic Landscape* (New York Museum of Modern Art, 1973)

Branzi, A. and De Lucchi, M. (eds). *Il Design Italiano degli Anni '50* (Milan, I.G.I.S., 1981)

Hillier, B. *Austerity/Binge* (London, Thames & Hudson, 1975)

Katz, S. *Plastics: Design and Materials* (London, Studio Vista, 1968)

McFadden, D. (ed). *Scandinavian Modern Design 1880-1980* (New York, Harry N. Abrams, 1982)

Meikles, J. *Twentieth-Century Ltd: Design in America 1925-1939* (Philadelphia, Temple University Press, 1979)

Teague, W.D. *Design This Day* (London, Academy Editions, 1975)

CHAPTER · SIX

THE AGE OF AFFLUENCE 1955-1975

Bernard, B. *Fashion in the 1960s* (London, Academy Editions, 1975)

Branzi, A. *The Hot-House* (London, Thames & Hudson, 1985)

Hillier, B. *The Style of the Century 1900-1980* (London, Herbert Press, 1983)

MacCarthy, F. *A History of British Design 1830-1970* (London, Herbert Press, 1983)

Melly G. *Revolt into Style* (London, Penguin, 1969)

Sparke, P. *Ettore Sottsass Jnr* (London, Design Council, 1981)

Kruskopf, E. *Finnish Design 1875-1975* (Helsinki, Otava, 1975)

CREDITS

CHAPTER·SEVEN

STYLE NOW 1975 – TODAY

Designer Magazine 1975-85 (London, Designer Publications)

Garner, P. *The Contemporary Decorative Arts* (London, Phaidon Press, 1980)

Hiesinger, K.B. and Marcus, G.H. *Design Since 1945* (London, Thames & Hudson, 1983)

Hillier, B. *The Style of the Century 1900-1980* (London, Herbert Press 1983)

ICSID Congress *Design Furniture from Italy* (1983)

Jensen, R. and Conway, P. *Ornamentalism* (London, Allen Lane, 1982)

Lucie-Smith, E. *A History of Industrial Design* (London, Phaidon Press, 1983)

MacCarthy, F. *British Design Since 1880* (London, Lund Humphries, 1981)

Murray, P. and Trombley, S. *Modern British Architecture Since 1945* (London, Frederick Muller/RIBA Magazines, 1984)

Phillips, B. *Conran and the Habitat Story* (London, Weidenfeld & Nicolson, 1984)

Wolfe, T. *The Purple Decades* (London, Jonathan Cape, 1983)

QED would like to thank the following for their help with this publication and for permission to reproduce copyright material (abbreviations used − *t:top, l:left; b:bottom; c:centre; f:far, m:middle*):

p.10 Bridgeman Art Library **p.12** *tc* Christie's Colour Library, *tr* Bridgeman Art Library, *b* Richard Bryant/ARCAID **p.13** *tl, bl, br* Bridgeman Art Library, *c* E.T. Archive **p.14** *l* © City of Cardiff Council, *r* Philippe Garner **p.15** *tl* Bridgeman Art Library, *tc* Alastair Campbell, *tr* Victoria and Albert Museum, *bl* Owen Jones 'The Grammar of Ornament' **p.16** *t* Bridgeman Art Library, *b* Lucinda Lambton/ARCAID **p.17** *t* Architectural Association, *b* Lucinda Lambton/ARCAID **p.18** *l* E.T. Archive, *t* Architectural Association, *b* Christie's Colour Library, *r* Bridgeman Art Library **p.19** *tl, bl* Christie's Colour Library, *tr* Giraudon, *bc* E.T. Archive, *br* Design Council **p.20** *t, b* Country Life **p.21** *tc* Design Council, *br* Bridgeman Art Library **p.22** Bridgeman Art Library **p.23** *tl, br* Bridgeman Art Library, *bl, tr, bc* E.T. Archive **p.24** *tl, br* BPCC/Aldus Archive, *bc* Christie's Colour Library, *tr* Design Council **p.26** *tl* Christie's Colour Library, *tr, bl, br* BPCC/Aldus Archive **p.27** *l* Michael Holford, *r* Bridgeman Art Library, *br* Richard Bryant/ARCAID **p.28** David Burch, QED **p.29** *t* Design Council, *b* BPCC/Aldus Archive **p.30** *l* Bridgeman Art Library, *tc, bc* Design Council, *br* E.T. Archive **p.31** *l, tr* Bridgeman Art Library, *cr* Design Council, *br* Richard Bryant/ARCAID **p.32** *tl* BPCC/Aldus Archive, *tr* Design Council, *br* Bridgeman Art Library **p.33** *t* Leicester Museum & Art Gallery, *b* Bridgeman Art Library **p.34** *All* Bridgeman Art Library **p.35** *l* Bridgeman Art Library, *tr* Design Council **p.36** *bl, t, br* Design Council, *c* Giraudon **p.37** *tl, tr* Design Council, *b* Christie's Colour Library **p.38** Christie's Colour Library, © SPADEM, 1985 **p.40** Ullstein Bilderdienst, © DACS, 1985 **p.41** *t, b* BPCC/Aldus Archive **p.42** *t* Liberty of London, *inset* Camera Press, London, *bc* BPCC/Aldus Archive **p.43** *l* Owen Jones 'The Grammar of Ornament', *tc* Victoria & Albert Museum, *tr* Cassina SpA, *c* Bridgeman Art Library **p.44** *l* Cassina SpA, *r* Architectural Association **p.45** *tl, tr, bl* Architectural Association, *br* Bridgeman Art Library **p.46** *l* E.T. Archive, *t* Design Aspects, *b* Giraudon, *r* Bridgeman Art Library **p.47** *tl* © SPADEM, 1985, *tr, b, r* Christie's Colour Library, *c* Cobra & Bellamy **p.48** Bridgeman Art Library **p.49** *tl, br* Architectural Association, *bl* Angelo Hornak, *tr* Cassina SpA **p.50** *All* Christie's Colour Library **p.51** *l, br* Christie's Colour Library, *tr* Architectural Association **p.52** *l* Giraudon © ADAGP, 1985, *tr* Angelo Hornak, *br* Cobra & Bellamy **p.53** *l* E.T. Archive © DACS, 1985, *tr* Bridgeman Art Library, *br* Cobra & Bellamy **p.54** *Both* Bridgeman Art Libary **p.55** *tl* Architectural Association, *bl* Bridgeman Art Library, *tr* John Vaughan, *br* Design Aspects **p.56** Architectural Association **p.57** *tl, br* Architectural Association, *tr* Bildarchiv Foto Marburg **p.58** *tl* E.T. Archive, *bl, tr, br* Christie's Colour Library **p.59** *Both* Bildarchiv Foto Marburg **p.60** BPCC/Aldus Archive, *c* Giraudon, *r* John Jesse/Irina Laski **p.61** *tl, bl* BPCC/Aldus Archive, *tr* Christie's Colour Library **p.62** *t* BPCC/Aldus Archive, *b* Christie's Colour Library **p.63** *tl, tr, b* Bridgeman Art Library, *tc* Angelo Hornak **p.64** *All* Christie's Colour Library **p.65** *tl, l* Bridgeman Art Library, *bc, tr, br* BPCC/Aldus Archive **p.66** Christie's Colour Library, © SPADEM, 1985 **p.67** *tl* © SPADEM, 1985, *bl* Christie's Colour Library, *tc* Bridgeman Art Library, *tr* BPCC/Aldus Archive **p.68** *l* Salmer Arte, *r* Giraudon **p.69** *tl, bl, c, tr, br* Salmer Arte, *cl* Deidi von Schaewen **p.70** David King Collection **p.72** *tl* BPCC/Aldus Archive, *tr* Georg Jensen Silver, *c, b* Peter Roberts **p.73** *tl* BPCC/Aldus Archive, *tr* Bildarchiv Foto Marburg © DACS, 1985, *br* Ullstein Bilderdienst **p.74** *tc* Tate Gallery, © DACS, 1985, *tr* Cassina SpA © DACS, 1985, *cl* Richard Bryant/ARCAID, *c* Japan National Tourist Organization/ARCAID, *br* David King Collection, *bl* Property of the French Nation, eventually to be housed in the Museum of Picasso © DACS, 1985 **p.75** *l* E.T. Archive **p.76** *t, bl, br* Peter Newark, *br* Peter Roberts **p.77** Architectural Assciation **p.78** *tl, br* © ADAGP, 1985, Deidi von Schaewen, *tr* Bridgeman Art Library, *bfl, bl* Architectural Association, *bfr* Christie's Colour Library **p.79** *tl, cr, cfr, br* Design Council, *tr* Bridgeman Art Library *tr* Gebruder Thonet, *cfl* Orrefors Glasbruk, *cl* Ecart International, *bl* Bildarchiv Foto Marburg, *bl* Georg Jensen Silver **p.80** Bridgeman Art Gallery **p.81** *tr* © DACS, 1985, *bl* Bildarchiv Foto Marburg, *cr, br* Design Council **p.82** *tl,tr, br* Angelo Hornak, *bl,* Design Council **p.83** *tl, br* John Jesse/Irina Laski, *tr* Angelo Hornak **p.84** F.R. Yerbury/ Architectural Assciation **p.85** *tl* Gustavsberg, *tc* Design Council, *tr, b* Orrefors Glasbruk **p.86** *l, tc, bc* Robert Opie, *tr, br* Design Council **p.87** *tl* BPCC/Aldus Archive, *bl* John Jesse/Irina Laski, *tr, br* Warner & Sons Archive **p.88** *t* Cassina SpA, © DACS, 1985 (photo Mario Carrieri), *b* Christie's Colour Library © DACS, 1985 **p.89** *bl* Cassina SpA © DACS, 1985, *c* QED **p.90** David King Collection **p.91** *All* David King Collection **p.92** *t* Architectural Association, *bl, br* © SPADEM, 1985, Deidi von Schaewen © SPADEM, 1985, *tr* Design Aspects, *b* Cassina SpA © DACS, 1985 **p. 94** *All* Design Council **p.95** *t* Tecta Mobel © ADAGP, 1985, *b* Design Council **p.96** *tr* DACS, 1985, *tr* Bridgeman Art Library, *br* Cobra & Bellamy **p.54** *Both* Bridgeman Art Libary **p.55** ...

Knoll International, *b* Ullstein Bilderdienst **p.97** *b* Andrew Clark **p.98** Bridgeman Art Library © ADAGP, 1985 **p.100** Rosenthal **p.101** Warner & Sons Archive **p.102** *t* Walter Rawlings, *bl* QED, *br* Owen Jones **p.103** *tl, tc* Christie's Colour Library, *tr* E.T. Archive © DACS, 1985, *bl* Peter Roberts **p. 104** Bildarchiv Foto Marburg © DACS, 1985 **p.105** *tl, bl* Cobra & Bellamy, *br* Topham **p.106** *l* Giraudon © ADAGP, 1985, *tr* Bridgeman Art Library © DACS, 1985, *br* Christie's Colour Library © DACS, 1985 **p.107** *tl* Cobra & Bellamy, *bl, tr* © ADAGP, 1985, Christie's Colour Library **p.108** *b* Christie's Colour Library, *tr* Angelo Hornak **p. 109** *l* Christie's Colour Library, *r* Aram Design Ltd **p.110** *t* Christie's Colour Library, *b* Cobra & Bellamy © SPADEM, 1985 **p.111** *tl* Christie's Colour Library, *cl, br* Bridgeman Art Library, *bl, tr* Cobra & Bellamy © SPADEM, 1985 **p.112** *Both* Christie's Colour Library **p.113** *t* Christie's Colour Library, *b* Giraudon **p.114** *tl* Bridgeman Art Library, *tr* Angelo Hornak, *bl, bc* Christie's Colour Library, *cr* E.T. Archive, *br* Robert Opie Collection © ADAGP, 1985 **p.115** *l* Giraudon © ADAGP, *tr, bl* Robert Opie Collection, *br* Peter Roberts **p.116** Ronald Grant Archive **p.117** Angelo Hornak **p.118** *All* Angelo Hornak **p.119** *c, bc, br* Andelo Hornak, *bl* John Margolies/ESTO **p.120** *l* Angelo Hornak, *tr* Design Council, *br* Architectural Association **p.121** *t* Topham, *b* BPCC/Aldus Archive **p.122** *background* Warner & Sons Archive, *tl, tr, br* Design Council, *bl* Angelo Hornak **p.123** *t, b* Christie's Colour Library, *cl* Angelo Hornak, *cr* Robert Opie **p.124** *tl, bl* Christie's Colour Library, *tr, cr,* Design Council, *br* Warner & Sons Archive **p.125** *tl* Hille International, *tr* John Jesse/Irina Laski, *br* Design Council **p.126** *tl, cl* Bridgeman Art Library, *tr,* Peter Mackertich, *b* Jessica Strang **p.127** *tl, tr* © SPADEM 1985, Christie's Colour Library, *bl* Bridgeman Art Library, *tc, br* Design Council **p.128** John Margolies ESTO **p.129** *tl, tr, bl* John Margolies ESTO, *c, br* Jessica Strang **p.130** Robert Opie Collection **p.132** *t, c* Peter Roberts, *b* Design Council **p.133** *All* Gaby Schreiber **p.134** *l* Seaphot Ltd: Planet Earth Pictures, *r* Motoring Picture Library **p.135** *t* Design Council, *cr* John Frost Archive, *c* Lufschiffbau Zeppelin GmbH Friedrichshafen, *b* Air Ministry **p.136** *t, bl* Steelcase Inc, *br* Walter Dorwin Teague Associates **p.137** *l* BBC Hulton Picture Library, *r* Design Council **p.138** *bl* Design Council © Sport and General, *cr, br* Design Council **p.139** *tl* Design Council, *tc* QED, *tr* Museum of Modern Art, NY © ADAGP, 1985, *bl* Museum of Modern Art, NY, *cb* John Jesse/Irina Laski **p.140** *tl,* Walter Dorwin Teague Associates, *bl* Peter Newark's Western Americana, *tr* (National Gallery of Canada) Design

Council **p.141** *bl* Design Council, *tr* Peter Newark's Western Americana **p.142** *tl, bl* BPCC/Aldus Archive, *cr* Fiesta Galerie, *br* 'The News' **p.143** *tl* Knoll International, *b* John Mills Jr, *tr* Peter Roberts Collection **p.144** *bl* F.R. Yerbury/Architectural Association, *remainder* Design Council **p.145** *tl, tr* Design Council, *b* Fritz Hansen **p.146** *br* Iittala, *remainder* Artek **p.147** *t* Design Council, *bl* Georg Jensen Silver, *br* Fritz Hansen **p.148** *t* Peter Roberts, *c b* Cobra & Bellamy **p.149** *t* Tecno, *c* Zanotta, *b* Topham **p.150** *t* Design Council, *b* Christie's Colour Library **p.151** *tl* Flos, *cl* Christie's Colour Library, *bl* Design Council, *tc* Arteluce, *tr, br* Cobra & Bellamy, *cr* Jessica Strang **p.152** *l* Braun, *r* Rosenthal **p.153** *tl* Design Council, *bl* Rosenthal, *r* Peter Roberts **p.154** *Both* Design Council **p.155** *t* E.T. Archive *remainder* Design Council **p.156** *tl* Gaby Schreiber, *cl, bl* BBC Hulton Picture Library, *tr* Design Council, *cr* Hille International, *br* BPCC/Aldus Archive **p.157** *tl, r* Design Council, *bl* BBC Hulton Picture Library **p.158** *tl* Fiesta Galerie, *tr* Artek, *cl* Motoring Picture Library, *cmt* Galerie 1900-2000, *cmb* Galerie Loft, *cr* Design Council, *bl* Peter Newark, *br* Herman Miller **p.159** *tl* Orrefors Glasbruk, *tr, cl, c* Design Council, *cr* Warner & Sons Archive, *bl* Tim Street-Porter/EWA, *br* Walter Dorwin Teague Associates **p.160** *tl, tr* Gaby Schreiber, *c* Practical Styling, *b* Topham **p.161** *tl* Design Council, *tr* Cobra & Bellamy, *b* Topham **p.162** Joe Clark, Life **p.164** *tl* Peter Roberts, *tr* Herman Miller Inc, *b* Peter Newark's Western Americana **p.165** *tl* Topham, *b* BPCC/Aldus Archive **p.166** *l* Richard Hamilton, *tc* Sony, *c* Bridgeman Art Library © DACS, 1985, *r* QED, *bc* Design Council **p.167** *tl* Tate Gallery, *tr* NASA (USA), *bl* QED, *bc* Sheridan Photo Library **p.168** *t* Rosenthal © DACS, 1985, *b* BPCC/Aldus Archive **p.169** *tl, cb* Angelo Hornak, *cl* Hille International, *bl* BPCC/Aldus Archive **p.170** *tl, bl* Design Council, *tr, cl* Daily Telegraph Colour Library, *cr* Whitmore-Thomas, *bc* Warner & Sons Archive, *br* Pentagram **p.171** *tl, tr* Daily Telegraph Colour Library, *b* Design Council **p.172** *cl* Tim Street-Porter/EWA, *bl, cr* Design Council, *tr* Topham **p.173** *tl, tc* Topham, *cl, bl* Design Council, *tr, br* John Adriaan **p.174** *tl* Peter Newark's Western Americana, *tr* Steelcase Inc, *br* Herman Miller Inc **p.175** *tl* Herbert Matter (courtesy Knoll International), *cl, bl* Herman Miller Inc, *tc* Peter Newark's Western Americana, *c* BPCC/Aldus Archive, *tr, br* Design Council **p.176** *tl* Walter Dorwin Teague Associates, *tr, bl* Herman Miller Inc, *bc* BPCC/Aldus Archive, *br* Topham **p.177** *t* Herman Miller Inc, *cl, cr* BPCC/Aldus/Research Reports Archive, *b* Topham **p.178** *tl* Angelo Hornak, *tr* Zanotta SpA, *b* Fiesta Galerie **p.179** *tl* Necchi, *cl* Design Council, *cr* Olivetti, *bl* Poltronova SpA, *tr, br* Cassina SpA **p.180** *t* Poltronova SpA, *c, bl* Zanotta, *br* Flos **p.181** *tl* Zanotta, *tr* Design Council, *b* Olivetti **p.182** *l* Iittala, *r* Rosenthal **p.183** *tl* Wärtsilä-Foto, *tr*

Oscar Woollens, *bl* Asko Furniture, Finland, *br* Oscar Woollens **p.184** *t* Sharp, *c* Pentagram Design, *b* Erwin Tragatsch Archive **p.185** *tl, cl, bl* Design Council, *tr* Canan **p.186** *l* Orrefors Glasbruk, *bl* Fiesta Galerie, *ct, inset* Daily Telegraph Colour Library, *br* Galerie Loft © ADAGP, 1985 **p.187** *tl* Daily Telegraph Colour Library, *tr* Pentagram Design, *bl* Design Council, *bc* Architectural Association, *br* Jessica Strang **p.188** *t, c, bl* Topham, *tr* Peter Roberts, *br* Daily Telegraph/Sacha © DACS, 1985 **p.189** *bl* Jessica Strang, *tc* Interni, *tr* Pentagram Design, *cr* Design Council, *br* Topham **p.190** Memphis/Milano **p.192** *t* R. Seifert & Partners, *cl* Boss Design, *cr* Greg Hursley, *b* Kinnear *b* Kinnear **p.193** *t* Mazda, *br* Branson Coates **p.195** *tr* Arcaid, *r* Sony, *cr* Memphis, *c* Apple Computer UK Ltd **p.196** *t* Architectural Association, *c* Enigma Graphics, *fl* Antonio Citterio, *l* Milton Glaser inc **p.197** *l* Design Council, *c* Greg Hursley, *r* Robert Harding Picture Library **p.198** *l* Olympus, *tr* Issey Miyake, *br* Sharp **p.199** *tl* Sharp, *tr* Kawasaki, *b* Sony **p.200** *t* Frank Spooner Pictures, *b* Niall McInerney **p.201** *t* Philippe Starck, *cl* Design Council, *c* Arcaid, *tr* Arcaid, *br* Moira Clinch **p.202** *t* Tecno, *cl* Santi Caleca, *cr* Krizia, *b* Cassina spa **p.203** *t* Design Council, *c* Olivetti, *b* Santi Caleca **p.204** *l* Georg Jensen, *r* Rosenthal **p.205** *tl* Georg Jensen, *c* Bang and Olufsen, *bl* Ergonomi Design Gruppen, *tr* Design Council, *br* Kolbjorn Ringstad/Stokhe Fabrikker AS **p.206** *t* Deidi von Schaewen, *b* Bulthaup **p.207** *t* Buch and Deichman, *bl* Ingo Maurer Design **p.208** *t* Deidi von Schaewen, *bl* Javier Vallhonrat/Emma Dent Coad collection, *br* Emma Dent Coad collection **p.209** *t* Emma Dent Coad collection, *b* Memphis **p.210** *t* Emma Dent Coad collection, *bl* Emma Dent Coad collection, *br* Arcaid **p.211** *tl* Design Council, *tc* One-Off Ltd, *tr* CZWG Architects, *bl* Arcaid, *br* Richard Davies **p.212** *t* One-Off Ltd, *c* SCP Ltd/Emma Dent Coad collection, *b* C and N Accessories **p.213** *tl* Ogle Design, *tr* Design Council, *cl* John Makepeace, *c* Terry Farrell, *cr* Ove Arup, *bl* Arc Design, *br* Malcolm Garrett **p.214** *tl* Arteluce, *tr* Memphis, *bl* Studio Dumbar, *c* Arcaid, *br* Duracell **p.215** *tl* Emma Dent Coad collection, *ct* Umbro International, *cl* Aspect, *c* Arc Design, *r* Din Associates, *bl* Aspect Picture Library, *br* Driade **p.216** *tl* Total Design, *bl* Studio Dumbar, *tr* Ninaber Peters Krouwel, *b* Studio Dumbar **p.217** *t* Science Photo Library, *bl* Allarts, *c* Intergraph/Productivity Computer Solutions Ltd, *b* Science Photo Library

Special thanks to Laura Beck and Mark Collard for typesetting, David Burch for photography, Mick Hill for illustrations, Kate Parish for additional picture research, Vicky Robinson and Hazel Bell for indexing, Iain Wallace for paste up and to Jack Buchan, Hazel Edington, Michelle Newton, Karin Skånberg and Liz Wilhide.

Every effort has been made to trace and acknowledge all copyright holders. Quarto would like to apologize if any omissions have been made.